Race, Jobs, and the War

Race, Jobs, and the War

The FEPC in the Midwest, 1941–46

ANDREW EDMUND KERSTEN

University of Illinois Press

URBANA AND CHICAGO

Publication of this book was supported by a grant from the
Humanistic Studies Unit, University of Wisconsin at Green Bay

Library of Congress Cataloging-in-Publication Data
Kersten, Andrew Edmund, 1969–
Race, jobs, and the war : the FEPC in the Midwest, 1941–46 / Andrew
Edmund Kersten.
p.   cm.
Includes bibliographical references and index.
ISBN 0-252-02563-6 (alk. paper)
1. United States Committee on Fair Employment Practice—History.
2. Illinois. Fair Employment Practices Commission—History.
3. Discrimination in employment—Middle West—History. I. Title.
HD4903.5.U58K47   2000
331.13'3'097709044—dc21   99-050488

For Fred

Contents

Acknowledgments

BEFORE LAUNCHING INTO the story of the FEPC in the Midwest, I must acknowledge the assistance of many people. First and foremost I am indebted to Roger Daniels, my mentor and friend, who suggested many years ago that I look into this topic. I will always appreciate his guidance and patience through the trials of graduate school. There is not a page in this book that does not show his influence on my thinking and writing. The other members of my dissertation committee, Professors Bruce Levine, Gene Lewis, and Allan Winkler, read an early draft of this book several years ago. Their suggestions and support improved it greatly. At various stages during this process a number of other scholars read either the whole or parts of the book and offered valuable criticism. A special debt of gratitude thus goes to Eileen Boris, Clete Daniel, Herbert Hill, David Macleod, August Meier, Paul Moreno, Zane Miller, Merl Reed, and Joe Trotter. I would like to acknowledge the following libraries and their staffs for allowing me to research and use their archival materials: Bentley Historical Library, Chicago Historical Society Library, Cincinnati Historical Society Library, Cleveland State University Archives, Illinois Historical Society Library, Indiana State Archives, Milwaukee Public Library, Milwaukee Urban Archives, Missouri Historical Society Library (St. Louis), National Archives and Records Administration (Great Lakes Region, Chicago), Ohio State Historical Society Library, Walter P. Reuther Library, Franklin D. Roosevelt Library, Harry S. Truman Library, University of Chicago Archives, University of Cincinnati Archives, University of Wisconsin at Eau Claire Area Research Center, University of Missouri at St. Louis Archives, Washington University Archives, and Western Reserve Historical Society Library. I would also like to gratefully acknowledge the special assistance given to me by Robert Horton of the Indiana State Archives, Archie Motley of the Chicago Historical Society, Robert Parks of the Franklin D. Roosevelt Library, and N. Charles Anderson of the Detroit Urban League.

I incurred other kinds of debts while researching this book. I would like to thank Hu English and Lineve McKie, Shelly and Russ Hayes, Linda and Pete Kersten, Steve Kersten and Michael Kingery, and Dave and Lindsay Morrison for letting me stay with them in various places in the Midwest. Another relative, Susan L. Finn, graciously did an extremely important research task for me while she was a student at the University of Wisconsin at Eau Claire. Thanks again, Susie. The interlibrary loan offices at the University of Cincinnati and the University of Wisconsin at Green Bay provided excellent service without which this book could not have been written. This book was also made possible by grants from the Bentley Historical Library, the Harry S. Truman Institute, the Taft Fellowship Program, the University of Cincinnati History Department, and the University of Cincinnati Research Council.

Finally I would like to thank those whose support helped me put the book in its final form, particularly Richard L. Wentworth, now-retired director of the University of Illinois Press; Emily Rogers, formerly an acquisitions editor at Illinois; Matt Mitchell, copy editor; and my new friends at the University of Wisconsin at Green Bay: Greg Aldrete, Gary Grief, Walter Herrscher, Harvey Kaye, Carol Pollis, Jerry Rodesch, and Joyce Salisbury. My parents, Fred and Karen Kersten, and my parents-in-law, Ted and Janet Finn, provided unflagging encouragement. My wife, Victoria, and our daughter, Bethany, offered comic relief and love. The book is dedicated to my father, whom we almost lost while I was completing work on the manuscript. The fact that he will see the book in print means more to me than I can express.

* * *

Some of the information in this book has been published earlier. The chapters on Detroit and St. Louis appeared in other forms in "Jobs and Justice: Detroit, Fair Employment, and the Limits of Federal Activism," *Michigan Historical Review* 25 (Spring 1999): 77–101, and "Stretching the Social Pattern: The President's Fair Employment Practice Committee and St. Louis," *Missouri Historical Review* 93 (January 1999): 149–64. I have written about Cincinnati and the FEPC in "Publicly Exposing Discrimination: The 1945 FEPC Hearings in Cincinnati, Ohio," *Queen City Heritage* (journal of the Cincinnati Historical Society) 52 (Fall 1994): 9–22.

Race, Jobs, and the War

Introduction

THE NOTION OF the Second World War as the "good" war is a powerful one. But as historians have recently pointed out, there was plenty of "bad news from the good war." For instance, in March 1942 the *Cincinnati Post* printed a story about Louise Boyd, a black Cincinnatian who had read a circular from the local United States Employment Service (USES) office looking for women to work in the defense industry. The job requirements listed a high school education, a height of at least five feet two inches, a physically fit body, and an age of at least seventeen years. Boyd applied but was rejected. As she later explained, "I met all the requirements but one . . . my face is black." When she complained to a USES official she was told, "sorry we have nothing for colored."[1]

Such stories of employment discrimination were common not only in the Midwest but across the nation. Employers often denied black and other minority workers war jobs because of their skin color, their religion, or their national origin. Private organizations such as the National Association for the Advancement of Colored People (NAACP), the National Urban League, and B'nai B'rith initially fought against job bias without many results. More successful were the wartime efforts of a new federal government agency devoted to eradicating employment discrimination, the President's Committee on Fair Employment Practice.

President Franklin D. Roosevelt created the Fair Employment Practice Committee (FEPC) in response to an intense lobbying campaign led by A. Philip Randolph, the head of the Brotherhood of Sleeping Car Porters and the leader of the March on Washington Movement. In January 1941 Randolph announced that if the Roosevelt administration did not deal with discrimination in the defense program, a hundred thousand African Americans would march down Pennsylvania Avenue on 1 July 1941. Throughout that winter and spring, Roosevelt and his advisors negotiated with Randolph without result. Finally on 25 June 1941—five days before the scheduled protest march—FDR issued Executive Order 8802 banning employment discrimination because of race, creed, color, or national origin for employers with defense contracts, labor unions, and civilian agencies of the federal government. To enforce the policy Roosevelt created the FEPC. The committee did not eliminate employment discrimination during World War II. In fact, it represents the limits of wartime liberalism. As Harvard Sitkoff once put it, the FEPC dented but did not overcome prejudice and discrimination. Nevertheless, I argue, by some basic standards concerning the level of activity, size of caseload, and number of adjusted complaints, the FEPC accomplished much. This tiny government agency—which never had more than 120 workers—exposed prejudice in the war industries and broke some racial barriers, processing over twelve thousand complaints and settling nearly five thousand (42 percent) to its satisfaction. The committee vigorously pursued an educational campaign in order to create more harmonious industrial relations between white and minority workers. Above all, the FEPC influenced the course of civil rights reform as it became a postwar model for city, state, and federal involvement in employment discrimination.[2]

This book examines the FEPC's experiences in the Midwest from 1941 to 1946. Taken in this context the Midwest is the Old Northwest, which includes Illinois, Indiana, Michigan, Ohio, Wisconsin, and parts of Minnesota and Missouri. The examination is further focused by the Fair Employment Practice Committee's own interests in the region. Committee officials were not concerned with the Midwest's rural areas but concentrated on what some scholars label "the Great Lakes Industrial Region." In general the FEPC's work focused on such cities as Chicago, Cincinnati, Detroit, Indianapolis, Milwaukee, and St. Louis.[3]

Scholarly attention on the Midwest is warranted for several reasons. Historians have renewed their interest in the nation's sections. Examinations of the Midwest, however, have lagged behind work on the South and the West. This book is intended as a contribution to midwestern studies as well as to the literature on the FEPC. Although there are histories of the FEPC at the national level, there are few regional studies and none of its midwestern activities. It cannot be said that the committee's successes and failures in the Midwest typified its results generally, which varied from region to region. In the South the committee generally failed to change biased employment patterns because of a lack of cooperation from employers, local organizations, and federal agencies such as the USES. The FEPC found its greatest successes in resolving complaints of discrimination in the Northeast, where it closed about two of every three cases (66 percent) that it received. In the Midwest, the committee settled fewer complaints than in the Northeast, closing about three out of every five cases (62 percent). This was, however, better than its success rate in the West, which was 55 percent. Despite the regional variation, the means that the FEPC used to fight employment discrimination were consistent throughout the nation. Unlike other New Deal agencies, the FEPC eschewed job quotas and relied on individual complaints and the case method system to create fair employment. Since its resources were limited, the committee leaned heavily on the support of local civil rights and labor activists, sympathetic employers, and governmental officials to complete its work. Where it found this assistance, change was indeed possible, especially in areas with tight labor markets.[4]

This book is thus a case study of the effectiveness of the FEPC's national goals and methods. It combines what some have called the "old" civil rights history—the history of national movements and federal government activities in civil rights—and the "new" civil rights history, which focuses on local movements. Although civil rights activism during the 1940s took place on many different levels, there were important intersections between local and national arenas. The experiences of the FEPC in the Midwest highlight the interconnections between the federal government, national associations, and community organizations. The FEPC was in part a response to a national association, Randolph's March on Washington Movement. The committee also acted as a catalyst, inspiring midwestern communities to rejuvenate and transform their own fights against employment discrimination. When federal officials and local activists cooperated job integration was often the result, particularly for male minority workers at the lower levels of employment.[5]

The activities of the FEPC in the Midwest were important for two other reasons. First, the committee devoted much of its resources to fighting employment discrimination in that region. Roughly 30 percent of its field staff, suboffices, and public hearings were in midwestern cities. FEPC officials focused attention there because they believed that gains were possible. In the committee's final judgement, "although there were conspicuous failures [in the Midwest], many large and small companies, through the effects of . . . the FEPC, brought their practices into line" with wartime federal fair employment policies. By the end of the war, experience had shown that, with the exception of a few places, job discrimination was not "dyed-in-the-wool" in the Midwest but something that could be extricated from the business and worker culture. The FEPC's efforts at times produced a modicum of success, but not always, which leads to the second point. The history of the FEPC in the Midwest is important because it illustrates the variations within that region. The FEPC integrated many companies in the northern parts of the Midwest but largely failed in the southern parts. Borderline cities, such as Cincinnati, East Alton, and St. Louis, provided the committee with its toughest cases, suggesting not only a strong southern influence but also a lack of support from local activists and government officials.[6]

This book engages in several scholarly debates. The first concerns the FEPC itself. Since the 1970s, many historians have denied the importance of the FEPC, suggesting that conditions in the labor market had a greater influence on minority employment. In *War and Society: The United States, 1941–1945* (1972), Richard Polenberg writes that minority workers' "most substantive gains seem to have occurred as a result of manpower shortages rather than FEPC action." Polenberg attacks Executive Order 8802 in his book, *One Nation Divisible: Class, Race, and Ethnicity in the United States since 1938* (1980), calling it a weak attempt to deal with employment discrimination. "That the executive order was regarded as a genuine breakthrough," he asserts, "showed only how accustomed most Americans were to observing the color line and how unaccustomed they were to federal efforts to erase it." Other historians, including textbook writers, have been even more negative. In *The Unfinished Journey: America Since World War II* (1995), William H. Chafe states that black employment increases resulted solely from the wartime manpower crisis, and in *American History: A Survey* (ninth edition, 1995), Alan Brinkley styles the FEPC as a "rare symbolic victory."[7]

Although there is no denying the importance of manpower shortages during the war, I maintain that mere job openings in no way guaranteed employment for minority workers. More often than not the FEPC's efforts were needed to break down unfair employment patterns even in areas with labor shortages, such as Detroit and Cleveland. In general I disagree with minimizing interpretations of the FEPC and agree with a group of historians who wrote the first monographs about the committee. Louis Ruchames, Louis Kesselman, Herbert Garfinkel, and others who published in the 1940s and 1950s viewed the committee as a significant civil rights advance, a major development in federal government policy against employment discrimination. Although these scholars acknowledged the limits of the committee's work, most judged the movement for permanent fair employment practice committees as a lasting and important legacy of the wartime FEPC. What this book adds to that literature is a perspective from the community level, something often lacking in the national studies. It chronicles the interaction between federal, state, and local activities in the fight for fair employment as well as the nexus between the FEPC and labor markets.[8]

Other debates related to this work concern the nature of the American home front during the Second World War. It contributes to the acrimonious debate among some labor historians about race and organized labor and the degree to which unions pursued racial egalitarianism. It is clear that during the war many white midwestern union workers, in both the American Federation of Labor and the Congress of Industrial Organizations, vigorously opposed the integration and promotion of African Americans and on occasion even Jewish Americans and other minority workers. Racism was a part of white worker consciousness, and at times employers hid behind it to avoid hiring or upgrading blacks.[9]

An infamous example that typifies the culture of rank-and-file racism is the Cincinnati "D-Day Strike" that began on 5 June 1944. The day before American and Allied troops landed in northern Europe, nine thousand white UAW-CIO workers at the Wright Aeronautical plant went on a wildcat strike to protest the upgrading of seven black machinists. Walter P. Reuther, army officials, and FEPC representatives helped to end the strike, which lasted almost ten days. This work stoppage reveals the depth of the racial animosity on the home front. According to the historian Stephen E. Ambrose, American workers "sacrificed their daily routines to make [the D-Day] invasion possible." This strike and dozens like it demonstrated that there was a racial limit to wartime sacrifice and patriotism. But the example also suggests that CIO union leaders were willing—and much more likely than their AFL counterparts—to work with the FEPC. The committee relied on the CIO leadership to support fair employment practices and to serve as a force for change. In many instances industrial union leaders assisted the Fair Employment Practice Committee because of their own commitment to interracial organizing and their dedication to the federal government's wartime policy to end employment discrimination.[10]

This book also relates to another homefront historiographical issue: the influence of the New Deal on American society. Historians tend to mark the end of the New Deal in the middle of Roosevelt's second term. As Alan Brinkley has written, "even Franklin Roosevelt must ultimately have realized . . . that by the end of 1937 the active phase of the New Deal had largely come to an end." I maintain that although Dr. New Deal had become Dr. Win-the-War, the former was still making house calls. Roosevelt set up alphabet agencies akin to those of the 1930s to handle such things as Japanese incarceration, wartime production, and employment discrimination. The FEPC was a quintessential New Deal agency, even though it is not often thought of as such. Moreover, like many other New Deal creations, the FEPC's impact outlived Roosevelt. Looking back over a half-century, it can be argued that the committee's most significant effect was moving the United States closer to a national fair employment policy. After Congress terminated the FEPC in 1946, civil rights activists continued to push for equal employment opportunity. Although frustrated at the national level, they achieved many successes at the municipal and state levels. By 1964 some two hundred cities and three dozen states had passed fair employment statutes. Ten of these states and the District of Columbia prohibited discrimination in employment because of race, color, religion, national origin, and sex. As Clete Daniel has written, "even as [the FEPC] fell far short of fulfilling the hopes that it inspired among millions of minority workers, [it] forced the American people to glimpse, if not to comprehend and accept, the . . . future that lay before them," a future that was slowly being realized even before the passage of the landmark 1964 Civil Rights Act and the creation of the Equal Employment Opportunity Commission. In a sense, the history of fair employment in the United States is another part of what William E. Leuchtenberg has called the "shadow of FDR."[11]

What this shadow has meant is the source of ongoing debate among historians and political scientists. Since the 1980s, new policy historians have arrived at several conclusions about the New Deal's legacy. To some, the expansion of the federal government in the 1930s and 1940s was another way to maintain the power of class-conscious, and perhaps race-conscious, elites and their bureaucratic allies. Another interpretation maintains that the state did not represent any particular interests and instead worked toward the common welfare of the nation. In this process, the state itself became a contested battleground for employers, labor unions, civil rights groups, and minority workers. The argument presented in this book reflects this latter position. The Fair Employment Practice Committee did not directly represent the interests of employers, labor unions, or civil rights groups. Rather the FEPC had two goals. The first was to assist minority workers in their quest for jobs. By realizing this goal the committee completed its second mission, which was to help win the war through the effective use of the nation's labor resources. The committee became the most embattled and controversial Roosevelt agency of its day. In the end, the forces of reaction dismantled the FEPC but could not destroy the spirit that led to its creation, which eventually resulted in a new federal fair employment agency that still exists today.[12]

* * *

The history of Roosevelt's Fair Employment Practice Committee is a tale of two committees. FDR created the first FEPC in June 1941, scuttled it in August 1942, and set up the second in May 1943. The two committees shared a name, mission, and methods. Both had an overriding concern for African-American workers, although the FEPC did spend some time on the employment problems of Jews, American Indians, Japanese Americans, and other minorities. The main differences between the two committees were size and organization.

Chapter 1 deals with the origins of the first FEPC, concentrating on midwestern support for and reactions to the committee. Chapter 2 focuses on the midwestern experiences of the first FEPC, particularly in Chicago and Milwaukee, where the committee set several key precedents for fighting job discrimination. In Chicago the committee publicly rejected quotas, adopted the case method system based on individual complaints, and utilized cease and desist orders. The third chapter describes the death of the first FEPC and the formation of the second committee, indicating the importance of reorganization for the Midwest.

Chapters 4 through 8 examine the second committee's activities in five states (Illinois, Indiana, Minnesota, Ohio, and Wisconsin) and two cities (Detroit and St. Louis). Taken together, these five chapters illustrate the real and potential progress against employment discrimination made possible by the partnership of local activists and the FEPC. They also reveal a midwestern pattern to job discrimination. The fight for fair employment was much more difficult in areas closer to the South. The final chapter discusses the end of the second wartime FEPC and summarizes its impact and legacy for the Midwest and the nation.

1. "A Refreshing Shower in a Thirsty Land": The Creation of the First FEPC

TO SOME CONTEMPORARY observers and to others long afterward, the late 1930s marked the end of the New Deal.[1] Roosevelt's alphabet agencies had accomplished much of their mission, bringing economic stability to areas such as the Midwest that suffered terribly during the early years of the Great Depression. President Franklin D. Roosevelt himself seemed to be preparing for retirement. In 1938 he created the first modern presidential library by deeding to the government part of his Hyde Park estate where he planned to write a history of his presidency. But the world would not let Roosevelt retire. When Adolph Hitler switched from "sitzkrieg" to "blitzkrieg" in Europe in April 1940, FDR slowly began to put the United States on a war footing. Suddenly questions about the nation's future prosperity and his own retirement were replaced by more pressing concerns of confronting European fascism and mobilizing the United States. As Roosevelt put it in his 1940 acceptance speech for the Democratic presidential nomination:

> Like most men of my age, I had made plans for myself, plans for a private life of my own choice and for my own satisfaction, a life of that kind to begin in January, 1941. These plans, like so many other plans, had been made in a world which now seems as distant as another planet. Today all private plans, all private lives, have been in a sense repealed by an overriding public danger. In the face of that public danger all those who can be of service to the Republic have no choice but to offer themselves for service in those capacities for which they may be fitted.[2]

Roosevelt's reluctant choice had a powerful impact on the nation. His wartime policies—in particular his policy on employment discrimination—influenced the lives of thousands of workers in the Midwest and elsewhere and changed the course of civil rights history.

Although FDR was well suited for the job of commander-in-chief, America was ill-prepared for war. Isolationists in Congress had kept Roosevelt's diplomatic hands tied and slowed military rearmament. On the eve of Pearl Harbor, America lagged behind European nations. Its army ranked eighteenth in the world behind, among others, Sweden and Switzerland. Furthermore, the United States had a small munitions industry. The nation's factories were devoted to the production of consumer goods, but Detroit's Ford passenger automobiles and Cincinnati's Crosley radios do not win wars. Roosevelt had his work cut out for him in the spring of 1940. Just a year after some had predicted that the Roosevelt years were over, a reinvigorated FDR took charge of the American mobilization effort.[3]

To prepare the United States for total war, Roosevelt created a new series of alphabet agencies. After Hitler's invasion of the Low Countries in May 1940, FDR resurrected the National Defense Advisory Commission (NDAC), an agency originally created by President Woodrow Wilson, to mobilize industry. Dissatisfaction with industrial mobilization led to the creation of the Office of Production Management (OPM) in late 1940, the War Production Board (WPB) in 1942, and the Office of War Mobilization (OWM) in 1943.[4]

The great experimenter had not lost his touch. By the time of the Pearl Harbor attack, American industry had begun to respond to the prodding of Roosevelt's agencies, and conversion was occurring nationwide. Gigantic factories were built, such as Willow Run near Detroit. The production of military airplanes jumped from six thousand planes in 1940 to nearly twenty thousand in 1941. American workers as well as businessmen profited from the increased economic activity. Unemployment rapidly decreased from 8,120,000 persons in 1940 to 5,560,000 in 1941 to 2,660,000 in 1942. Moreover, union membership rose from roughly 8 million in 1940 to 10 million in 1941.[5]

Not all felt the return of prosperity equally. Some Americans, blacks in particular, were left behind as the economy geared up for war. Since the 1920s African Americans had suffered from high rates of unemployment. Nineteen twenty was a high watermark for black employment in American industry. Industrial manpower needs created by World War I drew thousands of black southerners north, many to midwestern cities like Chicago, Cleveland, Detroit, and Milwaukee. George E. Haynes, the Negro Economics Director in the United States Labor Department, estimated in 1920 that over five hundred thousand were employed in northern industries. Although the majority of these workers entered unskilled positions, a small number achieved semiskilled and skilled status in industries such as shipbuilding and iron foundries. In the aftermath of the First World War most economic gains in northern industrial plants were temporarily lost. The prosperity of the late 1920s and the job experiences afforded during the war allowed some African-American workers in the North to reestablish themselves in a number of industries, including foundries.[6]

The Great Depression wiped out these advances. The downward trend in construction and manufacturing hurt black employment as did the 1930s pattern of hiring white workers to perform such traditionally "Negro jobs" as waiters, bellmen, porters, and garbage truck drivers. As Nancy Weiss has shown, the New Deal provided some blacks with relief from economic dislocation. Some of FDR's agencies were better than others. Although several agencies, such as the Civilian Conservation Corps, denied minority workers equal job opportunities, the Public Works Administration (PWA), the Works Progress Administration (WPA), and the National Youth Administration (NYA) trained and employed a large number of African Americans.[7]

Despite the New Deal's assistance, black and other minority workers languished through the lean years of the Great Depression and the stagnant years of Roosevelt's second term. There were some opportunities for African Americans, especially in those industries where they had been previously employed during the First World War. For instance, unskilled blacks found their way back into construction jobs not controlled by trade unions. Manufacturing jobs, however, were beyond the reach of most blacks. In late 1940, of the eleven thousand skilled and semiskilled positions open in the aircraft industry, fewer than 1 percent went to nonwhite workers. There were exceptions. In the fall of 1940, Cincinnati's Wright Aeronautical, which made bomber engines, announced plans to train and hire a thousand black workers. Generally, however, defense employers refused to hire black workers, claiming that white workers would strike if they did. Frequently union leaders and rank and file in the American Federation of Labor (AFL) and the Congress of Industrial Organizations (CIO) indeed opposed the hiring and training of black workers for production lines, but asserting union intransigence on racial issues was also a way for employers to mask their own prejudice.[8]

The refusal of white employers and workers to allow minorities war jobs created production bottlenecks. According to a 1941 Federal Security Agency (FSA) report, discrimination against black and Jewish Americans, as well as those of Italian, German, Mexican, and Asian descent, substantially reduced the available labor supply, causing unnecessary worker migration and delaying production schedules. The FSA report provided a telling example involving midwestern workers. In late 1940 the owner of a large foundry in Wheeling, West Virginia, ran out of local white labor for his plant. Rather than hire qualified blacks in Wheeling, the employer recruited skilled and semi-skilled white foundry workers from western Ohio, thus draining the supply of workers from cities such as Cleveland, Columbus, and Zanesville, and causing labor shortages and production problems in the Buckeye State.[9]

Because of discrimination in defense industries, some minority workers, especially blacks, felt left out in the cold and publicly expressed their anger. A July 1940 editorial in the NAACP's magazine, *Crisis*, nicely summed up the feelings of many. Noting that $4 billion had been earmarked for national defense, the author claimed that "one thing is clear to Negroes: all this is being planned without the opening of participation to colored people." Midwestern African Americans also held this view. Six months later, an editorialist in the *Cleveland Call and Post* lamented the lack of employment opportunities for able black workers and claimed, falsely but with some metaphorical truth, that "No Negroes Wanted" signs appeared in every government recruiting office for those interested in anything but "scullion" work. The author wondered if "the very government itself [wasn't] trying to make a traitor of him," and insisted that "the American Negro [was] loyal and true, able and capable."[10]

The executive secretary of the NAACP, Walter White, personally shared this last belief. In an article for the *Saturday Evening Post,* White proclaimed that "it's our country, too." Noting that blacks were largely excluded from service in the military and jobs in industry, he predicted that the "largest defense headache ahead of the United States Government" would be the status of "that 10 per cent of our population that is Negro." White provided statistics to back his claim, but perhaps his most compelling examples were anecdotal. He told of a wealthy, patriotic white woman who fired a gardener of German birth upon discovering that he was a member of the German American Bund. He was hired at a local airplane plant the next day. That plant refused to hire any blacks, including one graduate of a trade school whose grade average was 98 percent. At the time that the article was printed this person was washing cars in a garage. White's point was clear: loyal black workers were being denied the opportunity to participate in the national defense program.[11]

Despite the employment problems facing African Americans, White was optimistic. He noted that even some southern companies (such as the Newport News Shipbuilding and Dry Dock Company in Virginia) hired black workers, and cited the example of Seattle's Boeing Aircraft plant, where union and management were working together to integrate production lines. Furthermore, and perhaps most importantly, the United States government had begun to take steps toward a fair employment policy.

On 1 September 1940 the National Defense Advisory Commission had issued an admonitory statement that "workers should not be discriminated against because of age, sex, race or color," and appointed Dr. Robert C. Weaver as an administrative assistant in charge of implementing the nondiscrimination policy. The NDAC, Roosevelt's first defense advisory agency, was responsible for the coordination of industrial and manpower resources. Sidney

Hillman, the cofounder of the Congress of Industrial Organizations, a fervent New Dealer, and the head of the NDAC's Labor Division, viewed his task as supplying labor "sufficient to produce swiftly and without stoppages" everything needed for the defense of the nation. Hillman devised the NDAC's labor policies, including the one on nondiscrimination. To Hillman and the NDAC, all available labor was to be tapped in the defense emergency. The commission's fair employment statement was intended to pave the way for integration on the shop floor. It was Weaver's job to carry out that policy.[12]

At thirty-three, Weaver was perhaps the most influential figure in the field of fair employment. At the time of Weaver's appointment, Thurgood Marshall believed that he was "the only man to handle the job." One scholar has likened Weaver's pre-1941 stature in the struggle for black economic opportunity to that of the dean of Howard University's Law School, Charles Hamilton Houston, the NAACP lawyer who laid the groundwork to end the "separate but equal" doctrine. As an influential member of the New Deal's informal "Black Cabinet," Weaver, along with Clark Foreman and Harold Ickes, had devised a method of revealing and eliminating discrimination on PWA work projects. They applied a simple test based on the occupational census. The test rested on the theoretical assumption that in the absence of discrimination, the percentage of blacks employed on New Deal jobs should be equal to their "proportionate share" of those jobs in the occupational census. Using the results as *prima facie* evidence of unfair practices, Weaver created a quota system that increased black representation on PWA programs by requiring that the minimum percentage of blacks on the payroll equal one-half of the percentage of skilled black workers in a city's construction force as reported by the 1930 occupational census. Because of Weaver's experience in fighting employment discrimination, the seven-member National Defense Advisory Commission could not have made a better choice to execute a nondiscrimination policy for the defense industries.[13]

Working under Sidney Hillman's direction, Weaver helped shape the government's early wartime employment policies. He developed for the United States Office of Education a nondiscrimination policy for defense vocational training and secured fair employment pledges from the AFL and CIO. These labor agreements were of special importance to Weaver, who believed, rather naively, that since union leaders had signed the pledges, "labor [did] not intend to be an impediment to increased occupational opportunities for Negroes." Although NDAC press releases bragged about the occasional Weaver success (in the Midwest he helped to get jobs for 150 black carpenters in St. Louis, Missouri, and three hundred black bricklayers in Indiana) these had little impact on overall African-American defense employment.[14]

In addition to enforcing the advisory commission's nondiscrimination policy, Weaver tried to boost African-American morale. In articles for the black press, he answered the administration's critics and sought to drum up support for the defense program. One month after joining the NDAC, Weaver wrote an article for the National Urban League's *Opportunity*, which was also serialized in black newspapers such as the *Cleveland Call and Post*. The essay in effect challenged the assumptions of that midwestern critic who claimed that federal officials had hung "No Negroes Wanted" signs in offices for worker and military recruitment. Weaver maintained that the problem of minority employment was not one of "racial policy" but one of "securing the maximum production of necessary materials and equipment with existing factors of production." Moreover, according to Weaver, the successful resolution of this manpower question was certain. Months before the issuance of the executive order setting up the FEPC, he wrote that "sooner or later the use of Negroes in many of these industries and operations will, in all probability, be required . . . by economic factors or . . . by political pressure."[15]

Although Weaver approached his work with his characteristic enthusiasm, he was largely unsuccessful in easing employment barriers for blacks, let alone other minorities. Securing policy statements proclaiming nondiscrimination from the AFL and the CIO had not stopped union officials and employers from ignoring skilled and available African-American workers. Since reneging on one's word to the federal government carried no penalty, it was done frequently.

By early 1941 the problem of job discrimination had become so serious that civil rights leaders believed alternatives to traditional lobbying were in order. Asa Philip Randolph, the international president of the Brotherhood of Sleeping Car Porters (BSCP), proposed a militant action to fight the omnipresent prejudice in the defense effort. On 25 January 1941 he called on thousands of African Americans to join him on a massive protest march in Washington, D.C., to register extreme disgust with discrimination in defense industries and the armed forces.[16]

By 1941, Randolph, a pioneer in the civil rights and labor movements whose rich baritone voice spoke for thousands of black workers, had been fighting for social justice for nearly a quarter-century. In 1917 he and Chandler Owen cofounded the *Messenger,* a militant socialist magazine. In 1925 he founded and served as the first president of the Brotherhood of Sleeping Car Porters, which eventually became affiliated with the American Federation of Labor. As a member of the AFL, Randolph sought in vain to break down union prejudice and discrimination against African Americans. He also tried to improve the lives of black Americans via politics. In the 1930s he had served on Mayor Fiorello La Guardia's New York City Commission on Race Relations.[17]

Despite his national reputation, Randolph's proposal for a march on Washington received no public federal response. J. Edgar Hoover, the head of the Federal Bureau of Investigation (FBI), added paper to Randolph's already thick dossier, but President Roosevelt and his advisors did not appear concerned. Nevertheless, for the next three months Randolph worked to make the march a reality. He established an organization, the Negro March on Washington Committee (later renamed the March on Washington Movement [MOWM]), and opened a headquarters in Harlem and several regional offices, including three very active midwestern branches in Chicago, Detroit, and St. Louis. Randolph also picked up support from more traditional black leaders such as the historian and activist Rayford W. Logan, Lester Granger of the National Urban League, and Walter White of the NAACP. In a letter to Randolph, which included a ten-dollar check to the MOWM, White wrote that "it is time we Negroes stopped talking at the big gate and got down to business to demonstrate that we are not going to be satisfied with anything less than unqualified democracy for ourselves."[18]

By spring 1941, as support for the march grew, the pressure brought by the MOWM produced its first result. On 11 April 1941 Sidney Hillman sent a public letter to all defense contractors, warning that the next three months would be critical for war production and that employers would create a "serious situation" if they did not hire all available workers. Noting that the Office of Production Management (which had replaced the NDAC in December 1940) was "informed there are good workers available who are not being hired solely because of their racial identity," Hillman urged them "to examine their employment and training policies at once to determine whether or not these policies make ample provision for the full utilization of available and competent Negro workers. . . . [E]very available source of labor capable of producing defense material," he insisted, "must be tapped in the present emergency."[19]

Finally it seemed that the federal government—or part of it at least—had acknowledged the problems on which White, Randolph, and other black leaders had focused. Absent from Hillman's letter was the optimism and call for patience that had characterized the OPM's previous statements. Even stern words, however, could not satisfy the MOWM, the NAACP, or the black public. According to the historian Richard Dalfiume, "there was a built-in cynicism among Negroes" toward the defense crisis. Discrimination in the war industries gave rise to "a sickly, negative attitude toward national goals," including the OPM's desire to maximize manpower. Not surprisingly, the leaders of the MOWM called Hillman's message a "mere plea . . . [that would fall] on deaf ears," and continued to organize support for their march. Many black midwesterners also held this opinion. As the *Cleveland Call and Post* flatly put it, "letters to employers won't get jobs" for blacks. In an editorial to the *Chicago Defender,* an African American agreed and called Hillman's letter "a theatrical stunt intended only for the gallery."[20]

If that were the letter's true aim, it failed. More likely Hillman's goal was to use his OPM office to coax defense contractors into obeying the government's nondiscrimination policy. At the same time, Hillman did not want to disrupt factories by causing work stoppages over shop floor integration. His statement, which was not entered into the *Federal Register* and thus had no legal weight, was a weak attempt to propound administration policy while "avoiding vigorous intervention" that could slow defense production.[21]

Because of the half-hearted nature of the OPM's action, organizing for the march on Washington picked up after Hillman's statement. By May, most of the plans were set and the nation's black leadership appeared to rally behind Randolph. On 29 May 1941 Randolph notified the White House formally that the MOWM was assembling ten to fifty thousand blacks to march on Washington on 1 July to protest discrimination in the national defense effort. For the first time, Randolph issued his demands. He wanted the president to sign executive orders "to abolish discrimination in national defense and all departments of the Federal Government." Randolph's call for executive orders reflected the political realities in Washington. Lobbying Congress on behalf of fair employment was almost a waste of time. Southern Democrats and conservative Republicans blocked all legislative attempts to deal with the issue, including the first two federal fair employment practice bills introduced in early 1941. In March Representative Vito Marcantonio (ALP, N.Y.) was the first congressman to propose a permanent fair employment practice commission, and in April Senator Scott W. Lucas (D, Ill.) became the second. So forgettable were these initial attempts that in 1945 Lucas had to struggle to convince his liberal constituents that he had introduced such a bill. If the MOWM were to affect national policy, pressuring FDR was its only practical course of action.[22]

Sensing that the march might actually take place, President Roosevelt began to pressure Randolph to stop the demonstration. FDR feared that the march might disrupt industrial production, upset his political alliances in the South, become grist in the Axis propaganda mill, and perhaps incite a race riot in segregated Washington, D.C. Hence he ordered his top advisors on racial matters—Aubrey Williams, Fiorello LaGuardia, and his wife Eleanor—to meet with the MOWM leadership. After conferring with Randolph, LaGuardia recommended that the president see Randolph himself.[23]

White House secretaries arranged a meeting for June 18. In attendance were FDR, Phil Randolph, Walter White, Assistant Secretary of War Robert P. Patterson, Secretary of the Navy Frank Knox, and OPM heads William S. Knudsen and Sidney Hillman. As White wrote in his memoirs, Roosevelt tried skillfully but without success to convince the black leaders to end the march. Finally the president turned to White, the more conservative of the two activists, and asked, "'Walter, how many people will *really* march?'" White responded, "'no less than one hundred thousand.'" White later wrote that "the

President looked me full in the eye for a long time in an obvious effort to find out if I were bluffing or exaggerating. Eventually he appeared to believe that I meant what I said." "'What do you want me to do?'" FDR asked. Once again White presented the MOWM's six demands, including an executive order banning discrimination in war plants. Quiet until that point, Knudsen, who was also president of General Motors, burst out and said that he opposed any step by the president that would interfere with employers' rights to hire. Knudsen demanded proof that any corporation, especially GM, discriminated against blacks. White retorted that he did not have the information with him but would send Knudsen a copy of the NAACP's reports on his company. "'And send me a copy too of General Motors' record when you send it to Bill, won't you?'" FDR wryly interjected. The president then offered a deal. He would issue an executive order banning discrimination in defense industries if White and Randolph agreed to call off their march. According to Randolph, FDR also told them that "it was in his mind that it would be well to establish a board which would have the power to take action by way of making the necessary investigations and carrying out the measures of redress." Although they had not received everything they wanted, the leaders of the MOWM agreed to cancel the march.[24]

The job of writing the executive order fell to Joseph L. Rauh Jr., a White House assistant. He later described what happened on June 19 to Studs Terkel. "I got a call from my boss, Wayne Coy [the Liaison Officer for the Office of Emergency Management who said] 'Get your ass over here we got a problem.'" Rauh ran the ten blocks to Coy's office. Coy explained that "'some guy named Randolph is going to march on Washington unless we put out a fair employment practices order.'" He asked Rauh if he would write an executive order. "'Sure, any idiot can write an executive order, but what do you want me to say?'" Coy responded, "'All I know is the President says you gotta stop Randolph from marching.'" Rauh's first draft of the order was rejected by Randolph, who negotiated for a stronger one. The final draft became Executive Order 8802.[25]

On 25 June 1941 President Roosevelt signed Executive Order 8802, which promulgated a nondiscrimination employment policy for the federal government during the war years. Citing his worry "that available and needed workers [had] been barred from employment in industries engaged in defense production solely because of consideration of race, creed, color, or national origin," Roosevelt reaffirmed "the policy of the United States that there shall be no discrimination in the employment of workers in defense industries or Government because of race, creed, color, or national origin." Executive Order 8802 mandated that all departments and agencies of the federal government related to vocational and training programs for defense production adhere to the nondiscriminatory employment policy. Moreover, contracting agencies of the government were to include in all contracts a provision obligating the contractor not to discriminate against any worker. Finally, the Executive Order established the Fair Employment Practice Committee under the auspices of the Office of Production Management. Its task was to "receive and investigate complaints of discrimination in violation of the provision of this order and take appropriate steps to redress grievances which it finds valid."[26]

The executive order did not satisfy every MOWM demand. Roosevelt took no action on the request to end segregation and discrimination in the military, a move strongly opposed by Secretary of War Henry L. Stimson and Secretary of the Navy Frank Knox. Perhaps not wishing to overplay their cards, Randolph and White agreed to set aside this request. Nevertheless, both declared Executive Order 8802 a "Second Emancipation Proclamation." It was the first time since Reconstruction that the federal government had created an agency to assist black workers. Some had high hopes for the FEPC. As one committee member, Earl Dickerson, put it a year later, "This order has given new meaning, new vitality to the Emancipation Proclamation. Lincoln's proclamation of 1863 freed us physically; Roosevelt's proclamation of 1941 is the beginning of our economic freedom." Although disappointed at the narrow scope of the Executive Order, the Midwest's main black newspaper, the *Chicago Defender,* shared this sentiment and called the president's order "one of the most significant pronouncements that has been made in the interest of the Negro for more than a century." Mary McLeod Bethune wrote FDR that the executive order "has come to us as a refreshing shower in a thirsty land." According to the NAACP's *Crisis,* "the President [had] done, finally, about all he can be expected to do on this problem."[27]

These favorable opinions were not shared by all African Americans. Traditionally Republican newspapers were skeptical. The *Cleveland Gazette* called the committee "teethless," and the *Philadelphia Tribune* similarly wondered how the FEPC would work without enforcement powers. Equally wary was the *Baltimore Afro-American,* which asserted, "Good stuff, Mr. President, if you can make it stick!" Perhaps the group most disappointed by Randolph's deal with FDR was the MOWM's youth organization, led by Richard Parrish, Bayard Rustin, and others of similar radical bent, which repudiated Executive Order 8802 and demanded that the march proceed as planned in order to secure "full participation in American life."[28]

With all attention on the escalating war in Europe and Asia, the general public's reactions to the FEPC appeared to be more subdued. Major urban newspapers such as the staid *New York Times* carried the story but without analysis or commentary. In Congress politicians tended to ignore the creation of the FEPC. Senator Joseph F. Guffey (D, Pa.) was an exception. He publicly thanked the president for the FEPC and placed the text of Executive Order 8802 into the *Congressional Record.* Representative Arthur W. Mitchell (D, Ill.), the sole African-American legislator in Congress, made a passing reference to the FEPC on 24 July 1941, noting that he was "deeply gratified at the action of the President." Many whites and blacks, it seemed, suspended judgement on the FEPC until the committee members were appointed and began to work.[29]

After haggling with Randolph over the composition of the FEPC, Roosevelt appointed the committee members in August 1941. Mississippi-born Mark Ethridge, the editor of the *Louisville Courier-Journal,* was tapped as FEPC chairman. Ideally, Ethridge, who was a white southern liberal with excellent public relations experience, would ensure that the FEPC would not become too radical while honestly enforcing Executive Order 8802. Three members were from the Midwest. In addition to David Sarnoff, the white president of the Radio Corporation of America, the two African-American members of the committee were from Chicago—Milton P. Webster, Randolph's right-hand man in the BSCP and the March on Washington Movement, and Earl Dickerson, a prominent and outspoken civil rights leader and Democratic alderman. The remaining members were white: AFL president William Green and CIO president Philip Murray. Murray and Green quickly named alternates to the FEPC. Green appointed Frank Fenton, the AFL's director of organization, and Murray named the national director of the CIO, John Brophy. The FEPC's first action was to appoint an executive secretary and his assistant. Believing that an African American would have difficulty dealing with lily-white government agencies, the committee selected a white man, Lawrence W. Cramer, the former governor of the largely black Virgin Islands, as executive secretary in charge of daily operations, and a black man, George M. Johnson, the dean of Howard Law School, as assistant executive secretary.[30]

Although the mere creation of the FEPC was an important historical achievement, the committee's ability to provide significant employment opportunities for black and other minority workers was limited. Initially the committee had a part-time staff of eleven and a modest yearly budget of eighty thousand dollars. In addition, the committee could only handle cases of discrimination against departments and agencies of the United States government concerned with vocational training programs for war production, contracting agencies of the federal government, and employers and labor organizations engaged in war production. The FEPC had no power to deal with firms that did not have government contracts or were not engaged in activities essential to the war effort. Moreover, since the FEPC was created by executive order, it was not able to subpoena, fine, or jail violators of its directives. Instead the committee had to rely on what FEPC officials termed "quiet persuasion" to convince employers to hire workers regardless of race, creed, color, or national origin. The FEPC kept an especially low profile in areas with high racial tensions. The committee sought to redress discrimination complaints without exacerbating social conflicts. If moral suasion failed, hearings, directives, and even revocation of defense contracts were possible. This last step was never taken; no war contract was ever canceled because of racial discrimination. As the committee's last chairman, Malcolm Ross, reflected in his memoirs, "in theory the company's refusal to hire qualified Negro workers should have canceled its entire contract. But suppose American lives are dependent on the production [of that plant's war materials]? Who is to judge the present value of lives against the long-term value of democracy?"[31]

Ultimately, the test that faced the newly created President's Committee on Fair Employment Practice was in the field. Minority workers and civil rights groups were fed up with the empty platitudes that had come from the OPM. They were going to judge the committee by its results, and results would be very hard to come by. Although Executive Order 8802 was a major event, most Americans paid little attention to it. In late 1941 the FEPC had a two-front fight ahead of it. It had to not only attack job discrimination and ease employment barriers but also to raise awareness and win public support. Propaganda and public hearings were weapons of choice in what soon became a major publicity campaign. One of the most critical battlefields for the committee was the Midwest. By late 1941 the region was already feeling the pains of labor shortages due in part to the failure to hire minority workers. The two FEPC members from Chicago (Dickerson and Webster) ensured that the Windy City would be a focal point in the publicity campaign. It was a logical choice for another reason. Chicago had a well-established tradition of civil rights activism upon which the committee could draw. The community networks that the FEPC built in Chicago and its experiences there in 1942 set the tone for all of its subsequent midwestern and national activities.

2. The Publicity Campaign and the Chicago Precedents

THE FEPC's PRIMARY GOAL was to open the war industries for all workers regardless of race, creed, color, or national origin. Its task was daunting as were its initial problems. In addition to the difficulties associated with a small budget and staff, few employers and workers knew of Executive Order 8802 or understood how it applied to them. To solve this problem, the FEPC launched a publicity campaign from late 1941 through the summer of 1942, the centerpiece of which was a series of public hearings held in Los Angeles, Chicago, New York, and Birmingham. These proceedings not only drew attention to job discrimination but also to the new federal agency and Executive Order 8802. The publicity drive was more successful than the committee members could have predicted. By late 1942 few Americans did not know about the FEPC and the policy prohibiting employment discrimination. The public hearings proved to be the best announcement of the president's fair employment policy, and the hearings in Chicago established precedents for its enforcement. By the committee's final hearing in Chicago in 1942, the FEPC had committed itself to the case method system for redressing individual complaints, which was a break from the New Deal's prior reliance on quotas to achieve fair employment. It also adopted the practice of issuing cease and desist orders, modeling itself on other federal agencies such as the National Labor Relations Board.

The FEPC began its publicity campaign by sending posters carrying the text of Executive Order 8802 to federal agencies and employers with defense contracts. Chairman Mark Ethridge initially planned to distribute the seventy-five thousand two-foot square FEPC placards in late December, but events in the Midwest pushed up the timetable. On 30 November 1941, in Columbus, Ohio, sixty-seven white tool and die makers at a Curtiss-Wright Aeronautical plant walked off the job after a single black machinist was placed in their department. After intense negotiations between the FEPC, the OPM's Labor Relations Division, and the plant's management, an agreement was reached. The black worker remained at his post and more were to be hired. Curtiss-Wright also pledged to abide by the federal policy of nondiscrimination and promised to place the FEPC's posters around the plant.[1]

By the week after Pearl Harbor, most major war plants had their FEPC posters. The results were immediate. Scores of companies requested more. One per plant seemed not enough. For instance, a Toledo steel firm wrote the committee in early 1942 requesting six more posters, so "that we can cover each department in our plant." The irony of the FEPC's poster distribution was that the committee's message and actions were not substantially different from those of the NDAC and the OPM. In the cover letter that Ethridge enclosed with each poster, he explained that the FEPC was "sending these to facilitate the cooperation of your workers with you in your efforts to carry out a program of full utilization of all labor resources in defense production."[2] The goal remained full utilization of manpower, and the federal government was still promoting fair employment by word of mouth, not direct

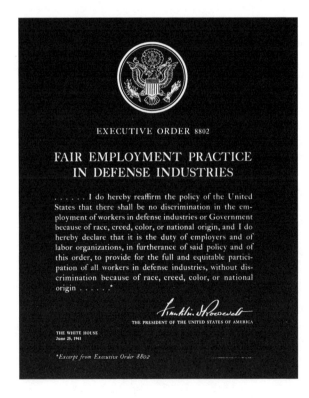

During its initial publicity campaign, the FEPC distributed thousands of posters of Executive Order 8802 to war plants throughout the Midwest and elsewhere in the United States. (National Archives, Records of the Office of War Information, Record Group 208; photograph by Ann Rosener, #208-NP-4NNN-1)

action. Nevertheless, the message was reaching more people, in part because more people were involved with the war effort. Some civil rights leaders, such as Walter White of the NAACP, were encouraged by this approach. Others were not. A typical black response to the FEPC's publicity campaign was to ask, "does it mean much?" The committee had announced its presence but it had not answered critics who feared that it did not have the teeth to back up its pronouncements. In other words, the FEPC had not differentiated itself from the NDAC or the OPM.[3]

To prove to employers and workers that Executive Order 8802 was to be obeyed, and to demonstrate the widespread existence of job discrimination, the FEPC decided to hold a series of public hearings in each region of the nation. The purpose behind the hearings was to collect information, demonstrate the power of the new agency, and attack employment barriers. The targeted cities were Los Angeles, Chicago, New York, and Birmingham. In late 1941 Ethridge dispatched FEPC field representatives to each of the four cities to collect evidence and prepare for the public hearings.[4]

The Los Angeles hearings were first, beginning on 20 October 1941. Generally speaking they were far from a complete success. The FEPC realized its main goal of increasing awareness about the federal government's fair employment policy. The hearings did not do much more than this, however. Bickering among FEPC members during the proceedings and sloppy staff work by Eugene Davidson, an FEPC field investigator and a former MOWM official, hindered the FEPC's cases against the industrialists and union leaders. Moreover, the committee issued no reprimands or directives to the violators of the executive order. As Dickerson and Ethridge stated during the hearings, the FEPC's motives were purely educational. In the absence of pressure on individual employers and unions, no one felt immediately compelled to drop color bars. In particular, the FEPC did not convince two major aircraft companies, North American and Vultee, to alter their unfair employment policies. It did not even persuade Vultee's president to retract his statement that "only members of the Caucasian race" would be employed at his plant. Thus the FEPC did not reap many rewards from its initial hearing, and perhaps damaged its fledgling reputation because of the conflicts within the agency.[5]

In Chicago the FEPC developed a better method of holding hearings. What happened there on 21 and 22 January and 4 April 1942, in effect, became the model for all subsequent FEPC hearings in the Midwest and elsewhere. The Windy City was an excellent site to begin attacking employment discrimination in the Midwest. Because Chicago was one of the region's main industrial centers, the committee directly reached many important defense contractors and their employees. With two members from Chicago, the FEPC could count on loyal contacts for accurate information about the city's war

industries. Earl Dickerson and Milton Webster were extremely well-connect-
ed. Dickerson, the Democratic alderman from the second ward, a member
of the Chicago NAACP, and the president of the Chicago Urban League, had
strong ties with the city's elite professional leadership. Webster, the vice president of the BSCP, had established networks among working-class African
Americans in the 1920s. There were several additional organizations and
activists who were willing to work with Dickerson and Webster and hence
with the FEPC. Chicago had a tradition of civil rights activism that came from
the black community and from the labor movement, particularly the CIO.
Several unions, especially those with radical leadership like the United Packinghouse Workers of America, had long-standing fair employment policies
and a history of supporting civil rights. The use of community contacts, including union leaders, liberal professionals, and local civil rights activists,
made the FEPC's job much easier and more productive. After two hearings,
the committee calculated marked progress in Chicago, demonstrating the
possibility for change on the home front during World War II.[6]

War in Europe had reshaped Chicago once before. On the eve of World
War I, the black population of Chicago was about forty-five thousand. Black
workers were concentrated in service jobs, such as waiters, cooks, maids,
porters, and janitors. Factory work had been generally off-limits as white
employers and workers upheld job color bars. This changed after war broke
out in 1914. As Chicago industries started to produce war matériel, migrants
began to flow into the city. War jobs attracted over fifty thousand southern
African Americans. By 1920 Chicago's black population was 110,000. Most
new black workers were confined to unskilled and domestic service jobs, but
an estimated ten thousand obtained semiskilled industrial work, many of
them in Chicago's stockyards.[7]

After the war, African-American workers experienced economic displace-
ment, although black women won a permanent place in garment factories
and black men remained an integral part of the steel and meatpacking industries. Blacks increased their industrial numbers slowly during the 1920s
as Chicago's industries maintained their need for workers. Job expansion was
also a result of the work of the Chicago Urban League, the YMCA, and the
Illinois Free Employment Bureau, which helped with placement. Equally
important were the responses of white workers and employers to the intro-
duction of blacks. Despite the fact that city-wide racial tensions were extremely intense following the First World War and that Chicago experienced a
major race riot in 1919, industrial race relations were often amicable. In its
massive study on the causes and consequences of the 1919 riot, the Chicago
Commission on Race Relations concluded that "racial friction [was] not
pronounced in Chicago industries."[8]

The Great Depression increased job rivalry between whites and blacks. The dramatic industrial downturn hurt all Chicago workers, but as laborers made their way down the economic ladder blacks were pushed to a lower rung than whites. New Deal work projects did not immediately help many unemployed black workers. Chicago employers hired whites to perform "Negro jobs." During the 1930s, hotels and restaurants, for example, replaced black bell-hops and waiters with whites. As J. G. St. Clair Drake and Horace R. Cayton demonstrated in their study of Chicago, black workers were "losing out" in the intense competition of the Depression years.[9]

What made Chicago and Illinois somewhat unique was the response to job bias during the Great Depression. Civil rights organizations in Illinois joined a national trend during the 1930s and struggled to break down the color barriers to employment through "Don't Buy Where You Can't Work" campaigns. They also strove to create equity for blacks on work programs through state fair employment practice laws. In January 1933 the Chicago branch of the NAACP had African-American State Representative Charles J. Jenkins of Cook County introduce a bill to prohibit "discrimination and intimidation on account of race or color in employment under contracts for public buildings or public works." The bill carried a penalty for violators. If the Illinois secretary of state determined that a company had discriminated it could lose its charter of incorporation. Although in 1933 the Illinois legislature passed the Jenkins bill and Democratic Governor Henry Horner signed it into law, it had little practical impact.[10]

Despite instances of unfair employment practices within New Deal programs, by the mid-1930s black Chicagoans in general benefitted greatly from them, particularly the NYA, PWA, and WPA. As one black leader wrote, "Mr. Roosevelt gave us work and bread. Our people will respond by giving Mr. Roosevelt most of their votes." Indeed they did. From 1932 to 1936 the number of black Chicagoans who voted for Roosevelt increased by 132 percent, illustrating the dramatic shift in African-American voting to the Democratic Party during the FDR years.[11]

It was not New Deal relief programs but the start of another war in Europe that revitalized Chicago's economy. The return of prosperity did not immediately help most black Chicagoans. To investigate the situation, in January 1940 Governor Henry Horner appointed the Illinois Commission on the Condition of Urban Colored Population. A year later, the Horner Commission spent two days in Chicago interviewing city leaders. Philip Flum of the Illinois State Employment Service told the commission that job placements were up for 1940 because of new defense contracts. In August, Flum's office placed 4,217 workers; 719 (17 percent) were black. In September 1940, 5,071 workers got jobs through the state employment service; 795 (16 percent)

were black. However, according to a 1941 survey of 358 Chicago defense industries, two-thirds refused to hire African-American workers. Analysis of
relief rolls also demonstrated that more whites than blacks were receiving
jobs. Leo M. Lyons, the head of the Chicago Relief Administration, reported
that the percentage of blacks on relief rolls was increasing despite the economic boom. Yet in general fewer people were on relief. From November 1939
to November 1940, the total relief population decreased 15 percent, from
229,305 to 193,721. However, Lyons also pointed out that 47 percent of those
on relief in November 1940 were black, roughly 5 percent higher than it was
the previous November, while the percentage of whites on relief had dropped
5 percent to 53 percent.[12]

In *Black Metropolis,* J. G. St. Clair Drake and Horace R. Cayton argued that
by 1940 black Chicagoans had hit a "job ceiling." Drake and Cayton used
Robert Weaver's test for fair employment to calculate the effects of discrimination. They reasoned that if all things remained equal during the recovery
period of the early 1940s, blacks should have attained their proportional share
of jobs. In Chicago in 1940 there should have been 18,500 skilled black workers. The census showed only 8,500. Similarly, there should have been 11,500
unskilled black workers. The Census Bureau calculated the actual number
to be over twenty-five thousand. Looking back at the two previous censuses,
Drake and Cayton concluded that the job ceiling had existed since the First
World War and had solidified by 1940.[13]

On the eve of Pearl Harbor, the employment problems in the Chicago
metropolitan area were difficult for African Americans. Skilled blacks rarely
found work in the city. African-American plumbers and steamfitters, for
example, were denied permits to work on the federally-funded Cabrini defense housing complex. The story of Quincy D. Jones, a skilled African-American carpenter, illustrates the problems faced by blacks in the building trades.
Jones began his career as a carpenter in the 1920s, and managed to practice
his trade during the Depression by working on WPA jobs in Chicago. In January 1941, on the recommendation of Jones's union, the Illinois State Employment Service offered him a construction job in Wilmington, a small town just
south of Chicago. Jones took the position, but when he arrived for work the
personnel manager of the construction company told him to go home because he would not "tolerate a Negro working with whites on this job!" For
Jones, returning to Chicago provided no relief from discrimination. As the
Chicago Defender editorialized, "many Negro workers qualified and available
for skilled positions on the job are being excluded" from defense jobs.[14]

Although employment discrimination was rampant in the Chicago area,
there were exceptions. In March 1941 Howard D. Gould of the Chicago Urban League reported that thirty-four city firms that had previously denied
blacks jobs were now employing them. According to Gould, this was due to

the tightening of the labor market and the activities of the Chicago Urban League. Most Chicago-area employers, however, opposed the idea of equal opportunity. In Melrose Park, a Chicago suburb, General Motors's Buick airplane engine plant expanded at a tremendous rate, but company managers refused to allow any blacks or Jews to work there. Gould worked for months to open that plant to blacks. He collected evidence from the Illinois Institute of Technology to show that trained African Americans were being denied jobs. When Gould could not get any response from Buick, he contacted the OPM's Negro Employment and Training Branch, headed by Robert C. Weaver. When Weaver's office failed to relieve the Buick situation, a few black leaders in Chicago suspected Buick of being on a secret OPM "exemption list" of employers who did not have to hire minorities. Because William Knudsen, the former president of GM, was the agency's codirector, the *Chicago Defender* speculated that Buick was off-limits to Weaver's office. Whether the exemption list existed or was a figment of a conspiratorial imagination, the OPM did not alter discrimination at the Melrose Park Buick plant or in Chicago.[15]

Some African Americans in Chicago responded to discrimination in defense industries with organized protest. In late 1940 Walter White wrote a letter to all NAACP branches calling for demonstrations against job bias in defense factories. On 14 February 1941 over a thousand people, white and black, paraded through the streets of Chicago in a march heralded as a "Demonstration for Democracy." Most local civil rights groups and some CIO locals participated. A few months later some activists formed the Chicago unit of the March on Washington Movement under the leadership of Dr. Charles Wesley Burton, the midwestern regional director of the MOWM. Although it had over twenty-five hundred members, the Chicago MOWM branch was not particularly successful. There was some friction between the Chicago MOWM and more established (and less radical) organizations, such as the NAACP. According to Roy Wilkins of the NAACP, Burton's "high-handed" style drove away local activists.[16]

Although black Chicagoans may have been wary of the local MOWM branch, they appeared satisfied with the creation of the Fair Employment Practice Committee. The editorials in the *Chicago Defender* were positive. One writer congratulated Roosevelt and "our brilliant leader A. Philip Randolph" for producing "one of the most significant pronouncements that has been made in the interests of the Negro for more than a century." Chicagoans, especially labor activists, had more to cheer about when FDR appointed two of their own to the committee. Frank McCulloch, a white labor lawyer and a liberal Democrat, was so inspired by the creation of the FEPC that he helped form a local organization to further the goals embodied in Executive Order 8802. The Fair Employment Practices Council of Metropolitan Chicago (Chicago FEP Council) was established in November 1941. Two white and two black men held the leadership positions. Its chairman was Dr. James M. Yard of the National Conference of Christians and Jews; McCulloch was vice chairman; Earl Dickerson was honorary chairman; Howard Gould of the Chicago Urban League was the secretary. The Chicago FEP Council seemingly took its charge from a *Crisis* editorial in August 1941 that called on local branches of the NAACP, offices of the Urban League, and other interested parties to pressure state employment offices and collect evidence of discrimination for the FEPC. From November 1941 to April 1942 the Chicago FEP Council did this and more.[17]

On 21 July 1941 the Illinois legislature passed and Republican Governor Dwight H. Green signed into law the nation's first general fair employment practices statute. In language similar to Executive Order 8802, the law—the author of which was again Representative Jenkins—banned discrimination in the employment or training of any person "on account of race, color, or creed." It also assigned a fine of not less than one hundred dollars and not more than five hundred dollars for violators. The fair employment act's one failing was that it provided no investigatory staff or adjustment agency. In late 1941 the Chicago FEP Council asked Francis B. Murphy, the head of the Illinois State Department of Labor, to assume the administration of the act. Despite plaintive letters and long-distance telephone conversations, vice chairman McCulloch was unable to secure any assistance from the Labor Department's director, who, McCulloch finally concluded, was "indifferent to the conditions" of Chicago's black Americans.[18]

Hope for governmental redress against employment discrimination in Chicago thus fell to the president's Committee on Fair Employment Practice. On 20 December 1941 Earl Dickerson wrote to McCulloch informing him of the opening of a Chicago FEPC office to prepare for the January 1941 hearings. Located in the Civic Opera Building, the office was initially operated by G. James Fleming, an African American from Philadelphia who had edited the traditionally Republican black newspaper, the *Philadelphia Tribune*, and who had been a member of Gunnar Myrdal's research group. The Chicago FEP Council wasted no time in collecting evidence for the hearings as did the FEPC. Fleming's office discovered that many Chicago businesses ignored Executive Order 8802. In December 1941 Fleming visited DuPont's Kankakee Ordnance Plant to check on an agreement that the OPM's Robert Weaver had arranged with the management to hire black workers. Fleming quickly discovered that DuPont was not living up to its pledge. When confronted, plant manager George Miller told Fleming that he talked "too much of the President's executive order." Miller stated further that he would decide when and where blacks were to be hired.[19]

The day the Japanese attacked Pearl Harbor, representatives from Fleming's office met with the Fair Employment Practices Council of Metropolitan Chicago to coordinate efforts. The meeting was successful in that the FEPC enlisted the council's full support. Yet the two organizations clashed over the issue of who was to lead the attack on employment discrimination. To the FEPC officials it seemed that the local group was too eager to help. Howard Gould wanted "to run away with the show." The council's secretary, Fleming reported, was "obsessed with the idea" that the council was to help gather evidence for the hearings. The FEPC needed that assistance but it wanted to take the lead and have the local organization merely assist in the hearings and follow-up afterward.[20]

Despite these minor differences, which were eventually ironed out according to the FEPC's liking, everyone concerned about fair employment in Chicago understood that the hearings would be of critical importance. The FEPC's work was essential for African-American, if not national, morale. No doubt the committee also wanted to redeem itself after its unsatisfactory efforts in Los Angeles. A few months before the Chicago hearings Milton P. Webster had told one of his friends that if the FEPC did not break down some employment barriers in Chicago, and if President Roosevelt did not give the FEPC his full support, "the committee will have to check out." Fortunately for the committee the hearings were a smashing success.[21]

On 19 January 1942, in city council chambers, Mayor Edward J. Kelly opened the Chicago hearings by welcoming the FEPC. In attendance for the committee were chairman Mark Ethridge, John Brophy, David Sarnoff, Lawrence Cramer, Frank Fenton, and Earl Dickerson. Ethridge called the Chicago hearings to order in front of an overflow crowd of two hundred people. In his opening statement Ethridge pointed out that "to draw lines of employment on any basis except that of fitness is to deny ourselves the full use of our manpower." He made it clear that those who "do not fall into line" with Executive Order 8802 were committing something "close to treason." The chairman also explained that the FEPC had come to Chicago in part because the Illinois law prohibiting employment discrimination had gone unenforced. The statements of civil rights leaders, including Howard Gould and Harry I. Barron, an educator and the executive secretary of the Bureau on Jewish Employment Problems, followed. In an example of black-Jewish cooperation, together they detailed the problems of minority workers in training and job placement and urged the FEPC to take "positive steps" against discriminatory hiring practices.[22]

The FEPC had asked eleven companies to attend the hearings, six from Chicago and five from Milwaukee. The first day of the hearings was devoted to the Windy City's employers. The Stewart-Warner, the Majestic Radio and Television, and the Studebaker corporations all failed to employ African Americans. Stewart-Warner's personnel director, R. W. Mathers, denied the charge of discrimination. The committee presented *prima facie* evidence that none of the company's eight thousand employees were black. Agreeing with the FEPC's findings, Mathers admitted that the company was in error and pledged that they would comply with Executive Order 8802 in every respect. H. R. Parkins, the counsel for Majestic Radio and Television, and H. A. Gates, the company's president, also promised to end unfair employment practices, agreeing that they had discriminated in the past. Gates discharged his employment manager to rectify the situation.[23]

Studebaker presented a difficult case because of some apparent lying by its attorney, Arthur A. Sullivan, and its industrial relations director, Walter S. Gundeck. They claimed that the reason that Studebaker required potential employees to identify race on job applications was not to facilitate discrimination. Rather, they asserted, the FBI had recommended this policy to gather information on potential employees. This answer to the FEPC's charge of discrimination disrupted the committee's case and delayed action against Studebaker until the FEPC executive secretary, Lawrence Cramer, contacted FBI director J. Edgar Hoover. A few months later Hoover responded to Cramer's inquiry and "categorically denied that the FBI recommend[ed] this procedure or that it or any of its agents recommended it to the Studebaker Company."[24]

Buick too seemed to lie to the FEPC. In September 1941 H. H. Curtice, general manager of the Melrose plant, had reported that his factory was complying fully with Executive Order 8802. *Prima facie* evidence submitted during the hearings revealed otherwise. Harry Barron reported that Buick refused to take qualified black trainees from the Illinois Institute of Technology (IIT). Barron backed his accusation with statistics that were corroborated by the FEPC's own numbers. Of 309 recent Buick hires who trained at IIT, forty-six (15 percent) had been Jewish but none were black. Buick's personnel manager, Carl E. Wooliever, admitted that the company asked for religion and race on its applications. Wooliever defended the policy, saying that it was to get "a picture of the men" they were interviewing. When asked why he had not hired the best student among the IIT graduates—who was an African American—Wooliever coolly replied that it was "just one of those things that could happen" when hiring a large group of people. At no point during the three hours of questioning did Buick's representative admit discriminating against blacks, and he continued to proclaim that the plant was operating within the executive order's intent.[25]

The remaining two Chicago firms, Bearse Manufacturing and Simpson Construction, both agreed to stop discriminating against Jews. Bearse's employment manager, James H. Erickson, promised to end the company's practice of specifying "Gentiles" on advertisements for power machine operators. Erickson said that he had been "foolish" in believing that Jewish operators could not work well on "heavy canvas goods." Simpson Construction, which had a number of Jewish and black workers in the field, refused to hire them in the office. Elmer Hansen, the company's president, promised the committee that he would instruct his personnel manager to allow all people to apply for jobs, not only "Gentiles [and] Protestants."[26]

The next day's cases against the five Milwaukee firms went quickly, in part because only four appeared. While attorneys for the Heil Company, the Nordberg Manufacturing Company, the A. O. Smith Corporation, and the Harnishfager Corporation came to the Chicago hearings, the Allis-Chalmers Corporation sent no representative, although members of the Communist-led UAW-CIO Local 248 attended to support the FEPC's actions. At the time, Allis-Chalmers was shut down because of a plantwide strike, and its management was in Washington, D.C., conferring with OPM directors Hillman and Knudsen in an attempt to settle the dispute with Local 248. Another aspect of the Milwaukee cases that expedited the proceedings was the fact that the companies shared a common problem—all refused to hire African Americans. The FEPC treated all five corporations in a similar fashion, demonstrating discrimination through *prima facie* evidence rather than by individual complaints. As soon as the committee dispensed with the Milwaukee cases it quickly moved to end the hearings.[27]

Unlike the Los Angeles hearings of October 1941, which ended without any directives from the FEPC, in Chicago Ethridge gave directives to each party. Every company—whether it admitted its past wrongs or not—was directed to change its employment policies to comply fully with Executive Order 8802. They were to "cease and desist" from submitting any further discriminatory orders from employment agencies. They were directed to give written notice to all employment agencies, including the United States Employment Service, of their new willingness to accept minority workers. Finally, each company was to file monthly reports with the FEPC demonstrating its progress in hiring without regard to race, creed, color, or national origin.[28]

By issuing these demands the FEPC improved over what happened in Los Angeles. The committee sent a clear message and blazed a path for advancing employment practices. In fact the Chicago hearings had been more successful all around. The committee's local contacts and the Chicago office's excellent staff work helped produce incontrovertible cases. Although there were recalcitrant employers such as Buick, the FEPC managed to alter the employment policies of five of the eleven companies at the hearings. Moreover, except for one incident, the bickering among the members of the FEPC did not resurface. Civil rights groups were pleased with the FEPC's results. Walter White wrote the committee to express "congratulations and appreciation" for the FEPC's directives to the eleven war plants. White felt that further follow-up action "should have very salutary effects." Even the conservative *Chicago Tribune* praised the FEPC and hoped that it would "assemble its facts with care and present them to the President forcefully," adding that "the abuses complained of make a mockery of our claim to be fighting a war for the four freedoms." "All editorials on the Chicago findings," an FEPC survey concluded, "were sympathetic with the purpose of Executive Order 8802 and the Committee."[29]

After the Chicago hearings, Mark Ethridge, who was tired of leading the agency with the "small[est] staff with the lowest budget in the government," resigned as chairman. Despite the shake-up of the committee and the addition of Malcolm S. MacLean of the Hampton Institute as the committee's second chairman, the FEPC wasted no time in holding the next set of hearings in New York from 19–20 February 1942. Less than a month later, the committee was back in Chicago to challenge two labor unions, the Chicago Journeymen Plumbers' Union Local 130 (AFL) and the Steamfitters' Protective Association Local 597 (AFL), which together made up the Pipe Trades Council of Cook County (PTC). This return visit to the Windy City was not part of the original publicity campaign. Local civil rights groups had called the committee back to redress individual complaints from several black plumbers and to enforce equal employment in the construction trades.[30]

The executive order that created the FEPC charged it with the responsibility of fighting discrimination practiced not only by employers but also by labor unions. The FEPC took this charge seriously and included unions as a part of its 1941–42 publicity campaign. In October 1941 FEPC chairman Ethridge spoke before the annual convention of the American Federation of Labor. He pleaded with the delegates to give the FEPC their "full support," and criticized them, stating that "there are still many unions which bar their fellowmen because of color. I would not be frank at all with you if I did not say that most of them are yours." Ethridge's speech earned him the praise of many influential civil rights leaders and newspapers. The *Chicago Defender* commended him for his "stand on the question of work opportunity for the Negro" and urged him to broaden the committee's struggle against union discrimination.[31]

The AFL did not receive Ethridge's speech in the same manner. At the 1941 convention all attempts to liberalize the federation's stand on racial discrimination were defeated. Convention delegates rejected a proposal by A. Philip Randolph to establish a permanent committee within the federation "to deal with discrimination on account of race, color, religion, and national origin." Like the other fair employment board that he helped to create, Randolph wanted this one to conduct investigations and hold hearings, especially in cases where AFL locals refused to admit black workers. William Green, the AFL president and an original FEPC member, attacked the proposal, which led to its defeat. William L. Hutcheson, the president of the carpenter union, also opposed it, bluntly telling Randolph to "mind his own business." Ethridge's words were similarly assailed at the convention and afterward. A few months later the *American Federationist* reprinted his convention speech. Editors added a disclaimer below the article stating that "we are reluctant to take issue with [Ethridge]. But in order that the record may be kept straight on a matter of vast importance it must be pointed out that his implication that discrimination by unions against Negro workers is widespread is not supported by the facts. The American Federation of Labor has always been most vigorously opposed to discrimination against any person because of race, color, creed, or national origin."[32]

During the early years of World War II it was AFL policy to espouse fair employment rhetoric at the national level while not practicing it at the local level. Agreements to create fair employment could be made but were rarely put into action. Until the creation of the FEPC the federal government did little to change the situation. Some government officials even helped to maintain the color bar. For example, OPM director Sidney Hillman's man in Chicago, Joseph Keenan, a native of the city, helped Weaver to orchestrate the fair employment deal with DuPont's Kankakee Ordnance Plant in late 1941. Before he was on the OPM's staff Keenan had been the secretary of the Chicago local of the International Brotherhood of Electrical Workers (AFL), which barred black workers from membership. As labor consultant for the OPM, Keenan looked the other way when Kankakee failed to live up to its agreement and in general allowed the construction unions to continue to bar minorities.[33]

African-American workers' problems with the AFL worsened in late 1941 when the OPM authored a stabilization agreement with the federation's Building and Construction Trades Department. The agreement, which affected eight hundred thousand workers, sought to determine wage and hour standards, forbade work stoppages, and otherwise stabilized labor relations to speed up the construction of defense plants. In return for no-strike pledges, the OPM gave the AFL a virtual monopoly over the construction industry. Since most AFL unions held closed shop contracts and maintained color bars, the pact locked out black workers. Civil rights organizations such as the NAACP complained about the stabilization agreement, but without result. Walter White even asked Attorney General Francis Biddle to have Thurman Arnold, the head of the Anti-Trust Division of the Justice Department, investigate the "monopolistic practices under the virtual closed shop granted by the Office of Production Management." Neither Biddle or Arnold took action. Roy Wilkins appealed to William Green, the AFL's leader, to stop the practice of discrimination in the AFL's construction unions. Green rejected the premise of Wilkins's letter and wrote back that "the American Federation of Labor has led in the fight against race discrimination." The AFL head also took the opportunity to suggest that the NAACP "remain neutral" in labor struggles between the AFL and CIO.[34]

Without support from the AFL, the OPM, or the United States Justice

Department, civil rights activists and black workers turned to the FEPC for help. In February 1942 the leaders of the Chicago-based American Consolidated Trades Council, an organization of black plumbers and steamfitters, sent a telegram to Earl Dickerson demanding FEPC assistance. The council also sent affidavits from four of its members—Edward L. Doty, Alex Dunlap, John Hopkins, and Harry Murphy—alleging discrimination. Because of closed shop agreements with the Pipe Trades Council, black plumbers and steamfitters could not work at the Great Lakes Naval Training Station, which was expanding its facilities. Dickerson and the black Chicagoan Elmer Henderson, who had replaced G. James Fleming as the head of the Chicago sub-office, requested that chairman MacLean set a hearing date to air the four grievances against the Pipe Trades Council. According to Henderson, the problem before the committee was how to force "the unions to either admit Negroes into their memberships or give clearance to Negroes for work on defense projects." Because of past failures in dealing with the union, Henderson suggested a hearing to "be devoted almost exclusively to the matter of the unions involved."[35]

The second round of Chicago FEPC hearings was held on 4 April 1942 at city hall. Earl Dickerson led the proceeding, which revealed in detail the tribulations of Chicago's black plumbers and steamfitters. The first witness was Edward L. Doty, an African-American plumber. As Doty explained, in 1939 the Pipe Trades Council had made a proposal to allow two "colored" delegates as representatives in the council, and to thereby allow blacks to work on union jobs. The catch was that black construction workers had to promise only to work on buildings owned or rented by blacks. The black plumbers and steamfitters of Chicago rejected the PTC proposal. As a result, black craftsmen remained outside the council and thus could not find jobs on defense or city projects.[36]

To obtain the Pipe Trades Council position, Dickerson called William Quirk, the business agent of the Chicago Journeyman Plumbers' Union Local 130 and an influential member of the PTC. Previous testimony had indicated that Quirk steadfastly opposed integrating his union. He had allegedly said, "I don't give a damn about the President and the OPM either. I am going to run my business." Such a position angered Dickerson, who argued with and attacked Quirk, who remained unshaken. When Dickerson asked if Quirk would lower the color bar, Quirk answered that until the black plumbers and steamfitters accepted the council's 1939 proposal, only those "who may be passing for white" would work on union jobs. Milton Webster provided follow-up questions. He wanted to know why the union refused black applicants. Quirk explained that until such a time when there were no unemployed white union members, whites would "come first."[37]

The FEPC similarly questioned Wilson Frankland, the president of the Steamfitters' Protective Association Local 597. Unlike Quirk, Frankland seemed less hostile to the idea of job integration. He maintained, however, that his hands were tied because of the "attitudes of the rank and file." Lieutenant Commander G. L. Lindeberg of the Great Lakes Naval Training Station made a similar argument. Lindeberg had not attempted to hire blacks because of his fear of "preventing the work from going forward." Moreover, as Lindeberg volunteered to the committee, he thought that the station was doing well in that it had "more than [its] quota of workmen of different races and creeds." At this Dickerson retorted, "there is no quota of employment, so that if the Naval Station has been operating under the theory of quotas, they must in the light of this order stop it." To Dickerson, Executive Order 8802 meant "that racial groups should not be quotaized on any basis whatsoever, but that these considerations of color should not be considered in the matter of employment."[38]

As in the previous Chicago hearings, the FEPC issued directives and cease and desist orders. The Steamfitters' Protective Association Local 597 and the Chicago Journeymen Plumbers' Union Local 130 were to stop discriminating against black craftsmen and permit them to be hired on city and defense jobs. They were also to report monthly to the committee, although it appears that they never did.[39]

In mid-April 1942 the FEPC conducted its last scheduled hearing in Birmingham, Alabama, which was notable for the courage of the committee's black members, whose lives were threatened during the proceedings, and for the racially conservative statements made by the former FEPC chairman, Mark Ethridge. Although the Birmingham hearing convinced only one business to break its employment color barriers (the Brecon Bag Company, owned by Coca-Cola), this hearing did capture the attention of the national press. Thus the FEPC's trip south had achieved its basic purpose and more. In fact, all of the committee's actions in 1941 and 1942 appeared to expand awareness of Executive Order 8802 and the agency set up to enforce it. Yet the campaign was more than a publicity coup. The hearings, particularly those in Chicago, set numerous precedents for future FEPC actions. After the first Chicago hearings, the committee adopted the methods of other established agencies, such as the National Labor Relations Board, and used directives and cease and desist orders. After the steamfitters and plumbers hearings the federal involvement in equal opportunity moved away from Weaver's quota system based on *prima facie* evidence of discrimination. As Dickerson explained, equal opportunity for the FEPC had to do with individual cases rather than numbers. Thus after completing the 1942 FEPC hearing schedule the committee began to function on a case method basis, relying less on *prima facie* evidence of discrimination and more on individual complaints.[40]

The FEPC's publicity campaign had generated tremendous controversy and thereby brought attention to Executive Order 8802, the FEPC, and the plight of minority workers. Northern and midwestern civil rights activists were pleased with the committee's actions. Shortly after the Birmingham hearings, Lester Granger, the head of the National Urban League, wrote to President Roosevelt that "the Fair Employment Practice Committee has now established national prestige that will enhance its effectiveness." Walter White praised the FEPC for "crack[ing] down" on the eleven firms in the Chicago area. The committee also found support among the radically left leaders of the Chicago Industrial Union Council (CIO), who wrote Chairman MacLean that they were "in full accord with the decision made by your committee" in the steamfitters and plumbers cases. The *Chicago Defender* also expressed its satisfaction, commenting that the FEPC "has given hope to millions of Negro workers whose morale would have been irreparably shattered were it not for their faith in the eventual realization of the Committee's main objective." This faith would be tested during the turbulent months of early 1943 when President Roosevelt reorganized the FEPC.[41]

3. Ruin and Rebirth: The Creation of the Second FEPC

As FEPC MEMBERS celebrated the first anniversary of Executive Order 8802 in the spring of 1942, they planned to expand operations. Wanting to build upon the publicity campaign, the FEPC scheduled a new round of hearings focusing on sixteen southern railroads and on employment practices in several midwestern cities, including Cleveland, Detroit, and St. Louis. The Midwest was a priority because, despite the committee's actions, job bias remained entrenched in the region. Because of economic necessity and the FEPC's activities, by the middle of 1942 black employment was generally increasing in all skill classifications, but barriers remained. Little over half—144,583 out of the 282,245—of prospective war-related job openings were for whites only. The situation in the Midwest was even worse than in the South. In Texas over nine thousand of the 17,435 openings (52 percent) for defense jobs were barred to African Americans. In Michigan the figure was 22,042 out of 26,904 (82 percent); in Ohio, 29,242 out of 34,861 (84 percent); and in Indiana, 9,331 out of 9,979 (94 percent!).[1] The FEPC had to expand its operations in the Midwest and elsewhere, because, as A. Philip Randolph pointed out, the committee had only "scratched the surface." Much more work remained.[2]

FEPC chairman Malcolm MacLean fully believed that President Roosevelt supported the planned activities in the Midwest and in the South. Owing in part to this belief, the committee members asked FDR to issue a new executive order giving the FEPC an expanded jurisdiction and the power to subpoena persons and records. They wanted additional legal means to adjust difficult cases. Moreover, FEPC officials wanted a larger budget and staff. A million-dollar appropriation would provide for twelve regional offices, modeled on the one led by G. James Fleming in Chicago, in order to facilitate the FEPC's work, particularly preparation for hearings in the Midwest. Many groups, including black civil rights organizations, supported the idea of a revamped FEPC. On its first anniversary, Walter White wired Roosevelt and urged him to "continue standing unequivocally behind the Fair Employment Practice Committee" and to "increase its machinery and authority to make more effective its edicts against discrimination." Lester Granger of the National Urban League made a similar request, calling on Roosevelt to invest the committee "with even greater powers in order to speed up the process that democratic Americans ardently desire." Some midwesterners shared White's and Granger's opinions. The *Chicago Defender* argued that broadened powers for the FEPC would "not only crack the walls of discrimination in the basic industries" but would "by the same token administer a much needed hypodermic to American democracy."[3]

When word reached the White House about the proposed increases in budget, staff, and powers, Paul V. McNutt, the head of the War Manpower Commission (WMC), and several other administration officials acted to thwart the FEPC's expansion plan and to rein in the committee. McNutt, a former Democratic governor from Indiana and a one-time presidential hopeful, opposed the FEPC. Although a New Dealer, McNutt was not liberal on racial matters. He was also an able but ambitious administrator wary of any infringement on his power. To him, the committee, which also dealt with manpower issues, was such an encroachment. To weaken the FEPC and prevent it from taking any additional powers, on 29 May 1942 McNutt requested that Roosevelt transfer the FEPC to the War Manpower Commission and thereby place it under his authority. After conferring with Harold D. Smith, the budget director and presidential confidant, and Wayne Coy of the Office of Emergency Management, President Roosevelt denied the FEPC's request for a new executive order and on 30 July 1942 transferred the committee to McNutt's War Manpower Commission. The formal WMC-FEPC agreement that followed explained that all policies were to be agreed upon and formulated by the committee and McNutt.[4]

Why Roosevelt made this move is not readily apparent. It was common for Dr. New Deal to reorganize his agencies, and perhaps Dr. Win-the-War was doing more of the same. In January 1942 FDR had replaced the Office of Production Management with the more powerful War Production Board, and later in April he had created the War Manpower Commission to deal with all issues of wartime employment. Perhaps the transfer was a part of the general reshuffling of the war agencies. It also seems reasonable that FDR wanted to clip the FEPC's wings in an effort to mitigate the level of racial tensions that had been rising nationally. In February there had been a racial incident in Detroit over the Sojourner Truth Homes, a federally funded public housing complex. Also in 1942 whites and blacks clashed on southern army bases. White southerners' racial animosity reached a peak with the FEPC's

Birmingham hearings. White supremacy groups, such as the Ku Klux Klan, and racially motivated violence were on the rise in the South as well as the Midwest. Presidential advisors gave Roosevelt comparable reports. In April 1942 FDR sent Supreme Court Justice Hugo Black to Birmingham and Mobile to look into the situation, and he confirmed the existence of heightened racial tensions. Some historians have thought that Roosevelt attempted to assuage the growing racial tensions by putting the FEPC under the careful watch of McNutt, so that it might not further disturb southern sensibilities.[5]

At first it was not clear what the transfer meant. If the goal was to rein in the FEPC, Roosevelt hid his intentions well. During his 7 August 1942 press conference a reporter asked, "what [was] the significance of the subordination of the Fair Employment Practices Committee to the War Manpower Commission?" Roosevelt responded, "I don't know. I doubt very much if there has been any subordinating of the Fair [Employment] Practices to the other." A. Philip Randolph and Walter White both objected to the transfer. Randolph called the move "a complete surrender to Ku Klux spirit." Midwestern reactions to the transfer were mixed. An editorialist in the *Cleveland Call and Post* wrote, "now that this agency has been put under the Man Power Commission [*sic*] which has branches throughout the nation, it should be possible to more vigorously attack the problem of racial discrimination in employment." Others expressed some misgivings at Roosevelt's action. In a letter to FDR, Ashby B. Carter, the Chicago branch president of the National Alliance of Postal Employees, wrote of his concern that the FEPC had been "shorn of its independence." He called on the president to "assure us" that Executive Order 8802 had not been thwarted.[6]

Most members of the FEPC opposed the move. Earl Dickerson thought McNutt would hamper the committee's work and asked his friends, including Frank McCulloch of the Fair Employment Practices Council of Metropolitan Chicago, to write McNutt asking him not to limit FEPC activities. Chairman Malcolm MacLean shared Dickerson's concern and told the president's secretary, Marvin McIntyre, that the transfer had been a reversal of policy "without discussion or warning." MacLean warned that African Americans and other minorities would see the transfer as a negation of Executive Order 8802, as the return of "discrimination as usual" to appease Southern whites, and as a sign of desertion by FDR. The FEPC field representative in the South, John Beecher, went public with his anger, writing in the magazine *Common Ground* that the transfer was similar to the "deal of 1876," when the North "let the South settle 'the Negro problem' in traditional ways."[7]

On 17 August 1942 President Roosevelt issued a press release to reassure the FEPC and civil rights leaders that the transfer was intended to "strengthen—not to submerge—the Committee, and to reinvigorate—not to repeal—Executive Order 8802." Under the WMC's aegis the FEPC would have access to its regional offices and the "friendly supervision of the Chairman of the Commission, Mr. McNutt, whose grasp of the whole problem of manpower utilization will be of great assistance to the Committee on Fair Employment Practice." By the winter of 1942–43, however, McNutt's "friendly supervision" had made it impossible for the committee to function effectively.[8]

McNutt slashed the FEPC's operating budget, denied the committee access to WMC field offices, refused to hire more FEPC staff workers, and failed to attend any committee meetings even when his presence was requested. More importantly, McNutt did not support FEPC activities. In November 1942 chairman MacLean referred the Chicago plumbers' and steamfitters' cases to McNutt. The FEPC wanted him to intervene directly and force the unions to abide by Executive Order 8802. No such action was taken. In December 1942 the FEPC issued cease and desist directives to the Capital Transit Company of Washington, D.C., which discriminated against blacks. McNutt and several White House officials became enraged at the FEPC's order, which to them demonstrated that the committee was going too far in its fight for fair employment. Roosevelt seemed to agree. Before leaving for the Casablanca Conference with Winston Churchill, FDR backtracked on his fair employment policy. On 10 January 1943 he called Mary McLeod Bethune and Earl Dickerson to the White House. Using the two influential black Democratic leaders as sounding boards, FDR announced that he wanted the FEPC's railroad hearings, scheduled for 25–27 January 1943, deferred until some later date. Dickerson asked for the president's reasons. Roosevelt merely responded, "I want it delayed until I return." The next day McNutt made the formal public announcement that the proposed railroad hearings, as well as the Cleveland, Detroit, and St. Louis hearings, had been "indefinitely postponed."[9]

A flurry of protests followed McNutt's statement. A. Philip Randolph called McNutt's move "a slap in the face of, and an insult to, upwards of twenty million Negro Americans." To him, the cancellation proved that the "FEPC was just a sop, an appeasement, in the first place to stop the March on Washington for jobs and justice." CIO locals and many metropolitan fair employment practice councils like Chicago's requested a return of the FEPC's powers, as did leaders of Catholic, Jewish, and Protestant groups. Walter White was more direct. By letter and telegram he expressed his outrage, accusing FDR's advisors of conspiring to sway the president away from fully supporting fair employment for minorities. To "surrender to such forces," White argued, was "disastrous not only to the Negro but to the principles of democracy itself."[10]

Many members of the FEPC agreed with White and tendered their resignations. When Roosevelt returned from Casablanca, MacLean's resignation was waiting on his desk. Ethridge, Sarnoff, and Cramer soon followed suit. By the end of February, Harold A. Stevens, Henry Epstein, and Charles H.

Houston, the lawyers hired as lead attorneys in the railroad cases, had left the FEPC. Houston told MacLean that McNutt had "made a mockery of the nation's war aims" and "in effect proclaimed that the four freedoms do not cover the Negroes and that the Atlantic Charter takes effect for Negroes at the bottom of the Atlantic Ocean." Houston said he was leaving to "rally the liberal forces of this country" to fight harder for fair employment.[11]

The departure of Houston and other key FEPC officials crippled the agency. The FEPC had not disbanded completely; John Brophy, Eugene Davidson, Earl Dickerson, G. James Fleming, and Milton Webster remained. Dickerson shouldered most of the burdens, acting as chairman and performing most of the daily operations. Fleming continued work on midwestern cases and hearings. Although McNutt was "ready to take the rap," blame for the dismemberment of the FEPC was directed at Roosevelt. In an article in *The Nation*, James A. Wechsler "put it bluntly" by saying, "the hopes of Negroes have been raised, and their disillusionment now will be far more disastrous than if the President had never shown a willingness to wage this battle" for fair employment. John Beecher, an FEPC field representative, wanted it remembered "that there was nothing wrong with the FEPC that strong White House backing could not have cured." To force Roosevelt to resuscitate the FEPC, A. Philip Randolph reinvigorated his March on Washington Movement, launching what he considered to be a "broad national program based on non-violent civil disobedience and non-cooperation modeled along the lines of the campaigns of Mohandas K. Gandhi." Claiming support from roughly fifty national organizations, the MOWM held "Save FEPC" rallies in New York and Chicago.[12]

Roosevelt found himself as usual between competing forces. On the one hand, the FEPC's existence created in the South and the Midwest "a state of emotional alarm," while on the other hand "there [was] widespread discontent among the Negroes" because of job discrimination. Attorney General Francis Biddle suggested to FDR that a solution might be reached if government officials conferred with civil rights leaders. The conference took place shortly thereafter in Washington, D.C. Randolph, White, and twenty-two other civil rights activists attended and argued for a resumption of FEPC activities, a new executive order to strengthen the committee, and a larger staff and budget. The president's advisors, including Francis Biddle, James Byrnes, and Jonathan Daniels, suggested that Roosevelt recreate the committee but not with the powers that civil rights activists wanted.[13]

By the end of May 1943 President Roosevelt had made his decision. Francis Biddle once wrote that FDR had "a way of sticking to old ideas in new forms." This was the case in Roosevelt's reorganization of the Fair Employment Practice Committee. On 27 May 1943 FDR issued Executive Order 9346, disbanding the first FEPC and creating the second. The new executive order strongly resembled the first, with a few important differences. First, the new FEPC consisted of six full-time members and was established as an independent agency under the Office for Emergency Management, the White House's administrative catchall unit. Second, it codified what had become FEPC policy of making fact-finding missions and conducting hearings. Third, it empowered the committee chairman to "make provision for such supplies, facilities, and services as may be necessary to carry out" Executive Order 9346. By September 1943 twelve regional facilities had been established.[14]

The new committee's personnel was also different from that of the old committee. Gone were Malcolm MacLean, Lawrence W. Cramer, Mark Ethridge, Frank Fenton, and Earl Dickerson. Unlike the other four, Dickerson wanted to remain but was not reappointed. Attorney General Biddle and other federal officials believed Dickerson to be an "extremist." Earlier in 1942 the FBI had investigated Dickerson on the suspicion that he was a communist or a communist sympathizer. Although the FBI was not able to substantiate its claim, Dickerson correctly predicted that it would hinder his "career as a person in public life." For the new FEPC chairman, FDR chose Monsignor Francis J. Haas, a white midwesterner originally from Racine, Wisconsin. Roosevelt's choice shows his renewed interest in solving the problems that job bias created. Unlike Ethridge and MacLean, who were in essence public relations ex-

In late 1943, Father Francis J. Haas (center), the FEPC's new chairman, held a meeting of the committee to discuss several critical issues, including the postponed hearings in Detroit. (National Archives, Records of the Office of War Information, Record Group 208; photograph by Roger Smith, #208-NP4TTT-1)

perts, Father Haas was a labor troubleshooter and former National Labor Relations Board official. As a graduate of the National Catholic School of Social Science, Haas had excellent training in the fields of social justice and labor relations and could act as a force to break job barriers and ease racial tensions. Like the first FEPC, the rest of the committee consisted of representatives from various social and political groups. International Harvester's Sara E. Southall, a Chicagoan with connections to Hull House and the Chicago Urban League, in some ways filled the void left by Dickerson. Other members were the African-American editor of the Norfolk *Journal and Guide,* Plummer Bernard Young; the Jewish entrepreneur Samuel Zemurray, head of the United Fruit Company; Boris Shiskin, an AFL economist; and the two carryovers Milton Webster and John Brophy.[15]

Executive Order 9346 was not hailed as another Emancipation Proclamation; reactions ranged from mild praise to outright skepticism. Lawrence Cramer, the outgoing executive secretary of the FEPC, reveled in the similarities between the two fair employment agencies and told Milton Webster that "imitation is the highest form of flattery." Others were disappointed at FDR's decision not to reappoint Dickerson. Although Dickerson was gone, he left an enduring influence upon the FEPC. His rejection of employment quotas and his advocacy of the case method system were adopted by the second FEPC, which concentrated on individual claims of discrimination to alter unfair employment practices. Perhaps the changes were too subtle to foster much enthusiasm. Mainstream papers such as the *New York Times,* which followed the FEPC, gave Executive Order 9346 little attention and no analysis. The NAACP's *Crisis* may have expressed the general lukewarm sentiment best when it announced that "the FEPC seems to be on its way again."[16]

With its proposed twelve regional offices and five regional suboffices, the FEPC was armed with a more effective means of fighting employment discrimination in the Midwest and across the nation. The added firepower in the FEPC's arsenal probably did not impress many because the new executive order did not seem to offer much help in ameliorating the severe racial problems of 1943. During that hot summer social tensions reached a crescendo. Black morale was at a low point; violent racial incidents occurred regularly; and employment discrimination was still commonplace even though workers were desperately needed.[17]

During the summer of 1943 some Americans, especially blacks, remained underutilized in the nation's tight labor markets. For example, in the Midwest, 42 percent of the region's urban industrial areas had stringent labor situations and expected shortages by early 1944. Roughly 10 percent of midwestern cities already had acute labor shortages. Only 22 percent of the Midwest had areas in which labor supplies met demands.[18] Employment discrimination kept blacks from filling the Midwest's labor requirements. Major defense corporations, such as Western Cartridge of East Alton, Illinois, McQuay-Norris Manufacturing of St. Louis, and Crosley Radio of Cincinnati, kept their doors closed to blacks although each desperately needed workers. Many labor unions, particularly AFL affiliates, made the situation worse. The Boilermakers, Machinists, and Teamsters thwarted attempts by many managers to fulfill the government's production and fair employment goals.[19]

Had Roosevelt not amended Executive Order 8802 and reinvented the FEPC, the committee would have handled less effectively the seemingly intransigent and omnipresent job discrimination in the Midwest and elsewhere. By recreating the FEPC Roosevelt had made it into a stronger, more quintessential New Deal agency. Like FDR's other alphabet agencies, the FEPC was created for a relatively short time for a specific purpose. Its leaders were, more or less, New Dealers who believed in the positive nature of the role played by federal government. More than this, it benefitted from a well-trained but small administrative staff and a clearly defined bureaucratic structure to attack employment discrimination. It was the bureaucracy that enabled the second FEPC to handle the widespread employment discrimination better than its first incarnation.[20]

Between May (when FDR issued Executive Order 9346) and September 1943 (when the second FEPC opened its regional offices), the committee developed an organizational structure to process discrimination cases. The foundation for the bureaucracy was a definition of discrimination. The FEPC considered employment discrimination to be what would later be known as disparate treatment—refusal to hire and upgrade because of race, creed, color, or national origin. In addition, subjecting employees to inferior working conditions and unequal pay for equal work constituted unfair employment practices. The FEPC also considered union segregation, refusal of membership, and denial of bargaining or voting rights to workers on account of race, creed, color, or national origin to be forms of job bias.[21]

The FEPC's jurisdiction fell into three categories: 1) complaints against all agencies of the federal government, 2) complaints against all employers and the unions of their employees having contractual relations with the federal government that expressly or by implication contained a nondiscrimination clause regardless of whether such contracts pertain to the war effort, and 3) complaints against all employers and the unions of their employees engaged in industries essential to the war effort, whether or not they had contractual relations with the government. The first two categories of the FEPC's jurisdiction were straightforward. The third, however, was more subjective. What constituted an "essential" war industry? The committee relied upon the War Manpower Commission's *List of Essential War Industries* as a guide, but reserved the right to expand the list. This policy often caused conflicts because not all employers, union leaders, or federal officials agreed with the FEPC when, for example, the committee determined that steamship lines, railway systems, and telephone and telegraph companies were essential war industries.[22]

The FEPC's *modus operandi* was as follows. In order for the FEPC to take action against an employer or union, the committee had to receive: "(a) a signed complaint, (b) against a named employer, union or Government agency, (c) alleging discrimination, (d) relating to employment, placement or training, [and] (e) because of race, creed, color or national origin." Once received at a regional office, an FEPC official would consider the complaint on its merits. If there was enough evidence to warrant further investigation the regional director would docket the complaint and meet with the party charged. If the regional office exhausted all avenues for settling the case locally, then and only then would the FEPC consider public hearings. "Satisfactory disposition" of the case was achieved "when the party charged complied with the requests of the FEPC representative that it take certain positive steps to correct present discriminatory practices or to guard against their future occurrence." In most cases the FEPC followed up to see that the violator had changed its unfair employment practices permanently.[23]

As was the case with the previous committee, the second FEPC welcomed assistance from other government agencies. Although many federal bureaus pledged to help the FEPC, the committee worked most closely with the War Manpower Commission. On 2 August 1943 the FEPC and the WMC signed a comprehensive operating agreement. Since the FEPC and the WMC had regional offices in the same cities, they were to work together to enforce the ban on employment discrimination. The agreement spelled out how this was to be done. The FEPC was given the lead in handling all discrimination complaints. When cases arrived at the FEPC first the WMC was to supply any assistance, including staff and records. If a case came to a WMC regional office first, via a USES office for instance, the WMC regional director had ten days either to settle the case or send it to the FEPC. Once the case reached the FEPC, the WMC was again to support the committee to the best of its abilities. Finally, the agreement called on both agencies to create and share all reports on employment discrimination.[24]

Although the FEPC welcomed—and sometimes solicited—assistance from private agencies, the second committee created strict guidelines for its relationships with local groups, intending to prevent misunderstandings and awkward situations. In particular the FEPC worried about organizations that used the words "fair employment practice" in their names. By 1943 there were several metropolitan fair employment practice councils, and a few, such as the ones in the Midwest (Chicago, Cleveland, Columbus, and Detroit), were quite active. Realizing that these councils had "large potentialities for good," the FEPC worked closely with them and encouraged "their local work." At the same time the committee feared that their similar names might bring "serious embarrassment" and confusion after it opened regional offices. Soon after the second committee was established, "it was agreed that the Committee should disapprove or oppose the use of the name locally of 'Fair Employment Practice Committee' without authorization." Nevertheless it was also FEPC policy to have the regional director act as a liaison with the metropolitan councils, which could investigate and handle discrimination cases as long as FEPC representatives approved and oversaw the activities. In general the FEPC wanted the councils to help foster local support for the committee's work while not taking unauthorized actions in the FEPC's name.[25]

By late September 1943 everything seemed ready once again. The nine regional offices and three suboffices were open, and staff and most major policies had been set in place. Yet by early October things were again in flux. On 1 October chairman Haas was called to become the Bishop of Grand Rapids, Michigan. In his place, FDR appointed Malcolm Ross, a mildly successful author and another former member of the NLRB. Ross, who had been Haas's FEPC assistant, did not have the same credentials as his superior. Although he was a New Dealer with sympathies for oppressed workers, Ross was a poor administrator with little experience in solving tough labor and racial problems. Walter White protested the promotion. He distrusted Ross, whom he called a "front man" for Attorney General Biddle, who in White's estimation failed "to act on numerous cases of mistreatment" of black Americans. Soon P. B. Young and Samuel Zemurray also left the committee for health reasons. FDR appointed Charles H. Houston and Charles H. Horn, another midwesterner, to replace them. Although the addition of Horn, the president of Federal Cartridge Company (Minneapolis), did not amount to much, the Houston appointment gave the committee one of the nation's best legal minds.[26]

By the fall of 1943 the FEPC was back in business. Because of Executive Order 9346, the committee was better prepared to attack discrimination in the nation's war industries and, for our purposes, in the Midwest. The FEPC had survived its first major political challenge. Moreover it had gained an important ally, President Roosevelt himself. As one historian has commented, "Roosevelt's commitment to the FEPC made it clear to Democrats below the Mason-Dixon line and in the border states that the Compromise of 1877 was off." More than that, his actions demonstrated that anti-FEPC forces would have to look outside the administration for support, thus moving Washington D.C.'s fair employment political battlefield from the White House to Capitol Hill. At the same time, the committee took its fight to America's factories in such critical production areas as Chicago, Detroit, Cleveland, Indianapolis, and St. Louis.[27]

4. The Chicago Office: The FEPC and Illinois, 1943–45

AFTER ITS REORGANIZATION, the FEPC picked up in Illinois where it had left off, albeit with some changes. When the Chicago office reopened in September 1943, Elmer W. Henderson had replaced G. James Fleming, who transferred to the FEPC's Philadelphia office. Although Fleming was an effective administrator, Henderson, an African American and a native of Chicago, was in some ways better qualified. As the former research assistant for the Illinois Commission on Urban Colored Population, Henderson had an intimate understanding of the employment and social problems in the Chicago area. He was also a member of the local NAACP with contacts among the city's elite reformers and labor activists, who proved to be a valuable aid in easing the employment color line. Two Chicagoans—Harry C. Gibson, an African-American attorney, and Joy Schultz, a white industrial relations expert— served as his full-time assistants. Henderson needed all the help he could muster in the difficult job ahead of him. The FEPC soon discovered that although job integration in the northern parts of Illinois was possible, eliminating job bias in southern Illinois was almost impossible. This pattern was not specific to Illinois but typical in the Midwest.[1]

Henderson began his work in Chicago by following up on the 1942 hearings. The city had changed quite a bit in the months that had passed. In late 1943 the Windy City was a microcosm for many of the problems plaguing the home front. As in other cities, in-migration had dramatically altered the urban ecology, intensifying some factors and rearranging others. Billions of dollars in war contracts drew thousands of workers. A Fisk University research study estimated that Chicago's black population had increased at least 25 percent, from 277,771 in 1940 to 350,000 in 1943.[2] Black and white migrants had come from the South mainly in search of jobs.[3]

In terms of employment, the basic pattern had not changed much since 1941. Compared to all groups in Chicago, African Americans had the greatest difficulty finding jobs. In late 1943 the War Manpower Commission designated Chicago a Group II area, meaning that the city had stringent labor conditions with shortages anticipated in six months. In general, any white Christian who wanted to work could. According to the Bureau on Jewish Employment Problems, Jewish workers were also "experiencing little difficulty in obtaining employment." The Bureau noted in early 1943 "with gratification that, due in large part to its efforts with the papers, discriminatory advertising decreased markedly, and [had] almost disappeared."[4] Mexicans and Mexican Americans in Chicago easily found low-skill jobs. Steel and packinghouse labor recruiters had brought Mexicans to Chicago in large numbers during the 1920s after the 1921 and 1924 Immigration Acts had cut off the flow of cheap labor from Europe. According to one employer they were brought to "dilute colored labor." In other words, they functioned as a type of "strike insurance" by creating competition for the lowest skill jobs. Like many black Chicagoans, Mexican workers performed the most disagreeable jobs. They also faced all sorts of social and employment discrimination. By 1943, however, there was full employment among the forty-five thousand Spanish-speaking people in the Chicago area. Government officials predicted in late 1943 that Chicago would need an additional 375,000 new workers by the end of the year. To fill the manpower requirements, employers were regularly hiring all job seekers—including some resettled Japanese Americans—but not blacks. The job situation for African Americans had improved since the proposed march on Washington in January 1941. Nevertheless, substantial barriers remained. Black men and especially black women still had trouble finding work. Even if they secured jobs, promotions and security were often out of the question.[5]

After investigating the employment situation, the FBI concluded that job bias was a primary factor responsible for low morale among Chicago's African Americans. Blacks were also unhappy because in addition to the difficulties getting a job, many had a hard time finding a decent place to live. As in other midwestern cities such as Detroit, while white migrants to Chicago easily found homes, blacks did not. In the city, African-American housing was confined to a seven-square-mile area between 14th Street on the north and 70th Street on the south, and between Cottage Grove Avenue on the east and Halsted Street on the west. The so-called Black-belt was formerly a white residential section. After blacks moved into the area, the once attractive and well-constructed buildings were allowed to deteriorate and become run-down. Homeowners broke up the larger homes into apartments for which they charged high rents and provided inadequate maintenance. Although it had numerous black churches and vibrant social and political organizations, the Black-belt had serious problems.[6] According to the FBI, the neighborhood averaged two to three murders a week, which were "seldom publicized in any of the newspapers."[7]

The combination of housing and job discrimination produced a situation ripe for a race riot. During the summer of 1943 social tensions in Chicago seemed to reach a peak. Anti-Semitism was reportedly on the rise as Jews had become a scapegoat for some in the black community. There was also anti-Semitism among whites. Some white workers at the Toolcraft Corporation were quoted as saying that "the Jews caused the war and did not belong in the U.S.," and that "Jews are niggers turned inside out."[8] There were frequent confrontations between whites and blacks on transit platforms and in residential areas. In early 1944 several white youths stoned a black church, the Little Zion Baptist, located on Wells Street. The situation was made more volatile when the assistant church pastor shot Joseph Alleruzzo, one of the stone throwers. Shortly afterwards, FBI director J. Edgar Hoover learned of rumors that persons of Italian descent planned to burn the church for revenge.[9] Despite the serious nature of these events, officials in the Office of War Information believed that "the race tension in the Chicago area is not as acute or as deep seated as it is in Detroit," and that "there is no immediate prospect that it will come to an open outburst of violence."[10]

Unlike some federal officials, leaders in Chicago were not willing to wait and see if a race riot developed. After the Detroit riots in July 1943, Fullerton Fulton, the radical head of the Chicago Industrial Union Council (CIO), called for a conference to discuss the potential for widespread racial conflicts in Chicago and to seek a solution to the problem of employment discrimination. The meeting was held at city hall. Present were Mayor Edward J. Kelly; A. L. Foster, the executive secretary of the Urban League; Oscar Brown, the president of the Chicago branch of the NAACP; the ex–FEPC member Earl B. Dickerson; Frank McCulloch of the Fair Employment Practices Council of Metropolitan Chicago; and about 170 other interested individuals. Because of the large number of labor representatives and because of Fulton's involvement, the FBI considered the meeting an example of "the Communist Party's exploitation of the Negroes."[11]

The conference was not, however, a rally for the Left. Perhaps to the FBI's surprise, the group made modest complaints and presented practical proposals. Speaking on behalf of the civic, fraternal, religious, and labor organizations present, Fullerton Fulton requested that Mayor Kelly's administration give more attention to racial tensions, arrest "ringleaders of racial hatred," arrange for more housing for migrant workers, and urge employers to hire without regard to race, religion, and creed.[12] Fulton also called for a municipal commission to investigate racial tensions. Before the meeting's end, Mayor Kelly announced his plans for a Mayor's Committee on Race Relations, heralded as the nation's first since the race riots following World War I.[13]

Kelly appointed civic, industrial, labor (including liberal CIO and conservative AFL unionists), and African-American leaders to the committee in equal numbers of whites and blacks. It was led by Edwin R. Embree, the president of the Julius Rosenwald Fund, and Robert C. Weaver, who had left his job in the War Manpower Commission, became its executive director. The committee's job was to "advise the city government in developing steps to eliminate racial tensions." During the war, the committee and its various subcommittees held several conferences and issued reports on various issues.[14]

Despite the dialogue, debate, and advice that the Mayor's Committee generated, its influence was limited. The committee had no legal power and more often than not gave the appearance of action while not actually altering the social structure of the city. Such was the case in the work of the Mayor's Committee Employment Subcommittee. The body was composed entirely of industrialists, led by James S. Knowlson, the president of Stewart-Warner. Although some of these employers adopted fair employment policies (often at the FEPC's behest), the Employment Subcommittee saw the employment situation among blacks as satisfactory and thus concentrated not on discrimination but on full employment. "No group can hope for job protection," the subcommittee wrote, "unless there are enough jobs for all." By leaving employment discrimination to the FEPC, the Mayor's Committee abdicated its responsibility in this area.[15]

Like Mayor Kelly, Illinois Republican Governor Dwight Green also created a government agency to investigate race relations. The Illinois Interracial Commission had no administrative powers, conducted no public hearings, and provided advice that was rarely acted upon. The commission, made up of seven white and seven black members and headed by a white social worker, Dr. Martin H. Bickham of Chicago, was most active in late 1943 when it fostered the creation of local race relation councils in Rockford, Peoria, Danville, Champaign, Evanston, and Springfield. On the whole, the Illinois Interracial Commission favored a policy of gradualism, which (as we will see) interfered with the FEPC's attempts to break down color barriers in employment.[16]

As a result, the only government agency in the field prepared and willing to handle employment discrimination in Illinois was the FEPC. Before Henderson had taken charge of the office, Francis J. Haas had sent a letter to the Fair Employment Practices Council of Metropolitan Chicago explaining the FEPC's reorganization and outlining the relationship that the committee would have with the Chicago Council. Haas stated that the FEPC welcomed the local group's assistance, especially with educational programs. Haas, however, "respectfully" requested that the local group change its name to avoid any "embarrassment." Furthermore, since the new Chicago office was "equipped to handle cases of alleged discrimination," the local council was to refer—and not settle unilaterally—any cases that they thought had merit.[17] Despite the FEPC's concerns, it did not have much to fear from the Fair Employment Practices Council of Metropolitan Chicago, which by 1943 was out of money and operating on a volunteer staff. As the Bureau on Jewish Employment Problems discerned in its 1943 annual report, without greater membership support and financial aid the council "cannot healthfully survive."[18] Perhaps the end of the Chicago FEP Council best illustrates how fighting for fair employment needed much more than good intentions.[19]

Even without the Chicago FEP Council the FEPC office had significant local support. In late 1943 St. Claire Bourne, the FEPC's information specialist, visited Chicago and concluded that "Elmer Henderson apparently has no public relations problems." Bourne marveled at the level of community cooperation. Henderson credited "a high degree of civil militancy in the Chicago area [which] provided a solid foundation on which to build up public support."[20] The FEPC had the backing of some labor unions and black organizations as well as the mayor's office. Mayor Kelly "extended [Henderson] the full cooperation of the city administration in whatever manner it could aid in the prosecution of [the FEPC's] work." Kelly tried to create a conducive atmosphere. A week before the FEPC's third birthday, he (like several other big city mayors across the nation) signed a proclamation designating 25 June "Fair Employment Practices Day in Chicago," so that "management, labor and all other segments of our population shall be stimulated to establish in our factories and places of business the democratic principle of equality of opportunity for which our fighting men of all races and creeds are at this time bravely sacrificing their lives."[21]

Many Chicago industrialists seemed to support the FEPC, which was rather unique in the Midwest. Even before the second FEPC reopened its office, the Employers' Association of Chicago sent a "warning" to all employers with defense contracts to abide by FDR's fair employment policies.[22] The only major government agencies that did not appear to wholeheartedly back the FEPC were the Chicago offices of the War Manpower Commission and the United States Employment Service. In contrast to other WMC and USES offices (for example those in Cleveland), both Chicago offices rarely referred cases of discrimination, which led Henderson to believe that the USES and the WMC were deliberately overlooking the problem.[23]

Henderson's first order of business was to visit the companies and unions that had attended the hearings in 1942. The most disappointing cases were those of the Chicago plumbers' and steamfitters' unions. Shortly after the hearings, Edward L. Doty, one of the original complainants, wrote to Mil-

ton Webster that despite several conversations with William E. Quirk, a rank-
ing leader in the Pipe Trades Council, no progress had been made in putting
blacks on construction jobs in the Chicago area. "Mr. Quirk still contends
that he has to place all of his men on the job before he can place any of we
men," wrote Doty. "He also uses the bottleneck in the material situation as
an additional reason for not placing we men on the job."[24] After its transfer
to the WMC, the FEPC referred the plumbers' and steamfitters' cases to
McNutt and the WMC for disposition. The War Manpower Commission
failed to improve the situation, and in 1944 Henderson recalled the cases. For
almost four years FEPC officials had labored without result. But in October
1945 William Quirk, a business agent for the Chicago Journeymen Plumbers' Union Local 130 (AFL) and a PTC official, was deposed from his position for embezzling union funds. Shortly after, black plumbers and steamfitters were hired on the first Chicago Housing Authority jobs. Two years later
the plumbers' union admitted black craftsmen for the first time.[25]

Henderson's office had a more immediate response from the other hearing participants. Compliance checks in December 1943 showed that ten of the
eleven companies that had attended the January 1942 hearings had hired
nonwhite employees (see appendix A).[26] Buick, which had proclaimed at the
hearings that discrimination was something that just happened, revised its
employment applications, removing questions about race and religion. It
hired Jews and African Americans and did not segregate them. Six months
after the hearings it was employing four times as many nonwhites. Studebaker
too practiced fair employment despite resistance from white employees.[27]
When management placed Maxwell Gleves, an experienced black tool- and
die-maker, formerly of Ford's River Rouge plant, in the machine shop, twenty-two white workers went on a wildcat strike. William Sennett, the education director of UAW-CIO Local 998 at Studebaker, brought the men back to
work after two hours, telling them: "We're making these airplane engines to
fight a war for democracy. Let's make that democracy a reality right here in
the shop by giving everybody a break without regard to color or creed."[28] A
year after this incident almost 6 percent of Studebaker's workforce was non-
white, as opposed to less than 1 percent when the war started.[29]

At the time of the racially motivated strike at Studebaker the FEPC had no
policy for dealing with such incidents. During the war, many work stoppages
occurred because disgruntled whites protested the hiring or upgrading of
blacks or other minority workers or because these industrial newcomers challenged racial discrimination in defense factories. Strikes against minority
workers—so-called hate strikes—were common in the Midwest (see appendix B). Although these work stoppages were a small percentage of the total
in any given year, they added to racial tensions and interrupted war production. The committee kept close track of these strikes, but until its reorgani-

zation it had coasted "along dangerously without [a] policy," as John A. Davis, an FEPC staff member, put it.[30] After the rash of racially motivated strikes in 1943, not only in Illinois but especially in Michigan and Pennsylvania, chairman Malcolm Ross devised guidelines for the FEPC. Lacking any direct jurisdiction, the FEPC was to assist government agencies in settling only racially motivated strikes while urging striking workers to return to their jobs. Ross and other FEPC officials believed that the committee had the confidence of most workers and could use that to settle the grievances involved. The policy worked well, and Henderson's office helped settle numerous work stoppages in Illinois, including one at the Allied Steel Company in Harvey, Illinois, just south of Chicago, in which whites struck when management removed a partition between white and black toilets.[31]

For some employers, union leaders, and workers, the threat of racially motivated strikes became an excuse to deny blacks and others defense-related work. A case in point was the George L. Detterbeck Company of Chicago, whose 145 workers made precision tools and cams. In March 1944 the United States Employment Service referred a few black workers to the company. The plant manager sent them back to the USES, claiming that the "present staff would quit if colored workers were employed" in any categories but janitorial. After futile negotiations between the USES and Detterbeck, the War Manpower Commission revoked Detterbeck's clearance to recruit workers outside of the city and sent the case to the FEPC. In July 1944 Elmer Henderson visited Mr. Detterbeck who said, "flatly and categorically," that he would not "risk losing a single one of his present employees." According to Henderson, he was "convinced that the employment of Negro workers would entail that risk" because "a number of his women workers would leave rather than work with Negroes." Detterbeck stated further that he had tried to integrate his company, but black women had proven "lazy" and "incompetent," and that he had "dismissed that as an unsuccessful experiment."[32] Although there had been such strikes in Illinois, Henderson did not believe Detterbeck's assertions since few Chicago war plants experienced racially motivated strikes.[33]

Despite Henderson's suspicions, there was a thread of truth to Detterbeck's claims. Some Chicago unions used the threat of a wildcat strike to prevent the hiring of black workers. The Chicago Boilermakers (AFL) were notorious for this. Unions also deterred some employers from hiring Japanese Americans. In 1944 the Illinois Central Railroad fired fifty-five newly hired Japanese-American workers because the Brotherhood of Maintenance and Way Employees (AFL) voted to strike if management did not discharge the workers. Illinois Central caved in to the union's demand. Henderson looked into the situation and decided that since the War Relocation Authority had declared the Japanese-American workers loyal, the union had "no reasonable excuse" for its actions. The committee's records do not indicate if these workers were rehired.[34]

In contrast to the AFL unions such as the Brotherhood of Maintenance and Way Employees, most CIO locals, many of which were on the Left, tended to promote fair employment. Chicago's UAW-CIO and Packinghouse Workers' locals struggled to break down job barriers and open up union leadership to blacks. In 1944, for example, a Douglas Aircraft UAW-CIO local protested the promotion of a white worker over the head of an African American. The department's white unionists held a meeting and had the promotion reversed and successfully got the job for the black man.[35]

Because of the strong support of CIO unions and liberal employers, Henderson and his staff integrated numerous war industries in Chicago. They helped to open the Dodge plant—one of the largest war plants in the nation—to black workers. Similarly, after the FEPC negotiated with them, Campbell's Soup, Argo Corn, Illinois Bell Telephone, and Chicago's mass transit companies removed their job barriers. The FEPC met with more success than frustration in Chicago. Its downstate experiences, however, would prove much different, demonstrating the pattern not only within Illinois but in the Midwest. Generally the committee found the color line in employment more malleable in northern areas than in southern. As Henderson discovered in 1944, Springfield was the exception that proved this rule.[36]

In 1940 African Americans comprised 5 percent of Springfield's population of eighty thousand. Perhaps because of their small number, blacks did not live in a segregated area. Rather they were interspersed throughout the city. There was even a Friendly Neighborhood Mixed Club, an organization composed of white and black housewives who worked together to improve the vicinity surrounding an integrated federal public housing project. Public accommodations, however, adhered to Jim Crow standards as did theaters, hotels, and restaurants. When federal defense contracts sparked job growth in the city, employment patterns reflected the town's Jim Crow traditions. In January 1942 the executive secretary of the Springfield Urban League (SUL), William M. Ashby, reported that despite conferences with the city's industrialists in which "solemn promises of cooperation and fair play were given," blacks were locked out of defense jobs. Springfield had five large war plants—Allis-Chalmers, Baker, Hummer, Shaklin, and Sangamo Electric—that by April 1942 employed 4,650 workers, of whom only ten were black. All worked as janitors.[37]

In the absence of unemployment and under pressure from the Springfield Urban League, there was a dramatic reversal in black employment by early 1943. In June 1944 L. Virgil Williams, Henderson's part-time assistant who was African-American, made a trip to Springfield to check on complaints that had been filed in 1942. Williams interviewed Ashby, who was at that time a consultant to the War Manpower Commission as well as the executive secretary of the SUL. All the major war plants, including Sangamo and Baker, were hiring black men and women. Even the local Piggly-Wiggly grocery store had broken with traditional hiring practices. Many AFL unions, which were more active in the city than the CIO locals, allowed blacks to become members, not members of auxiliaries. Ashby was especially enthusiastic about the Teamsters, which developed a good record in race relations. In contrast to their Detroit counterparts, black truckers in Springfield joined the union and hauled war goods on local and intercity routes. The town's United Association of Journeymen, Plumbers, and Steamfitters also let blacks work on defense jobs—one of the few such instances in the nation. The only organization in Springfield that did not support fair employment was the local United States Employment Service, which (like many USES offices across the nation) routinely referred black women to domestic and other service jobs when they applied for defense work. Williams investigated the Springfield USES and lectured the office's manager about Executive Order 9346 and the binding agreement with the WMC, but with little result. Despite USES intransigence, Williams reported to Henderson that the overall picture of black employment was "good." In fact, in terms of fair employment, Springfield exhibited some of best employment practices in Illinois. As in Chicago, cooperation among employers, civil rights organizations, labor unions, and the FEPC made this possible.[38]

The worst violators of Executive Order 9346 in Illinois were not far away. The southwestern corner of the state was dotted with small towns that had been transformed by the war. East St. Louis, Granite City, Hartford, Wood River, and East Alton all became vital war production centers, making a variety of materials, including shells, bullets, chemicals, and steel. The war had invigorated the region's economy and revived racial tensions. The root of heightened racial tensions was often competition between blacks and whites for war jobs. Whereas Springfield had some of the trappings of Jim Crow, these small towns along the Missouri border had well-entrenched racist traditions. As had happened during World War I, wartime social transformations created challenges to caste structure, resulting in confrontations.[39]

During World War II there was no repeat of the 1917 race riot in East St. Louis. Although rumors were rampant that one might develop, racial frustrations were channeled through job actions. Several of southwestern Illinois's major manufacturers employed blacks. The working conditions, however, were often discriminatory, and African-American workers frequently protested by conducting wildcat strikes. In March 1944, in East St. Louis, over three hundred struck to change Monsanto Chemical's discriminatory segregation policies. Four months later, three hundred black chippers tried to shut down Granite City's American Steel Casting Company for similar reasons. White workers also used wildcat strikes. Shortly after D-Day in June 1944, for example, white workers struck the American Steel Foundries Company in East St. Louis because management upgraded a black worker to a crane operator. The reaction of management at the American Steel Foundries Company to the strike was atypical—it fired all striking workers and kept the promoted black worker. The general employment pattern in southwestern Illinois was to exclude black workers or to keep them in low-skill, menial positions.[40]

In late 1944 Henderson's assistant, Harry H. C. Gibson, made two investigative visits to the area. Some of what he found was encouraging. Monsanto Chemical had integrated its plant and, since the strike of early 1944, relations between white and black workers had improved. This was not the case at the Key Company, which had been stonewalling the FEPC for two years. In 1942 it had promised to hire African Americans, but Gibson found none there during his second visit. He also discovered that the War Manpower Commission and the United States Employment Service were facilitating the discriminatory employment practices. The WMC's area director for southwestern Illinois, Glenn Filley, instructed the local USES manager, C. R. Hughes, to fill labor referrals regardless of any discriminatory requests. Filley justified the practice to Gibson, telling him that vital local companies, such as Key and Continental Can, had been given high manpower priority ratings and therefore needed workers at any cost. In his report Gibson recommended action against the local WMC and suggested that the FEPC take immediate steps against the seemingly intransigent employment patterns in the area. Although East St. Louis's Key Company seemed a likely choice for a public hearing, the FEPC's target was southwest Illinois's largest munitions manufacturer, the Western Cartridge Company of East Alton.[41] After years of fruitless negotiation with Key's management, FEPC officials concluded that the committee's "time and energy would be better spent elsewhere."[42]

In 1940 East Alton was a small town of forty-seven hundred located a few miles from where the abolitionist newspaper editor Elijah P. Lovejoy had been murdered in 1837. Not much had changed in a hundred years. East Alton folklore held that in the 1890s a black resident "outraged a white girl." In defense of her honor, the town's white men rounded up a posse and hunted the alleged offender. Luckily for the black man, he was able to escape during the night. African Americans had not resided in East Alton since then. At the town's train station, a sign read: "Nigger, don't let the sun set on you in East Alton."[43]

Western Cartridge—East Alton's primary employer—bowed to local tradition. Western Cartridge was an essential factory, and its parent corporation, Olin Industries Incorporated, was one of the largest small-arms ammunition manufacturers in the world. Roughly every third bullet fired by American forces had Olin's stamp on it. Western Cartridge alone produced over 3 billion shells during the war. There were no blacks among its twelve thousand workers. According to Franklin W. Olin, the eighty-five-year-old president of Olin Industries, management did not discriminate against blacks; it only carried out the wishes of the community. Charges of unfair employment practices at Western Cartridge first reached the FEPC in November 1943. In an apparently rare action, the Illinois WMC's regional director, William Spencer, notified Elmer Henderson that he had received numerous complaints from black workers who had been turned away from the plant after being referred by the USES. Henderson investigated and decided to hold a public hearing in Chicago on 7 December 1943.[44]

Five days before the hearing, Spencer called Henderson to his Chicago WMC office for an informal meeting. Spencer was concerned that the FEPC was proceeding too fast and that job integration might result in work stoppages. An agreement was hatched to slow the process. Before blacks were to be hired, Western Cartridge pledged to carry out an educational program for its white workers. After the indoctrination Western Cartridge was to begin hiring blacks. Henderson agreed to the plan and canceled the scheduled hearing.[45]

Two months after the agreement, however, Western Cartridge had not begun the educational program. Henderson then asked the Illinois Interracial Commission to help the FEPC integrate Western Cartridge. The commission's chairman, Martin H. Bickham, refused and wrote Henderson that "this is not the time to integrate Negro employees" into the plant. Bickham proclaimed his "good will" and "understanding," and said he was committed to "the processes of employment for Negroes and other minorities without interruption or discrimination." Nevertheless, Bickham asserted, "this Commission is persuaded that it must move in directions indicated by its own advisers and processes, and not be activated by the decisions and activities of other units of government." In other words, if the FEPC pursued the Western Cartridge cases, it was on its own.[46]

On 23 February 1945 the FEPC took unilateral action and held a public hearing in East Alton's town hall to air grievances against Western Cartridge. FEPC members Malcolm Ross, Sara Southall, and Milton Webster made the trip, as did staff workers Emanuel Bloch, Maceo Hubbard, and Elmer Henderson. Bloch and Hubbard, who was an African American and a former lawyer for the NAACP, were the FEPC trial examiners. The scheduled two-day hearing almost ended before it began. Shortly after opening statements, about one hundred members of Western Cartridge's Brass Mill Operators' Union Local 1632 (AFL) stormed into the town hall and threatened to run the committee out of town. As Malcolm Ross stated in his memoirs, the mob was particularly upset at Webster, Henderson, and Hubbard, whose presence flaunted community standards. "For two dubious hours it was touch-and-go between words and action," wrote chairman Ross later, but "words it turned out to be."[47]

The hearing was an exercise in futility. The FEPC and Western Cartridge's attorney, R. H. McRoberts, exchanged old charges and arguments. McRoberts claimed that Western Cartridge did not discriminate and that Olin Industries had a good record of hiring black employees nationwide. He admitted that no African Americans worked for Western Cartridge. However, because the possibility of a wildcat strike still existed, McRoberts argued, no one could expect management to integrate the plant. Western Cartridge employees, union leaders, two of the town's ministers, and the mayor of East Alton, C. A. Van Preter, supported McRoberts's position. Lucille Barker, an employee and union stewardess at Western Cartridge, stated that all white workers "would walk out if Negro help came in." Chris Meisenheimer, another worker, predicted that the effects of integration would be the same as "if you drop a match into a powder keg." According to McRoberts, the company's position was that it did not want "bloodshed."[48]

Chairman Ross let Milton Webster lead the attack on the company and union. Ross "secretly dubbed" Webster the "Keeper of the White Conscience." If a white worker, employer, or FEPC member "failed to realize exactly how it feels to face the indignities and injustice habitually met by Negroes, his deep, baritone voice was off on a twenty-minute speech to make the matter clear." Webster directed his talent toward W. C. Hambleton, the head of the joint council of AFL unions that held the bargaining rights with Western Cartridge. After some probing questioning, Hambleton admitted that the threat of strikes was often a union ploy. In this case, he declared, it was not.[49]

Writing after the war, Malcolm Ross called the two days in East Alton one of "the FEPC's total failures." The committee was unable to change the employment patterns at Western Cartridge. Perhaps chairman Ross could have lobbied President Roosevelt for assistance, but with larger matters, such as the shape of the postwar world, on FDR's mind, it was uncertain that anything other than the creation of another ad hoc committee—akin to the Stacy Committee that sought to settle the FEPC's charges against sixteen southern railroads—would have resulted. In his memoirs Ross blamed the failure at East Alton on the town's southern whites, who brought their racism from the "backwater" of the "sluggish [and] cut-off bends of the Mississippi and the Missouri." In part, he was correct, but it was more than only the racially conservative white workers and employers. Unlike Chicago, where the FEPC made measurable progress, East Alton lacked a strong civil rights tradition, liberal employers, radical labor unions, and a local government willing to help the committee complete its work.[50]

Despite frustrations in southern Illinois, by the end of the war Henderson and his staff had made an impact in the state as a whole. The FEPC had its greatest success in the Chicago area, which is indicative of a pattern in the Midwest. The committee discovered first in Illinois and later in other states such as Ohio and Indiana that it was easier to adjust complaints of discrimination in cities in the upper parts of the Midwest. In Chicago FEPC officials docketed over five hundred complaints, making the city's FEPC office the third most active behind New York and Philadelphia. Henderson settled nearly 60 percent of the cases. The FEPC, with the cooperation of local labor, civil rights, and government leaders, changed the general employment pattern in Chicago. As had been the case during the First World War, the city's black workers won a place in the area's industries. The percentage of blacks in the labor force rose from 8.6 percent in 1943 to 13.1 percent in 1944.[51] Black workers found jobs—skilled and unskilled—in manufacturing, transportation, construction, and government. As the Chicago Urban League proudly and justifiably reported toward the end of the war, "industrial democracy has come to be the accepted pattern in the Chicago area. . . . From one end of the city to the other—in hundreds of plants both large and small—in almost every industry of any kind, we can cite actual cases" of fair employment. Testifying before the Senate Subcommittee on Education and Labor in late 1944, the chairman of the Chicago Council against Racial and Religious Discrimination, Arnold Aronson, who would later participate in the postwar push for a permanent federal fair employment law, credited the FEPC with opening job opportunities in the city. "As a result of the activities of the FEPC," Aronson maintained, "employment [has] been secured for thousands of workers in jobs which previously had been closed to them." He publicly thanked the FEPC, and in particular Henderson's office, for their diligent efforts. The committee had not acted alone. Cooperating with local activists, it had united the fight for fair employment and illustrated the possible advances, especially in the upper Midwest, that such combined efforts could make.[52]

5. The Limits of Activism: The FEPC in Indiana, Wisconsin, and Minnesota

In ADDITION TO Illinois, Elmer Henderson and his Chicago-based staff were responsible for the rest of the FEPC's Region VI and Region VIII, which included Indiana, Minnesota, and Wisconsin. In these states Henderson continued the work of the first FEPC but did not systematically attack Jim Crow as he did in Illinois, where he devoted most of his staff and resources. Henderson only had a budget of a little over fourteen thousand dollars, two full-time and one part-time assistant field investigators, and two secretaries. The limits of the FEPC's activism were, in part, a direct result of the financial constraints imposed first by President Roosevelt and later by Congress. Henderson also held back when the committee's work might exacerbate racial tensions. Nevertheless, he tried to combat discrimination, mostly by sending his investigators to Indiana, Wisconsin, and Minnesota to probe complaints and prod employers and union leaders.[1]

Henderson's field investigators, Joy Schultz and Harry H. C. Gibson, visited Indiana for the first time in 1944. The Second World War had changed Indiana much as it had other states. War production created labor shortages, spurred migration, and altered social relations. One constant amid the transformations was job discrimination against minority workers. The situation was typical of the Midwest; blacks and other minorities had an easier time finding wartime employment upstate rather than downstate. The efforts of the FEPC and the state government did little to alter this pattern.[2]

Early in the 1940s the Indiana state government tried without much success to ease color barriers to war production jobs. Shortly after A. Philip Randolph called for a march on Washington in early 1941, J. Chester Allen, a black Democratic state representative from St. Joseph County, introduced House Bill 445 to outlaw employment discrimination on account of race, creed,

color, or national origin by Indiana companies that held federal defense contracts. Unlike the similar Illinois fair employment statute, this bill called for
enforcement machinery. A state commissioner would administer the fair
employment law by fining violators from one hundred to five hundred dollars per incident of discrimination. Although the Indiana House of Representatives passed H.B. 445 by a vote of ninety-one to zero, the bill died in the
state Senate because of intense lobbying by the state Chamber of Commerce,
which believed the proposed law to be "dangerous and undemocratic," and
which generally stood "unalterably opposed to any legislation either state or
federal, on the subject of anti-discrimination between the races."[3] After the
bill's defeat, a public battle over fair employment developed, the result of
which was a compromise. The state Chamber of Commerce and civil rights
supporters agreed to a "bi-racial plan of co-operation," the centerpiece of
which was a new state committee, appointed by the Democratic Governor
Henry F. Schricker, to monitor black employment in war industries. The
Indiana State Bi-Racial Committee, headed by State Representative Allen, was
created on 27 June 1941, two days after Executive Order 8802 was issued. It
worked with twenty local biracial committees to ease the color bars to employment.[4]

The problems facing Allen's committee were significant. Although the
Indiana State Industrial Union Council (CIO), the State Federation of Labor,
and the state Chamber of Commerce paid lip service to fair employment, in
practice white Hoosiers clung to old ways.[5] In August 1941 Allen conducted a
survey of the state's major manufacturers. Of the 1,026 inquiries sent, only
246 (24 percent) were returned. Out of the 79,524 workers employed at those
plants, 2,451 (3 percent) were black, and they generally held low-skill jobs.[6]
Akin to the national trend, many blacks remained unemployed while whites
received defense jobs. Analysis of Work Projects Administration statistics also
pointed to the problem. In April 1941 the WPA in Indiana employed 36,407
people, 3,792 (10 percent) of whom were black. According to the 1940 census, blacks comprised only 3.5 percent of Indiana's population. In other words,
African Americans were overrepresented on the state's relief rolls.[7]

By 1942 the State Bi-Racial Committee apparently had made progress
against job discrimination. In its fourth report the committee announced
that from July 1941 to July 1942 firms reporting black employees showed a
net increase of 82 percent in the number that they employed.[8] Investigations
by federal officials revealed similar encouraging news. Indiana "exceeded the
national average of 46.6% in increased placements of black workers . . . as
compared to 1940." The Indiana increase was 51.9 percent.[9] Yet these numbers, which generally showed the gains in plants that hired blacks before the
war, hid the presence and pattern of employment discrimination where job
opportunities existed, largely in the northern part of the state.[10]

Since the turn of the century black Hoosiers had been employed in the steel industries near Gary. In 1906, when construction work on the Gary mills began, about one hundred black workers were brought from Chicago. The black population of Gary at the time was under five hundred. Over the next twenty years, African Americans came by the thousands to the Steel City in search of high-paying jobs. Typically they found low-skill employment as foundry workers and handlers. Nevertheless, the labor shortage during World War I caused employers to hire in unprecedented numbers. The percentage of blacks in the Gary Works, for example, never dipped below 14 percent from 1922 to 1934. By 1930 the 17,900 blacks in Gary—an increase of 238 percent in ten years—constituted 17.8 percent of the city's population. In 1940 there were 20,394 blacks in the city, comprising 18.2 percent of the population.[11]

As happened nationally, the Great Depression wiped out the employment gains of Gary's blacks. They were among the first fired as a result of the economic disaster. In 1933 National Urban League investigators reported that about 50 percent of the city's African Americans were on full relief, while the other 50 percent were on partial relief.[12] New Deal programs provided some assistance, but many, including the CWA, CCC, NYA, and WPA, discriminated. Shelters for the unemployed were designated for whites only, as were FERA-sponsored recreational activities. By the New Deal years Gary had become a fully segregated city. Blacks and whites did not have equal access to parks, schools, housing, and public accommodations.[13]

Black steelworkers reclaimed their economic place during the Second World War. From the beginning to the end of the war Gary remained one of the War Manpower Commission's critical labor shortage areas. By 1943 black workers again constituted an important segment of the steel mills' labor force. Many white workers, however, resented their return. Although the United Steelworkers' leadership supported fair employment, rank-and-file whites frequently did not. On 17 July 1943 white and black workers shut down the American Steel Foundries plant in East Chicago, a few miles from Gary. Whites left their jobs to protest the promotion of a black worker to crane operator. Blacks walked out to protest employment discrimination and segregation at the plant. American Foundries was closed for an entire week. Despite the resistance of some white workers, however, black employment in the steel mills expanded rapidly.[14] In May 1943 African Americans made up 14 percent of the workforce at Gary Works, increasing to 24 percent by September 1945.[15]

The dramatic gains were mitigated by the reluctance of Gary's steel employers to put blacks in skilled positions. Some feared hate strikes like the one in East Chicago, while others simply objected to the idea. The local branch of the Indiana Bi-Racial Committee got nowhere in talks with steel mill managers. When local activism failed to achieve redress, the FEPC stepped in to handle grievances.[16]

By late 1944 Henderson had received numerous complaints originating in Gary. Many came from black male steelworkers who were disgusted with the "impossibility for Negroes to obtain promotions or any type of advancement."[17] Black women in Gary were outraged that the mills would not even consider hiring them. As the historian Eileen Boris has pointed out, employment discrimination against African Americans is not merely a matter of racism but also of "racialized gender," racial notions of manhood and womanhood that kept black women from industrial work. Dozens of black women in Gary had encountered this first-hand. As one complained to the FEPC, "they hire these Polish girls but tell black women to go home."[18] Henderson sent Harry H. C. Gibson and Joy Schultz to Gary to investigate these cases. They interviewed James C. Fannery, the assistant area director of the WMC, and Tom Webster, the head of the Gary USES. Fannery and Webster told the FEPC officials what they already knew. Mills were willing to employ black men because of the labor shortage. But African-American women, who made up 90 percent of the persons available for referrals, were not being utilized.[19] Some employers, such as American Bridge, had experimented with black women welders, but when whites protested the companies immediately backed down. Despite the obvious presence of job bias, the FEPC refused to pursue vigorously these complaints from African-American women. The reasons why are unclear. Perhaps Henderson did not believe that Executive Order 9346 gave him the authority to attack the double-binds of sex and race discrimination. Or perhaps his decision rested on pragmatism. The Chicago FEPC office's resources were limited, and since Harry Gibson reported to Henderson that "the prospects for [Gary] are fairly good and we do not expect any serious unemployment problem except among Negro women in the near future," Henderson may not have seen the Gary steel cases as critically important.[20] Not until late in the war would the FEPC change its policy and attack job bias against black women more wholeheartedly.[21]

Henderson was similarly lax in attacking employment discrimination by the Gary Street Railway. FEPC officials considered the nation's public transportation systems essential war industries and demanded fair employment practices from urban mass transit systems and interstate railroad and trucking firms. Thus the investigation into the Gary Street Railway was one in a series that included the infamous Philadelphia Transit System case, where Roosevelt forcibly integrated the company, and the Capital Transit System case, where President Truman ordered the FEPC not to issue directives against its management.[22]

Breaking the employment color barrier at Gary Street Railway had the potential to ease rising racial tensions in the city. It could have been a tangible as well as a symbolic advance in the battle against Jim Crow. It might have also served as a means to quell rumors floating about Gary that some blacks had formed a bumper club, the members of which rode the buses and pushed whites off whenever an opportunity presented itself. These rumors, like those of the mythical Eleanor Clubs, had no basis in fact but were, as Howard W. Odum demonstrated, borrowed from southern folklore.[23]

In November 1944 Gary Railway's top two officials met with Henderson in his Chicago office. They claimed that the large in-migration of white southerners dictated a policy of caution. They also indicated that the responsibility for discrimination rested with the union, the Amalgamated Association of Street Electric Railways and Motor Coach Employees of America (AFL), which steadfastly refused to work with blacks. Aside from this initial contact Henderson did little to integrate Gary's transit system, deciding to focus his attention on the Indianapolis Railway System instead.[24]

By the end of the war the FEPC had been barely more active than Gary's Bi-Racial Committee in addressing employment discrimination in Gary's urban transit system, not to mention in the city's steel mills. Henderson demonstrated a reluctance to pressure employers to adhere to the president's fair employment policies. An explanation for this is not forthcoming in the records of the FEPC. In addition to Henderson's strained resources and limited authority under Executive Order 9346, another reason became clear late in the war: Gary was a racial powder keg. There were several incidents during the war that could have precipitated a race riot. In June 1944 thirty black patrons of a downtown bar took to the streets, demanding that the saloon fire its white bartenders and hire black ones. The Gary police quickly dispersed the crowd, preventing any larger conflict. Another more serious incident began on 18 September 1944, when white students at Froebel High School went on strike demanding that the public school system become completely segregated. Froebel and two elementary schools were the only integrated schools in the city; the rest were for whites only. The Froebel strike lasted two months. Shortly after a goodwill visit from the popular crooner Frank Sinatra, on 12 November the students returned without having won their objective. As a Federal Security Agency official put it at the time, "the disturbances around the Froebel High School . . . indicate a growing spirit of unrest and irritation."[25] It might have been this "unrest" that caused Henderson to reconsider any further action in Gary.[26]

During the war, race relations in Indianapolis, a city where blacks comprised 7.6 percent of the population, were markedly less tense than in Gary. Problems in the state capital did not center on such issues as public education or housing.[27] As Turner Catledge explained to the FEPC in late 1943, "racial tension here developed over the matter of employment in defense industry."[28] As late as June 1941, the city's blacks made up 44 percent of the "employables" on relief. About 20 percent of these persons were classified as skilled or semiskilled laborers. "Therefore," the *Monthly Labor Review* observed, blacks had "a rather specialized problem regarding their chances of employment in the future."[29] During the national defense mobilization program it was often assumed that a highly trained person had a better chance of obtaining a position than an unskilled laborer. Yet despite the level of training, entering into defense jobs was difficult for blacks in Indianapolis.[30]

There was some hope for improvement. One of Indianapolis's major industries was the Radio Corporation of America, whose president, David Sarnoff, was a member of the first FEPC. In December 1941 the executive secretary of the FEPC, Lawrence W. Cramer, sent G. James Fleming to check on RCA. Fleming reported that the plant employed twenty-six hundred people, but not a single African American. He also told Cramer that the Associated Negro Press (headquartered in Chicago) had asked him what steps Sarnoff was going to take to modify RCA's employment practices. Fleming warned Cramer that "it appear[ed] that some publicity is going to break around his membership on FEPC and the lily-white employment practices of his company."[31] By January 1942 the situation had changed slightly. RCA hired one black janitor. After learning this, Fleming wrote Cramer, "please inform me whether we dare ask RCA to [the Chicago] hearing."[32] RCA was not invited to the Chicago hearings. Shortly after the hearings, however, David Sarnoff distributed a memo to all RCA plants across the nation asking employment managers to "review the forms now used for applications" and remove any blanks with respect to the race, religion, or color of the applicant. He also reminded his managers that "the policy of the Radio Corporation of America and its subsidiary companies agrees with the spirit and letter of the policy set forth" in Executive Order 8802.[33] The results were less than one might expect from an FEPC official's company. RCA did become a leading employer of African Americans in Indianapolis, but limited their numbers, fearing, in the words of one FEPC staffer, that the company "would acquire the reputation of being a 'Negro plant.'"[34]

RCA was not the only company to break the color bar. The Lukas Harold Corporation hired hundreds of black men and women in comparable numbers. Three other major defense plants—GM's Allison (the city's largest), Chevrolet, and Curtiss-Wright—employed black workers to varying degrees. Allison hired its first black unskilled laborers in October 1940. In mid-1943 a few black mechanics were added, prompting white workers to walk out. They returned when it became clear that Allison's management was not going to fire the black workers. Although they had won the strike, employment managers decided not to risk another and made no further attempts to upgrade its black employees during the war. Chevrolet, too, became more cautious about hiring skilled black workers when whites staged a wildcat strike in the spring of 1943. Only Curtiss-Wright maintained its commitment despite protests from white workers. By March 1944 the plant employed many black men and a handful of black women in all skill categories.[35]

These successes and good racial conditions encouraged FEPC officials to pressure Indianapolis's recalcitrant employers. In particular the FEPC sought to open Indianapolis Railways, the local transit company, to blacks. The FEPC might have been more successful had it not been for the Chamber of Commerce, which proved a hindrance to the FEPC. The head of the state Chamber, Clarence Jackson, and the president of Indianapolis's Chamber, William H. Book, viewed Executive Order 8802 as an unwelcome interloper interfering with local affairs. In December 1942 Book wrote a blistering "Dear Governor" letter to the head of the WMC, Paul V. McNutt, complaining about the FEPC's investigations in Indianapolis. Book explained that complying companies, including Allison, had been falsely accused of discrimination. He also thought that the FEPC's requests to post notices and make monthly reports was "burdensome to already overworked plants" and "amount[ed] to punishment."[36] Finally Book requested that McNutt have the FEPC refer cases to the WMC for adjustment. McNutt forwarded the letter to Cramer, who penned a forceful reply. He told Book that the FEPC's investigations were warranted and that it did not use unofficial bodies to carry out the policy of the United States government. Cramer did acknowledge that "so-called Metropolitan Councils of Fair Employment Practice" had helped the FEPC, but these were "democratic" organizations that represented a broad spectrum of the community, unlike conservative, one-sided chambers of commerce.[37]

After Cramer's rebuke Book publicly mollified his views on the committee and even later praised the FEPC's "substantial beneficial results."[38] But the overtures at friendship and the pledges of cooperation that followed were disingenuous. Book offered to work with the FEPC in order to manage its activities in Indianapolis and thereby slow or stop progress against discrimination, particularly within the city's transit company. In this he was quite successful.

The Indianapolis Railways employed over twelve hundred workers, including 117 white women and 93 blacks. Despite a stringent labor supply in the city, however, the railway would not hire blacks as drivers and operators. In late 1944 Joy Schultz visited Indianapolis in an attempt to ease the color bar. She first met with William Book, who told her that the Chamber backed the FEPC's work and that the railway's management was willing to hire blacks but the union, the Amalgamated Association of Street Railway and Motor Coach Employees of America (AFL), objected to the idea. Book suggested that a hate strike would result if the issue was pressed too hard. He encouraged the FEPC to proceed cautiously and to stay away from a new black organization, the Citizen's Committee, which had formed under the leadership of E. Louis Moore, a prominent black attorney. Moore, Book claimed, was "more interested in his own financial welfare than the welfare of his group" and was seeking to be bought off.[39]

Not taking Book at his word, Schultz met with representatives of the Citizen's Committee and the union and management of the Indianapolis Railways. Schultz found the Citizen's Committee to be more disorganized than radical or corrupt. After meeting with several members of the local group she secured support for the FEPC's actions. Book's claims were echoed at a meeting with transit company officials, as management blamed the union for discrimination. "The company contends," an FEPC official later commented, "that it cannot afford to train operators unless it has reason to believe that the Negro operators would be accepted by the Association and contends further that some of the members of the Association are opposed to the employment of Negroes as operators." Indeed the threat of a strike gave cause for caution. However, the union's president, James F. Greene, argued in a meeting with Schultz that "the major opposition to the employment of Negroes lay with the company which was being hypocritical and was passing the buck to the union."[40]

After meeting separately with each party, Schultz held a conference with James F. Greene and Harry Reid, the president of the railway, and it was agreed that blacks would be employed after an educational program for white workers. Black activists and left-wing labor leaders opposed this agreement. The National Domestic Workers Alliance of Indianapolis, comprised of black women, the local NAACP branch, and the Indiana State Industrial Council (CIO) criticized FEPC chairman Malcolm Ross for failing to do more. Walter Frisbie, the secretary-treasurer of the Indiana State Industrial Council, sensed that the delay in action would be "damaging" to the movement to end employment discrimination.[41]

Frisbie and the other activists were right. The conservative elements in Indianapolis had succeeded in thwarting the FEPC's goals. The delay and the educational program had only clouded the process. By spring 1945 the FEPC was no closer to integrating the transit company. Furthermore, its support was dwindling. William Book in the end proved to be more a wet blanket than an aid. When Schultz recommended that a hearing be held in Indianapolis to air grievances against the railway, Book tried to scare the FEPC off by saying that he hoped "very much that there won't be trouble, but it looks to me like there might be; still, if the company shows it means to carry out the order—and I am sure it will—I would guess that it would really obviate real trouble."[42] The FEPC's proposed action against Indianapolis Railway was slated to be a part of a final series of midwestern hearings that would have attempted to settle many remaining cases collected by the Chicago, Cleveland, and St. Louis regional offices. But the hearings were canceled when Congress cut the FEPC's budget in 1945.[43]

Although the FEPC failed to integrate either Indianapolis's or Gary's city transit systems, both cities witnessed some easing of employment barriers. This was decidedly not the case in Evansville, an industrial city of 97,062 people (6,862 blacks) near the Indiana-Kentucky border. During the war it was a major war production center. Chrysler's Plymouth plant built army tanks; Republic Aviation made P-47 Thunderbolts; and the Evansville ship- yards manufactured and repaired landing craft. At peak production over fifty thousand war workers were employed in the city.[44]

As blacks and whites migrated to defense jobs in Evansville, numerous social tensions—especially dealing with race—surfaced. The city's transpor- tation system was crowded, often bringing unwanted contact. Racial friction seemed to heighten on the weekends when white soldiers from the nearby Camp Breckinridge (Kentucky) rode into the downtown. Recreational facil- ities, which were segregated, were insufficient, particularly for black work- ers and soldiers. Housing was also a serious problem. The Evansville Hous- ing Authority adamantly refused to put blacks in public wartime housing projects. Such attitudes among local officials created resentment among the city's black residents. Blacks were also upset by the labor situation. UAW-CIO Local 705 forced Chrysler to hire African Americans. By late 1944 blacks com- prised 16 percent of the plant's 3,070 workers.[45] Much to the chagrin of com- pany officials, Chrysler became the only major employer in Evansville to practice fair employment. Plant managers complained to Joy Schultz of the FEPC about carrying the "load of employing, training, and upgrading Ne- gro workers."[46] They had also become "jittery" after a discharged "colored employee dared to murder a white Chrysler foreman."[47] In late 1943 liberal religious leaders formed the Evansville Interracial Commission to attempt to improve the situation, but city leaders paid little attention to its recom- mendations.[48]

By some accounts the Evansville city government was a mere facade. C. B. Enlow, the president of National City Bank, purportedly ran the town. Be- cause Executive Order 9346 and the FEPC seemed to threaten his control of Evansville, Enlow was not in favor of the government's antidiscrimination activities. Moreover, because he managed the local Chamber of Commerce, the town's major bank, the newspapers, and the antiunion Evansville Coop- erative League, Joy Schultz noted, Enlow "was not disposed to take the FEPC program too seriously." When she made her initial visit to Evansville, her first appointment was with Enlow, who feigned interest and pledged "help if [she] encountered knots which [she] could not untangle." As it turned out, most of the town was knotted and Enlow gave no help.[49]

The employment difficulties of Evansville's black workers were in part the result of the local USES, which refused to refer black applicants to plants that had color bars, and routinely filled white-only placement requests. In the few plants where African-American workers were welcome they were segregated and confined to menial labor. Such was the case at Chrysler, which refused to upgrade blacks despite UAW-CIO support for such action. Republic Aviation's management shared Chrysler's attitudes toward black workers. Plant officials told the FEPC, "it was decided that a cautious policy . . . was wise, since Republic did not want to put itself in the position of operating counter to community custom."[50] The employment manager at the Evansville shipyards feared the possible violent repercussions of integration. The mere rumor that the shipyards planned to hire three hundred black welders resulted in the formation of white protest groups. Joy Schultz tried to convince Clyde Birdsong, the president of the Evansville Metal Trades Council (AFL), which had bargaining rights at the yard, to accept black workers. After months of negotiations Schultz indicated to her superiors that more discussion would be fruitless and no further FEPC action was taken. Aside from the gathering of information, the committee's efforts did not bring immediate results.[51]

In comparison to Indiana, the Fair Employment Practice Committee had a much easier time in Wisconsin. As in other midwestern states, the Second World War spurred tremendous industrial growth in Wisconsin. In 1944 the annual manufacturing output of Milwaukee alone was worth $1 billion, an increase of 75 percent over 1939.[52] Although Milwaukee captured 60 percent of all war contracts in the state, other cities, such as Green Bay and Appleton, also benefitted from wartime production. The main industrial problem—one common to that region—was labor. In September 1943 Beloit, Kenosha, Manitowoc, and Milwaukee all had stringent labor situations. The demand for factory workers made the integration of war plants a necessity. Although there was some resistance, Wisconsin employers and workers did not object strongly to the integration of war plants. By 1945 Wisconsin had become a leading state in terms of fair employment.[53]

Employers in northern Wisconsin adopted fair employment practices faster than those around Milwaukee. In other words, American Indians—who lived mostly in the northern part of the state and who by 1940 accounted for 3.9 percent of the state's total population—found war jobs more quickly than other minority workers.[54] In the July 1942 issue of *Employment Security Review,* James F. Wallace, an information specialist for the Wisconsin United States Employment Service, praised state employers for putting "minorities to work." Focusing most of his attention on northern cities, Wallace reviewed the employment patterns of the state's major manufacturers. Citing anecdotes from local USES managers, he reported that white workers and employers "have largely succeeded in overcoming whatever opposition" they had to employing Native Americans.[55] For example, in Ashland, a town that borders Lake Superior, shipbuilders regularly hired and upgraded workers from the Chippewa Reservation. Shipbuilding yards and ordnance plants in Eau Claire, Green Bay, and Sturgeon Bay also employed Indians from the Oneida, Menominee, and Lac Oreilles Reservations. The FEPC apparently received no job-related complaints from Wisconsin's Native Americans.[56]

Most of the committee's cases came from southeastern Wisconsin. In Milwaukee during the Second World War employers were slow to adopt fair employment practices. This was nothing new. Milwaukee's industrialists, supported by the AFL unions and the city's socialist mayors, Victor Berger and Daniel W. Hoan, had long helped to maintain the color bar. Joe W. Trotter has argued that from the 1910s through the 1930s, "blacks in Milwaukee . . . experienced greater confinement to domestic and personal service than blacks in other northern cities of various sizes."[57]

There had been an easing of the color barriers in employment during the 1920s. Some black migrants—mostly men—entered industrial jobs performing the hottest and dirtiest work. As news of these employment opportunities reached the South, more blacks came to Milwaukee. By 1930 the black population of Milwaukee had increased 237 percent to 7,501, only 1.2 percent of the city's total population.[58] Job discrimination was still common. Employment in the city's breweries, for example, was out of the question, as were many high-paying jobs in Milwaukee's manufacturing companies such as A. O. Smith and Heil.[59]

During the Great Depression the job situation became much worse. As happened elsewhere in the nation, blacks were the first laid off and the last called back to work. Black unemployment in Milwaukee was higher than in other midwestern cities, including Chicago and Detroit. As late as 1940, 29.3 percent of Milwaukee's black workers were unemployed. The comparable percentage for Detroit was 15.7 percent, and 19.3 percent for Chicago.[60]

Unemployment among blacks remained high in January 1941 as Milwaukee industries geared up for war. By the mid-1940s the city had received over $2 billion in nonfood war contracts and increased industrial employment from 110,000 in 1940 to 200,000 in 1943.[61] African Americans, however, did not benefit from the economic expansion. In December 1940 William V. Kelley, the executive secretary of the Milwaukee Urban League (MUL), surveyed fifty-six local defense contractors and found that only twenty-eight employed blacks, generally in unskilled positions. Unfair employment practices sometimes created pathetically ironic situations. For instance, in the early 1940s some black women in Milwaukee worked as NYA instructors, training white women to be machine operators for defense jobs. Milwaukee's industrialists hired these students but not their teachers.[62]

Milwaukee's black leaders actively protested employment discrimination in the city's war plants. In response to A. Philip Randolph's call for a march on Washington, black Milwaukeeans organized a short-lived branch of the MOWM. In addition, William V. Kelley, the conservative executive secretary of the MUL, and James W. Dorsey, the vocal head of the local branch of the NAACP, worked closely together to fight job discrimination. Through letters and meetings Kelley and Dorsey managed to secure the support of nonpartisan Mayor Carl F. Zeidler, who, three weeks before Pearl Harbor, delivered a radio address appealing for equal treatment for Negroes in the war industries. The two black leaders who set aside their political differences during the war also enlisted the backing of the Milwaukee County Industrial Council (CIO) in the fight for fair employment.[63]

At first Milwaukee's employers refused to listen to black leaders, CIO officials, or the mayor, and did not relax Jim Crow employment policies. As a result, Kelley and Dorsey sent the FEPC many signed affidavits from black workers alleging job discrimination in hiring and promotions. As noted in chapter 2, the committee responded by including five of the largest Milwaukee firms—Allis-Chalmers, Harnischfeger, Heil, Nordberg, and A. O. Smith—in the first Chicago FEPC hearings. At the January 1942 proceedings, Nordberg and Harnischfeger officials admitted that they did not hire blacks, and a representative from A. O. Smith added that the company "never did and didn't intend to employ" them.[64] Allis-Chalmers and Heil were charged with failure to promote African-American workers. Julius F. Heil, later the company's executive vice president and Republican governor of Wisconsin, vehemently denied the FEPC's accusations and defended his position that restricting some jobs, such as office boys, to whites only was not discrimination.[65]

The employers who had attended the Chicago hearings initially resisted the FEPC's directives to cease and desist their unfair employment practices and to hire and promote black workers. Heil was perhaps the most publicly recalcitrant. Shortly after the hearings he threatened the FEPC with a libel suit. Others made clear their intentions to ignore Executive Order 9346.[66] When William Kelley paid a visit to Harnischfeger, the company's president, Arthur Coppin, told him that the plant's employment practices were "none of [the Urban League's] business," and added that he "resented that fact that [the organization] had participated in the Chicago hearings."[67]

A few months after the hearings, as the white-male labor supply in Milwaukee disappeared and under continuing pressure from Henderson's FEPC office, the city's defense contractors began to change their policies. In early February 1942 a group of Milwaukee employers announced that they would hire skilled and semiskilled black workers. This news was followed by reports from Kelley and the MUL showing that black employment was on the rise. By the end of the war, Heil's percentage of minority workers had increased from .1 percent to 3.9 percent. Allis-Chalmers also showed marked improvement, employing over six times as many nonwhite workers as it did in early 1942. FEPC investigators were particularly impressed with A. O. Smith, which by the end of the war had hired over eight hundred African Americans. Harnischfeger and Nordberg also increased the number of black workers in their plants, but to a much lesser degree than the others (see appendix A).[68] Nevertheless Kelley and Dorsey were quite satisfied with the FEPC's actions in Milwaukee. In June 1943 Dorsey wrote to the head of the Chicago FEPC office, "we feel that through no other force than the very effective work of your committee, Negroes were placed in jobs that they never had before, and the employment problem here so far as Negroes getting jobs today is concerned is very good."[69]

Economic conditions continued to improve as the war came to an end.[70] In 1945, for example, the FEPC integrated the Milwaukee Road, which began to hire black stewards. Although a small victory, Henderson was "greatly pleased with the action taken by the Milwaukee Road," and thought that it would assist the FEPC in its "negotiations with other railroads" that it had been battling since 1941.[71]

As the Federal Bureau of Investigation reported, partly because of the favorable job situation, racial tensions in Milwaukee were lower than in most cities across the nation. Milwaukee had some problems due to the large number of migrants and the shortage of good housing. In addition, the FBI received some reports that Milwaukee's Communist leaders were "raising hell" and trying to agitate in the black community.[72] Nevertheless, in its famous RACON report, the bureau trusted the positive reports from one of its primary informants, William Kelley of the MUL, and concluded that "Negroes as a whole feel they are getting along well at the present time and have no desire to cause trouble."[73]

The rosy picture painted by the MUL, the FEPC, and the FBI hid some problems. Milwaukee employers with defense contracts generally refused to hire black women. In April 1942 William Kelley first alerted the FEPC to the employment problems of African-American women. Again the committee did little to redress these grievances until late in the war. When Joy Schultz, Henderson's assistant, investigated the problems of black women workers in Milwaukee in 1944, she found that the MUL no longer sought to redress their grievances. In fact Kelley actively discouraged black women from complaining, telling them not to be "sorehead[s]" or so "touchy."[74] Because by 1944 a few Milwaukee firms, such as Hansen Glove and Rhea Manufacturing, were employing black women and because Henderson did not receive many more complaints from them, the issue of genderized racism and prejudice against black women was allowed to go unresolved—at least for the time being.[75]

Because of Milwaukee's close proximity to Chicago, Henderson and his staff could give it some attention. The major industrial cities of Minnesota, however, were too remote. Henderson's resources were stretched too thin to devote time, money, and effort to job discrimination in Duluth, St. Paul, and Minneapolis. Therefore it was up to Minnesotans to settle the issue of fair employment.

Minnesota's industrial as well as agricultural sectors revived shortly after the start of war in Europe. Minnesota Mining and Manufacturing (3M), Honeywell, and Northern Pump expanded rapidly even before the Japanese attack on Pearl Harbor. Although these firms were making new products, they retained the old patterns of employment. Discrimination against Jewish and black workers was common despite state laws in 1939 and 1941 prohibiting unfair employment practices.[76]

Although dubbed the "Twin Cities," St. Paul and Minneapolis did not have identical employment patterns. Whereas employers in St. Paul generally did not discriminate, those in Minneapolis did. "Minneapolis," Carey McWilliams wrote in 1946, was "the capitol [*sic*] of anti-Semitism in the United States." McWilliams argued that conflicts over religion and jobs had allowed an "iron curtain" to separate "Jews from non-Jews."[77] Blacks in Minneapolis had an equally hard time finding employment. With the lone exception of the Federal Cartridge Company, owned by Charles L. Horn of the FEPC, discrimination was common in all types of jobs from manufacturing to retail. Most blacks during the early war years were either unemployed, on relief, or working in the railroad industry in traditional occupations.[78]

To battle employment discrimination, several groups in St. Paul and Minneapolis organized the Twin City Council on Fair Employment Practice (TCCFEP) in August 1942. Among the members of the TCCFEP were the executive secretaries of the Minneapolis and St. Paul Urban League branches, officials from the Minnesota Jewish Council, and representatives from the United States Employment Service. A local white magistrate, Judge Vincent A. Day, was chairman. The most important role that the council played was resolving instances of discrimination. On its own, without FEPC assistance, the TCCFEP's Case and Clearance Committee adjusted several complaints concerning a Minneapolis aircraft manufacturer (most likely Consolidated Aircraft) and Northern Pump. In both cases the council threatened to take the matter to the FEPC, a warning that the employers took seriously. Despite these advances, the council, which did not have any legal powers or governmental sanction, had only limited success.[79] The leadership of the TCCFEP recognized this weakness early on, and in its constitution wrote: "It is our hope that the matters of discrimination can be ironed out within the Case and Clearance Committee, but if not the Committee will be prepared to recommend certification to the Federal Government."[80]

The Twin City Council on Fair Employment Practice sent the FEPC affidavits and general information on current employment patterns. The FEPC was grateful for the local assistance, although it maintained some distance as it did with all metropolitan FEP councils. It used the information gathered by the TCCFEP to break down job barriers created by major manufacturers. For the most part, Minnesota's defense employers freely adopted fair employment practices. In an October 1943 meeting, Charles W. Washington, the head of the Minneapolis Urban League, told Elmer Henderson that the need for workers had opened the industrial gates of the Twin Cities to both blacks and Jews. The War Relocation Authority also had a good record in placing relocated Japanese-American workers. There were some instances of discrimination, however. One Japanese-American typesetter was unable to get a job because of the attitude of a secretary of a Typographical Union. Despite an agreement with Sidney Hillman of the War Production Board to integrate its plants, 3M refused to hire blacks and Jews, and later, when pressed, hired only token numbers of each group. Nevertheless the general picture was good. In its 1943 report on the performance of Negro workers in three hundred war plants, the National Urban League singled out Minnesota employers for their nondiscrimination policies. The state's business leaders maintained equal job opportunity through the end of the war. As a result, Henderson and his two assistants, Joy Schultz and Harry Gibson, each made only one trip to the Twin Cities. Presumably not much more was needed.[81]

If employment discrimination had been more severe in Indiana, Wisconsin, and Minnesota, Elmer Henderson probably could not have done much more than he did without a larger staff and more money. In any case, considering the level of racial tensions in areas such as Gary and his disregard for such issues as genderized racism, it is doubtful that he would have pursued all cases equally. Henderson, Gibson, and Schultz, nevertheless, had been quite active during the war. During its first year, the staff of the Chicago office handled 609 complaints of discrimination and closed 327 (54 percent) of those cases. Only 13 percent of the cases closed were satisfactory adjustments, meaning that in the FEPC's own account "the party charged complied with the requests of the FEPC representative that it take certain positive steps to correct present discriminatory practices or to guard against their future occurrence."[82] This low rate was a reflection of the lack of resources and the entrenched nature of discrimination, especially in the lower parts of the Midwest. Nonetheless, in the midst of tight labor markets, when the FEPC combined forces with local groups such as the Indiana Bi-Racial Committee, the Milwaukee Urban League, and the Twin City Council on Fair Employment Practice, modest progress was made. Henderson partially overcame the limits of FEPC activism by relying on local civil rights groups, employers, and labor organizations.

6. The FEPC in the Buckeye State

COMBATTING JOB BIAS in Ohio was another top priority for the FEPC. By 1945 it had two regional offices there and had conducted three separate rounds of public hearings. The FEPC's experiences in Ohio demonstrate not only the midwestern pattern but also the success that was possible when the committee had strong local backing, as it did in Cleveland. By the same token, when local support was lacking or when opposition overpowered support the FEPC was frustrated. The committee's experiences also show that fair employment was more than a federal issue. In Ohio government officials at all levels, activists, workers, and employers wrestled with employment equity in battles that took place in the state house, in the courts, in city halls, in the factories, and in the streets.

Despite the importance of fair employment practices in Ohio, the FEPC was a relative latecomer to the state. Because of the limited resources and political conflicts of the first committee, the FEPC did not make a concerted effort in Ohio until 1943. By then, local organizations, the state government, as well as many city governments had grappled with fair employment, although without many tangible results. The Ohio story begins with the actions of state politicians and local activists to create equal employment opportunities in the early 1940s.

Governmental involvement in fair employment practices originated from an unlikely source in Ohio, Republican Governor John W. Bricker, who was elected in 1938. Bricker opposed "the paternalism of the New Deal," which he thought "had weakened the old homey virtues of initiative and self-reliance."[1] In his first term Governor Bricker sought to remove the government's presence in everyday life by slashing the state's budget and dramatically reducing programs that aided the poor and unemployed. Bricker's uncompromising anti–New Deal efforts prompted his biographer to dub him the "defender of the old guard." Yet despite being a paragon of Republican conservatism, Bricker used the power of the state to assist Ohio's black workers.[2]

African Americans, who were 5 percent of the population of Ohio in 1940, were a traditional part of the Republican political base in the Buckeye State.[3] This was the result, on the one hand, of the influence of several black Republicans in Ohio, such as George Washington Williams, a state representative from Cincinnati, who in the late nineteenth century helped to draw blacks into the GOP's camp. On the other hand, many blacks joined the Republican Party because of the reactionary nature of Ohio's Democratic Party, the leaders of which, such as Frank J. Lausche of Cleveland, were not strong supporters of civil rights issues. Although there were many racial conservatives among Ohio's Republicans, such as Robert A. Taft, Bricker nursed the relationship with black voters and leaders in order to keep them within the Party.[4]

Almost a year after being sworn into office, on 7 January 1940, Governor Bricker convened a statewide conference on African-American unemployment problems. Over 250 people, including black activists, labor officials, industrialists, and government representatives, attended the meeting. In a statement to Governor Bricker the assembled group called for the creation of a state body to investigate the employment difficulties of Ohio's black population. Nine months later, in November 1940, Bricker established the Advisory Commission on the Employment Problems of the Negro. The twelve-person commission was directed by Fred G. Bennett, a white personnel director at Columbus's Buckeye Steel Castings. Chester K. Gillespie, a black Republican state representative, attorney, and one-time president of the Cleveland NAACP, was its vice chairman. Dean S. Yarborough, the chairman of the sociology department at Wilberforce University, and Constance R. Heslin, an instructor in race relations at the University of Toledo, were the two other African-American members.[5]

On the surface, at least, the commission appeared to run counter to Bricker's gubernatorial goals. It was an expansion of state government designed to aid a specific and disadvantaged social group. Why did Bricker set up a such an agency? Political expediency is one answer. Although a majority of blacks voted for Republican gubernatorial candidates from 1932 to 1938, the percentage had dropped consistently in each election, especially in Cincinnati, Cleveland, and Columbus. In 1936 and 1940 Ohio's black voters overwhelmingly chose FDR over his Republican opponents. Ohio's African-American political leaders, including Gillespie and David D. Turpeau of Cincinnati, remained loyal to the GOP, but some influential black Republicans, such as William O. Walker, a Cleveland city councilman and the editor of the *Cleveland Call and Post,* a black newspaper, seemed to waver and lean toward the Democrats. By creating the Advisory Commission, the governor was appealing to Ohio's black voters and leaders who were abandoning the Party of Lincoln.[6]

The commission's objectives were to encourage employers and unions to relax job barriers confronting black workers in Ohio. Through newspapers and speeches, commission officials, along with the governor, urged employers to hire African Americans, especially in defense plants.[7] By July 1941 commission director Bennett was claiming that tremendous progress had been made. Quoting from Ohio State Employment Service (OSES) statistics, Bennett maintained that there had been a 100 percent increase in black job placements from 1940 to 1941. In 1940 the OSES had placed 23,396 blacks. In the first six months of 1941 it found jobs for 23,818 black workers. Such results brought some black Republicans back into the fold.[8] In October 1942 William O. Walker editorialized in the *Cleveland Call and Post* that he did not "see how any Negro voters can do otherwise than solidly support John W. Bricker for re-election."[9] Although civil rights and fair employment were not issues in Ohio's 1942 gubernatorial campaign, Bricker captured the support of black voters and was reelected, beating his Democratic opponent John McSweeney handily and becoming Ohio's first three-term Republican governor.

Despite the job advances and admonitions to employers, not all of Ohio's black Republicans were impressed with the activities of the Advisory Commission or the governor on behalf of black workers. The commission did not seek the aid of or work with Roosevelt's FEPC, and it did not pressure defense employers who resisted fair employment to change their ways. By late 1942 the Advisory Commission, which had served its political function, was practically defunct. As a result, in January 1943 Chester Gillespie submitted a bill to the General Assembly (H.B. 11) that would have outlawed discrimination in employment by Ohio's defense employers. Gillespie's bill provided penalties for violators, with fines ranging from one hundred to five hundred dollars or imprisonment and hard labor for no less than thirty and no more than ninety days. Bricker did not support the bill, which died in the House Judiciary Committee.[10]

In the early 1940s most civil rights activists and organizations in Ohio relied less on the state government and more on direct action to break down color barriers in employment. Since the 1850s there had been a strong tradition of African-American activism in Cleveland that lessened prejudice and produced unusual economic opportunities for blacks. By the 1910s local civil rights groups had created what Frank U. Quillin, an African-American educator, described as a "Negro's Paradise."[11] Blacks were not only employed in a wide range of occupations but also enjoyed access to most public accommodations and some private clubs. The "interdependence and independence [of Cleveland's] white and colored races," Quillin commented in 1912, furnished "the world at large an ideal condition of affairs."[12] Although Quillin's remarks were overstated, pre–World War I Cleveland, as the historian Kenneth L. Kusmer has written, avoided "the more virulent forms of racism."[13]

Conditions in Cleveland changed dramatically after the First World War. In 1910, 8,448 blacks lived in the city; in 1920 there were 34,451, a 308 percent increase.[14] With the rise in black population came segregation, discrimination, and violence. Although southern black migrants found new freedoms in Cleveland and won a permanent place in the factory life, as Kusmer has written, their opportunities were limited because of racial prejudice.[15] Unions, particularly the AFL locals, contributed to the problem. Most labor organizations, including the railroad brotherhoods and the restaurant unions, barred blacks from membership. Another difficulty was education. Although Cleveland's public schools were integrated, blacks were denied technical training unless jobs were lined up in advance.[16] Writing in 1930, the noted black author and attorney Charles W. Chesnutt concluded that "there is a race problem in Cleveland but it is not acute." Cleveland still offered more opportunities than other cities of its size.[17]

Discrimination became a more immediate and severe problem during the Great Depression. In the 1930s the black population, which accounted for 8 percent of the population at the start of the decade, lived through awful hardships.[18] In October 1933 black workers comprised 10 percent of Cleveland's labor force but 27 percent of the unemployed. At the same time nearly 80 percent of Cleveland's black population received some form of relief. According to Christopher G. Wye, New Deal agencies ameliorated the situation, giving some of them a chance at training and skilled work.[19]

African Americans organized and agitated to create more economic opportunities. The local chapters of national organizations such as the NAACP and the National Urban League made some advances, as did unaffiliated local groups, such as the Future Outlook League (FOL), perhaps Cleveland's most militant civil rights association. The FOL was founded on 4 March 1935 by John O. Holly, a man who had held odd jobs in the city before the Great Depression radicalized him. His organization was fiercely independent, largely working by itself and engaging in new forms of protest. Whereas the NAACP and the Negro Welfare Association (an Urban League affiliate) preferred traditional private negotiation, the FOL favored direct action. Holly led his group on "Don't Buy Where You Can't Work" campaigns. Both techniques were sometimes successful but did not substantially change unfair employment practices in Cleveland.[20]

In 1940 blacks comprised 10 percent of Cleveland's population, but represented 21 percent of the unemployed, 45 to 50 percent of the relief cases, and over 30 percent of the WPA workers.[21] As the local NAACP branch observed, "this problem [had become] accentuated because recent figures as to trends of employment serve to indicate that the Negro percentage on the relief rolls will rise in direct proportion to the percentage of white persons leaving, so that eventually Negroes will comprise by far the largest proportion of those on relief."[22] As defense contracts flowed into Cleveland, whites easily found work at major firms such as GM's Cleveland Diesel Engine Division, Cleveland Standard Tool, Thompson Products, Warner and Swasey, and White Motors. Fred Long of Cleveland's Associated Industries surveyed the situation in late 1940 and found that two-thirds of the city's industrial employers had never hired and had no intention of hiring African Americans.[23] Blacks were denied employment except in traditional places such as foundries, where they could get mostly "Negro jobs," those usually refused by white workers when other work was available. Even in the foundries there was discrimination. On average, black foundry workers earned twenty-five to thirty-five cents less per hour than whites.[24]

According to the *Cleveland Call and Post*, the story of Fred Mance, a twenty-year-old machinist, reflected the experiences of many skilled black workers. Mance, a high school graduate, received over four hundred hours of training in blueprint reading, trigonometry, and practical machine shop skills. At the time that Mance began his job search Cleveland's tool and die manufacturers were hiring white workers with ninety hours of training. He failed to obtain employment at Cleveland Twist Drill, Thompson Products, Cleveland Pneumatic Tool, Ferro's Foundry, Warner and Swasey, Chandler-Price, American Steel and Wire, National Acme, and Fulton Machine and Foundry. After reading in the *Cleveland Call and Post* that the Ohio State Employment Service was placing black workers, he went to the Cleveland office where Elliot Young, the OSES's black aide, told him that he did not qualify for skilled work because he lacked apprentice experience.[25]

Months after the issuance of Executive Order 8802, Mance, like many black workers in Cleveland, remained unemployed.[26] Most defense firms and their unions initially ignored the president's order. One tool manufacturer told a local NAACP investigator, "I don't care what Roosevelt says, I am not hiring any Negroes." Some plant managers claimed that they favored fair employment but that their hands were tied because of deep-seated prejudice among their workers.[27]

There was some truth to that assertion, especially among AFL affiliates who, akin to the national trend, paid lip service to fair employment while not practicing it. One of the city's largest and most influential unions, the International Association of Machinists (IAM-AFL), had a constitutional clause against the acceptance of black members. The Cleveland Machinist Lodge 233 tried to end the practice at the 1940 IAM national convention. Joseph F. Reddish, the financial secretary, introduced a resolution to strike the word "white" from the ritual. The motion failed, but two months later Matthew De More, the head of the IAM in Cleveland, and Frank Evans, a black AFL organizer, submitted a resolution to the Cleveland Machinists' Executive Council removing the ban on black members. This passed unanimously but was never implemented.[28]

The CIO's leadership in Cleveland faced similar rank-and-file prejudice. It maintained a rhetorical commitment to fair employment, which white workers often opposed. The Cleveland Industrial Council announced its official position in September 1941 via the organization's newspaper, the *Cleveland Union Leader*. "We can be proud that the CIO has been, from the first, a leader in the rising movement to wipe out the disgrace of 'Jim Crowism' which turns colored Americans against white Americans. But we can't rest on our laurels. . . . It is the duty of all CIO members to fight every act of discrimination . . . and thereby to put teeth into the President's expressed policy."[29] But putting teeth into Executive Order 8802 proved difficult. For example, in early 1942 the membership of the Textile Workers of America (CIO) Local 17 at the American Rock Wool Company passed a resolution by a vote of forty-five to twelve banning "Negroes from jobs." Vigorous protest from the Industrial Council as well as local groups such as the Future Outlook League produced a retraction of sorts. A few weeks later the local passed another resolution stating that the union "does not object to the employment of any workers because of their race." The motion also stated that "the union . . . will vigorously contest any practices through employment [that] in any way lowers or destroys or tends to destroy the wage standards and working conditions which they have built and which they are continuously striving to improve." Some black leaders, including William Walker, the editor of the *Cleveland Call and Post*, believed the latter statement to be a veiled threat against the employment of blacks.[30]

A few industrialists in Cleveland were adamant about hiring without regard to race, creed, color, or national origin. One prominent example was John L. Schmeller, the president of the National Bronze and Aluminum Foundry Company. About a week after the creation of the FEPC, in July 1941, Schmeller wrote the OPM requesting more aluminum scrap so that his plant could expand operations. Schmeller promised that as soon as the OPM agreed to his plans he would train and hire five hundred black workers in all skill categories. Until the Second World War National Bronze, established in 1908, had employed mostly unskilled black foundry workers. To check on the possibilities for job integration, Robert C. Weaver of the OPM investigated the plant, along with Harry E. Davis of the Cleveland NAACP branch and Sidney R. Williams of the Cleveland Urban League. The three concluded that Schmeller's proposal was genuine and that the company's employment record was good. In his report Davis noted that Schmeller had even hired Fred Mance after he learned of the machinist's plight. On the recommendation of Weaver and the NAACP, the OPM agreed to Schmeller's expansion plans, which were delayed after the plant was completely destroyed by fire in October 1941. National Bronze was rebuilt and two thousand blacks worked there in 1942.[31]

During the early 1940s liberal industrialists like Schmeller were the exception. Cleveland's civil rights groups had to fight to make employers obey Executive Order 8802. Sidney Williams of the Cleveland Urban League wanted to localize the president's order. In conferences with plant managers and union leaders Williams urged the employment of black men and women. At times he was successful. In June 1941 Spero Electric Corporation opened its doors to black women for jobs as sprayers. The Urban League also tried to enlist the support of city government in the fight for equal employment opportunity. In this arena Williams often worked with Harry Davis and Charles W. Quick of the local NAACP.[32] As the 1941 mayoral elections approached, Republican Mayor Edward Blythin responded to the pressure by issuing a public statement urging "all employers, labor organizations and fellow employees within the City of Cleveland [to] do all within their power to give effect to the letter and spirit of the Executive Order of the President of the United States under date of June 24, 1941 [*sic*], relating to employment of citizens of the United States without regard to race, creed, color or national origin."[33] The statement had little practical effect. Nevertheless Blythin used it in his campaign to distance himself from his opponent, Democrat Frank J. Lausche, who ignored the issue. The tactic worked well in the black wards but not in the white ones. Lausche was elected mayor, becoming the first Democratic mayor in more than a quarter-century.

Lausche was slow to respond to the needs of Cleveland's black workers. As a result, the Future Outlook League forced the mayor to examine the plight of African Americans. Although John Holly had supported the March on Washington Movement, during the war the FOL maintained its independent strategy, albeit with a new twist. It tried to enforce Executive Order 8802 without any contact with the FEPC. For instance, in May 1942 the Future Outlook League got the mayor's attention by picketing one of the city's largest employers, the Standard Tool Company, which refused to hire black women. Holly and a dozen FOL members marched in front of the plant on 9 May. According to the *Cleveland Call and Post*, the demonstration was "so orderly that police could find no grounds upon which to halt the march."[34] Mayor Lausche persuaded the FOL to stop picketing after promising to meet with plant officials to work out a plan to achieve compliance with Executive Order 8802. A meeting was held a week later but no agreements were made about increasing the number of blacks in Cleveland's war industries. Holly was not discouraged, and threats of an FOL picket to enforce Executive Order 8802 began to open more job opportunities. In October 1942, for example, Holly announced plans to march against the National Biscuit Company (NABISCO), whose management agreed to hire black women to avert the protest.[35]

More than any other black organization in Cleveland, the FOL was dedicated to ending the color barriers for black women, who faced even more discrimination than black men. Even in 1944, when Cleveland's industry was at peak production, out of the thirty-five thousand African Americans working in war plants fewer than six thousand were women.[36] Holly used other methods in addition to picketing. In late November 1942 he retained three black attorneys (Chester Gillespie, Clayborne George, and Harvey J. Johnson), who filed a petition for an injunction in Common Pleas Court against three factories, Warner and Swasey, Thompson Products, and Thompson Aircraft Products (TAPCO). The lawsuits were filed on behalf of two black women, Claretta Jean Johnson and Effie Mae Turner, trained machinists who had been denied employment. Eschewing cooperation with the FEPC, the FOL's intent was to enforce Executive Order 8802 through the courts. If the judge in the Common Pleas Court agreed with the FOL's arguments, the lawyers reasoned, then Warner and Swasey, Thompson Products, and TAPCO would have to abide by the executive order and hire and promote black women.[37]

Because of the efforts of the Cleveland Urban League, Warner and Swasey, Thompson Products, and TAPCO were employing African-American men and women, but only in unskilled positions. Moreover, Warner and Swasey and TAPCO segregated plant facilities, including cafeterias and toilets. Plant managers blamed the International Association of Machinists, in particular Matthew De More, the head of the IAM in Cleveland, for the discriminatory policies. De More defended his union's resistance to the promotion of black workers by stating that the companies wanted to hire skilled African Americans in order to break the union and replace white workers with cheaper black labor.[38] "Both privately and publicly," De More told the *Cleveland Call and Post,* he opposed discrimination.[39] Yet he also opposed the FOL's lawsuits and any attacks on the IAM. Others also came out against Turner's and Johnson's cases. The *Cleveland Press* called the actions "ill advised" and accused the FOL of trying to establish a "quota system" for black workers. Similarly, Frank Evans, a black AFL organizer in Cleveland, said that the suits were "unfair" to Thompson Products.[40]

Judge Frank J. Merrick heard the two lawsuits on 15 and 16 December 1942, and found against the plaintiffs on 26 December. He lectured the FOL lawyers for an hour before coming to the heart of the matter. "Now for Executive Order 8802," he stated, "I have doubts as to its interference in this issue. It was written to encourage full participation in national defense. In wartime most of our rights are taken away from us. The defendants must keep maximum production in mind. If they have strikes and disunity in their plants, the government can take over the plants."[41] In other words, not only was the executive order unenforceable in court, but even if it were enforceable "maximum production" outweighed individual "rights." Although they lost the cases, FOL leaders felt that they could win in the appellate courts. By late 1943 the Johnson and Turner suits had made their way to the Ohio Supreme Court, which on December 1 dismissed the cases because "no debatable constitutional question" was involved.[42]

The Johnson and Turner cases represented both a victory and a defeat for the FOL. Even before the December ruling Warner and Swasey, Thompson, and TAPCO began hiring and upgrading black skilled workers. By late 1943 the FOL's attempt to enforce Executive Order 8802 through Ohio's courts had produced significant nonjudicial results. Nevertheless, Holly's continued pursuit of the cases was perhaps self-defeating. Unlike his lawyers, Gillespie and George, who left the cases in August 1943, Holly never seemed to understand that as a part of administrative law Executive Order 8802 had little legal weight in court. Furthermore, while he focused most of his organization's energies on court battles, the FOL's prominent role in the fight for fair employment in Cleveland was supplanted by another group, the Cleveland Metropolitan Council for Fair Employment Practice (Cleveland FEP Council).[43]

In March 1942 forty-five civic organizations in Cleveland, including the Ohio Consumers' League, the Cleveland YWCA, the NAACP, the Urban League, and the B'nai B'rith had formed the Cleveland FEP Council to "obtain a broadly representative and democratic community approach to the problem of discrimination in war industry because of consideration of race, creed, color, or national origin, and to coordinate efforts within this community designed to aid and abet the letter and spirit of Executive Order 8802." The Cleveland FEP Council differed from the FOL in almost every way. It was interracial and sought to secure fair employment through close cooperation with the Fair Employment Practice Committee rather than through independent, direct action.[44]

Daniel E. Morgan, a local white judge and former Republican mayor, initially led the Cleveland FEP Council. Like similar metropolitan organizations such as the Fair Employment Practices Council of Metropolitan Chicago, the Cleveland FEP Council's efforts focused on redressing individual complaints of discrimination. In general it was unsuccessful. For instance, in the summer of 1942 the council took up the complaints of three Jewish men who had received WPA training but were refused employment at the Parker Appliance Company. Their WPA instructor had warned the three that Parker discriminated and suggested that they put either "Catholic" or "Protestant" on their job applications. In July 1942 officials of the Cleveland FEP Council met with Parker's personnel director, who denied being anti-Semitic and insisted that his plant hired Jews but not blacks. Because the Cleveland FEP Council had reached an impasse, Morgan decided to contact the FEPC, which until then had not concerned itself much with Cleveland.[45]

To help the council settle the grievances it had collected, Lawrence W. Cramer, the executive secretary of the FEPC, sent Daniel B. Donovan, a white FEPC investigator and former CIO organizer from Lakewood, Ohio (a town near Cleveland), to meet with the group. Donovan found that although the Cleveland FEP Council had been aggressive it had not resolved many cases and in some instances, as the FEPC had feared, it had made matters worse. For example, in late 1942 George Segal, the executive director of the Bureau on Jewish Employment Problems who had replaced Morgan as chairman, visited the Osborn Manufacturing Company only to find out that the FEPC had already contacted plant officials. The company's employment manager was angered that the local group had made demands when the company was struggling to meet the FEPC's requirements.[46] As Segal told Donovan, the "embarrassing situation" had occurred elsewhere and often resulted in "no opportunity for positive action locally."[47]

In an attempt to avert further awkward situations and to coordinate efforts in Cleveland, the FEPC chairman, Malcolm S. MacLean, met informally with the council on 23 May 1942. After the meeting Donovan became the liaison between the local council and the FEPC. It was the Cleveland FEP Council's job to collect complaints. Almost weekly during the summer of 1942, William Walker, who was a member of the council, published in the *Cleveland Call and Post* blank forms to be filled out by those who had been refused a job because of race or color. These were compiled and sent to Donovan, who used them to prepare for hearings in Cleveland. In November 1942 the FEPC set tentative dates for those hearings and others in Baltimore, Detroit, Philadelphia, and St. Louis. As we have seen, however, in January 1943 Paul McNutt, the head of the WMC, canceled all planned FEPC hearings, believing that the committee was becoming too aggressive in attacking employment discrimination.[48]

Although the FEPC hearings were canceled, fair employment efforts in Cleveland had not been in vain. By January 1943 job opportunities for black Clevelanders were improving. When Cramer scheduled the hearings there had been only token employment of minority groups in the city. Tokenism gave way to fair employment practices at large plants, such as White Motors, and at smaller ones, such as the Railley Corporation. Although most gains involved black men, black women were also finding defense work. The FEPC and the Cleveland FEP Council successfully integrated black women into Republic Steel and the Aluminum Company of America (ALCOA). Warner and Swasey not only employed African-American men and women but also stopped segregating toilet and lunch facilities.[49] Commenting on the economic gains of 1943, the president of the Cleveland NAACP branch, Clarence L. Sharpe, wrote that "the economic conditions of the Negro have seen tremendous improvement" and that "employment and wages were high."[50]

In addition to the efforts of the FEPC and the Cleveland FEP Council there were several other reasons for the transformation. A primary reason was the tightening of Cleveland's labor market. In late summer 1943 the WMC described Cleveland as an area of "labor stringency" and expected things to get worse. George Segal of the Cleveland FEP Council maintained that many firms relaxed their color bars "due to manpower needs [and] nothing more."[51] Other firms adopted fair employment because of pressure from federal officials. B. C. Seiple, the manager of the Cleveland USES, denied his office's services to several firms, including Fisher Body bomber plant and Cleveland Pneumatic Tool, that had discriminatory employment policies. J. Lawrence Duncan, a black investigator for the OPM and later the WMC, was responsible for some important advances in Cleveland, including the initial integration of White Motors. WMC officials also educated employers about job integration and helped settle complaints from black workers.[52] The WMC was so effective in redressing grievances that when the second FEPC opened its office in Cleveland in September 1943, William T. McKnight, the black regional director based in the city, complained to his superior, Will Maslow, that "the War Manpower Commission has practically resolved all the complaints of discrimination, leaving no action for the Fair Employment Practice Committee except one of reporting."[53]

McKnight was exaggerating; there was plenty of work for him. When he opened his office there were over one hundred docketed cases from Cleveland. McKnight, who was apparently appointed on the recommendation of J. Lawrence Duncan of the OPM, was prepared to handle his assignment. He was a native of Cleveland, where he practiced law after receiving a degree from Yale Law School in 1927. McKnight was also a member of the local NAACP branch, but unlike many black activists in Cleveland—and in Ohio—he was a Democrat. Such credentials led to several government positions, including Assistant Attorney General of Ohio (1937–38), attorney for the United States Department of Labor (1939–43), and regional director for the FEPC (1943–45). McKnight had three assistants. Joining Daniel B. Donovan as investigators were Olcott R. Abbott, a white man, and Lethia W. Clore, a black Clevelander with ties to A. Philip Randolph's National Council for a Permanent FEPC.[54]

McKnight's primary tasks were to improve employment opportunity for minority workers and to relieve social tensions. The two issues were inseparably linked. The FBI considered race relations in Cleveland a critical problem. In the judgement of its agents in the city, "the great amount of discontent" in the black community was a function of "the inability to obtain employment for which they are qualified."[55] Heavy in-migration of southern whites and blacks, housing shortages, and vicious and unfounded rumors about black bumper clubs on local transit lines exacerbated racial animosity. Cleveland Mayor Frank Lausche tried to alleviate the situation in August 1943 by creating the Mayor's Committee for Democratic Practices, a powerless—and hence largely ineffectual—advisory body on race relations. Almost by default the job of mitigating social tensions fell to McKnight, who carried on an impressive public relations campaign, giving dozens of speeches on how to improve race relations.[56]

McKnight and his staff also reduced tensions by helping to integrate the city's war plants. According to George W. Washington of the Cleveland Urban League, job integration significantly lessened racial animosity. In December 1944 there were over thirty thousand black workers employed in defense factories in unskilled and skilled positions. One in five was an African-American woman. In all, blacks made up 12.5 percent of the workers in war plants.[57] The change in employment practices during the war was so dramatic that the Cleveland Urban League believed "the treatment of the Negro in industry" to be "far beyond his treatment in civil life." Thus it concluded that "it [was] about time . . . that schools, the government, the Christian associations, and the churches . . . catch up."[58]

Some white workers objected to job integration and protested with wildcat strikes. According to McKnight, this was the region's "number one problem."[59] Clevelanders witnessed several racially motivated strikes during the war. On 10 May 1943 dozens of white workers at Timken Roller Bearing struck to protest the training of twenty-seven black workers. At Republic Steel on 23 June 1943 one hundred whites walked off their jobs when two blacks were upgraded into jobs in which they would share the same locker room with whites. McKnight helped settle many of these industrial disputes, resulting in more blacks working in defense factories.[60]

White worker resistance notwithstanding, the favorable situation in Cleveland caused by the cooperation between local groups and the FEPC allowed McKnight to concentrate on other areas of Ohio with varying success. In general the FEPC did better in the northern parts of Ohio than in the southern and had mixed results in central Ohio. Columbus, the state capital, where 35,765 African Americans made up 11.6 percent of the population in 1940, had a reputation for poor race relations. Frank U. Quillin, who had sung the praises of Cleveland, wrote of Columbus in 1913 that "in all my travels in the state I have found nothing just like it. It is not so much a rabid feeling of prejudice against the Negroes simply because their skin is black as it is a bitter hatred of them because they are what they are in character and habit. The Negroes are almost completely outside the pale of white sympathy."[61] Although there had never been a race riot in Columbus there had been a few serious incidents. For example, in 1919, the same year in which the city witnessed a brief revival of the Ku Klux Klan, a riot nearly erupted when the Pennsylvania Railroad brought in black strikebreakers to replace striking white employees.[62]

Through the work of such groups as the Columbus Urban League and the local YMCA, relations between whites and blacks slowly improved following World War I. The situation for blacks in Columbus, however, did not. By 1940 blacks were segregated into the worst sections of the city, such as the American Addition and Bronzeville, and labored mainly as unskilled workers and domestic servants. Despite the necessities of war production, African Americans were kept from industrial jobs, skilled or unskilled. Employers were not entirely to blame. When the management of Curtiss-Wright tried to hire skilled black workers in November 1941, Carl Copeland, the plant's chief organizer for the UAW-CIO, led a walkout in protest. Owing to swift action by Curtiss-Wright's management, the FEPC, R. J. Thomas and Richard Frankensteen of the UAW, and Walter White of the NAACP, the weeklong strike ended after Thomas transferred Copeland out of Columbus.[63]

Curtiss-Wright was the only major employer in Columbus to initiate a fair employment policy and hire black men and women in skilled and unskilled positions. Most Columbus employers refused to lift the color bar, especially in skilled jobs, and some boasted after the war that they had "never hired Negroes."[64] Matters were not improved by the city's civil rights organizations, including the NAACP and the Columbus Urban League, which did not place much pressure on employers to hire minorities. Moreover, like Cleveland's Future Outlook League, the Columbus Metropolitan Council on Fair Employment Practice, an organization formed in November 1942 by the Columbus Urban League, the local Chamber of Commerce, and the Young Women's Christian Association, rebuffed FEPC attempts to coordinate activities. In a conference with McKnight, council leaders explained to the FEPC that all cases in Columbus could be settled locally without federal assistance.[65] Without local support from these moderate organizations, McKnight worked with a more radical group, the Vanguard League, a short-lived Congress of Racial Equality affiliate founded in 1940. The Vanguard League generally remained aloof from FEPC activities, although the two managed to cooperate to help integrate Columbus's Curtiss-Wright plant and fight discrimination at Ohio Bell Telephone.[66]

The lack of local support and success in Columbus led McKnight to focus on other areas of the state. Although in late 1944 the Columbus Metropolitan Fair Employment Practices Committee changed its policy and requested the FEPC's assistance, McKnight and his staff were too busy preparing for hearings in Zanesville, Cincinnati, and Akron to take more action in Columbus.[67]

In Zanesville, a town located sixty miles east of Columbus, the FEPC focused its efforts on the Line Material Company, which refused to hire black women. Although no explanation is forthcoming in the FEPC records, by late 1944 several FEPC officials, including William McKnight, had decided to tackle the tough problem of sexual and racial discrimination against women. Perhaps the sheer number of cases from black women guided the committee's actions. By late 1944 the FEPC had received twelve hundred complaints from African-American female workers.[68] In any event, Line Material was in essence a test case to challenge job barriers against black women. And a challenge it was. Plant managers were not obliging and devised a clever plan to subvert the FEPC's demand that they hire and upgrade black women by using Executive Order 9346 against the committee.

Line Material gained the reputation of being a good employer during the war, hiring black as well as white men. The plant managers, however, refused to employ African-American women. The company's personnel director and union leaders believed that if black women were hired the plant's white women would walk out, shutting down the vital factory. After receiving complaints from several black women who had been denied jobs at Line Material, the FEPC immediately dispatched investigators to the plant in an attempt to reach an agreement about job integration. These private meetings failed to ease race-based sex discrimination, so on 12 January 1945 the committee held a hearing in Zanesville to pressure Line Material into hiring black women.[69]

Shortly after the proceeding began, Harold V. Schoenecker, the company's attorney, filed a motion to stop the hearing, arguing that "the Fair Employment Practices Committee is exceeding its authority . . . by applying its provisions to a particular sex or a whole group of workers." The FEPC's hearing commissioner, Maceo Hubbard, a Harvard-trained African-American lawyer, denied the motion and directed Line Material to "recruit and hire new employees, including Negro women, without discrimination because of race, creed, color or national origin."[70] The FEPC's efforts in Zanesville were successful; management was apparently swayed by the committee's arguments. Within a month Line Material had integrated African-American women into its production line.[71]

In contrast to the Zanesville hearing, which was designed to change the employment policy of one company, the Cincinnati hearings two months later were an attempt to ease the color barriers, particularly against black women, in an entire city. Despite the fact that it sent Ohio's first black legislator, George Washington Williams, to Columbus in 1879, Cincinnati had long-standing customs that handicapped African Americans. Almost every institution, from schools to hospitals to public recreational facilities, discriminated against blacks. The worst of all prejudices, Frank U. Quillin had concluded in 1910, was "the one that strikes at the law of self-preservation, strikes indeed at one of the basic principles of our life, namely, that every man should be permitted to earn his bread by the sweat of his brow."[72] According to Quillin, job bias in Cincinnati was worse than in many southern cities. At least in the South blacks could find unskilled and sometimes skilled work. Generally, this was not the case in Cincinnati.[73]

At the beginning of the Depression decade life for black Cincinnatians was harsh.[74] In 1930 Theodore M. Berry, a black attorney and activist, conducted a survey of the economic status of blacks in the Queen City and found that as the number of blacks in the city had increased their economic opportunities had remained limited. In 1910, 19,639 blacks lived in Cincinnati. By 1920 that number had grown to 30,079, a 53 percent increase. By 1930 blacks comprised roughly 10 percent (47,818) of Cincinnati's population. The percentage of blacks working in industry, especially in skilled occupations, had failed to rise accordingly. Berry sent 475 questionnaires to Cincinnati employers and received answers from 234. One hundred seven businesses (46 percent) openly refused to hire black workers. The other 127 Cincinnati businesses utilized some black labor, but, as Berry noted, the questionnaire "seemed to provide evidence of a low occupational status for Negro workers." Over 80 percent of black women were engaged in domestic service and had "very little opportunity" to work in industry. Roughly 70 percent of black men worked as unskilled laborers, many of them as porters or janitors. A few found a place in some branch of industrial production, but these jobs were rarely skilled.[75]

Berry concluded from his survey that Cincinnati employers were "first, not interested in employment problems of the Negro; and second, that there was not much desire to have Negro workers advance above a certain low level of occupations." Still Berry hoped that Cincinnati employers would offer more jobs, especially skilled ones, to blacks and called on city officials, employers, and social organizations to band together and eradicate job discrimination.[76]

By 1940, when the black population had risen to 55,593 (12 percent), this had not happened.[77] As in other midwestern cities, blacks remained on relief and WPA projects while whites went to work on new defense jobs. Of the more than two hundred Cincinnati industries with defense contracts in 1942, fifty-five hired blacks.[78] Only two companies, Wright Aeronautical (a subsidiary of Curtiss-Wright) and Cincinnati Milling Machine, employed African Americans in large numbers. Wright, however, kept its black workers confined in a segregated building.[79]

Because so many Cincinnati industries with defense contracts had not, as officials in the Division of Negro Welfare (an Urban League affiliate) stated, "heeded the President's exhortation to industry to 'open the doors,'" several black organizations tried to create more jobs for blacks.[80] In early 1942 over twenty groups formed the Cincinnati Metropolitan Fair Employment Practices Council (Cincinnati FEP Council) under the leadership of J. Harvey Kerns of the Division of Negro Welfare in order to make Executive Order 8802 effective. The Cincinnati FEP Council attempted to ease job barriers by contacting local federal officials in the WMC and the USES and pleading for action. Both agencies turned a deaf ear to the complaints. In December 1943 the Double Victory Council of Cincinnati, led by Anne E. Mason, a local reporter for the *Pittsburgh Courier,* took more direct action and picketed the Cincinnati USES because its manager, Dillard Bird, refused to refer black women to war jobs. The march against the USES resulted in a meeting between the Double Victory Council's leaders and James M. Baker, the director of the WMC in Cincinnati, who told the black protesters that the solution to discrimination was not protest or forced integration but "a well-planned educational campaign."[81] Neither an educational campaign nor the hiring of black women followed.[82]

In September 1943 Ernest G. Trimble, a white FEPC investigator, visited Cincinnati to report on the status of blacks in war industries and found that discrimination was widespread and supported by the local WMC and USES. Trimble's conference with James Baker of the WMC was not productive. Baker told the FEPC official that blacks were only suited for foundry work and that "they were using the war as an opportunity to demand jobs for which they were not qualified."[83] Even if the WMC and the USES had referred blacks to Cincinnati's war plants, however, most would not have taken them. Trimble interviewed fourteen personnel managers from the city's largest firms. All refused black, and sometimes Jewish, workers. The managers explained that integrating their companies would produce work stoppages and perhaps a race riot. Although employers clearly hid behind these assertions, there was some truth to them. In addition to the unsubstantiated rumors about violent black bumper clubs on the local transit system there had been many racially motivated strikes at the handful of companies that hired African Americans. Wright Aeronautical was the scene for several strikes by whites protesting the employment of black skilled workers. The small walkouts in late 1943 and early 1944 culminated in a major strike on 5 June 1944 over the upgrading of seven black employees to idle machines in a building where only whites worked. The so-called "D-Day Strike" lasted nine days, and over nine thousand white workers participated.[84] Because of the social tensions in the city, the widespread discrimination, and the complicity of federal officials, Trimble believed that "the time [had] come for vigorous action." He suggested a series of hearings in Cincinnati that would "single out a few of the larger companies." If the major firms adopted fair employment policies, Trimble reasoned, the "smaller companies would then fall into line."[85]

FEPC chairman Malcolm Ross agreed with Trimble, and in late 1944 he announced the creation of a Cincinnati suboffice in order to prepare for the hearings. Ross appointed Harold James, who came to the FEPC via the War Relocation Authority, to head the office and transferred Lethia Clore and

Olcott Abbott from Cleveland to assist him. Before the Cincinnati FEPC office opened, as the state's black newspaper, *The Ohio State News,* recorded, the city's major industrialists had met to discuss a strategy to deal with the FEPC. During the meeting, which was reportedly attended by Ohio's Republican Senator Robert A. Taft, it was decided, in the words of an FEPC official, "to present a united front in resisting the hiring of non-white persons."[86] Not all Cincinnatians opposed the FEPC. In January 1945 an anonymous editorialist in the *Cincinnati Post* asked rhetorically, "can we afford the luxury of a color line at the factory front where arms are made for Americans whose skins are white or black or yellow?"[87] To most Cincinnatians, however, the answer was yes, and they challenged the easing of job discrimination at every turn. The mere opening of the suboffice was difficult. In late February 1945 James faced possible cancellation of the lease to the downtown FEPC office when white women complained to the building's owner that Alice Lewis, James's black secretary, was using "their" toilet. According to James the situation "apparently solved itself" after two weeks. Similar problems confronted the FEPC office directors in Atlanta and Dallas, and, as McKnight commented to James, it was typical of the "attitude of Cincinnati in all things racial."[88]

The Cincinnati hearings were held from 15–17 March 1945 in the city hall. With the help of Theodore Berry of the local NAACP, James and his staff had built good cases against Crosley Radio, Baldwin, Cambridge Tile, F. H. Lawson, Kirk and Blum Manufacturing, Schaible, Streitmann Biscuit, and Victor Electric. The immediate goal of the hearings was to redress sixty-two complaints of discrimination. Forty-six of them (72 percent) were from black women. Before the hearings, two companies, Schaible and Kirk and Blum, settled with the FEPC, promising to hire and upgrade black workers, including women. The rest refused, hiding behind their labor unions, which threatened to strike if the plants became integrated. At the hearings the threat was made clear by Fred Ross, the head of the International Brotherhood of Electrical Workers (AFL) local at Crosley. Emanuel Bloch, the FEPC's white trial examiner, asked Ross if his "union [had] taken any affirmative position on the issue of the employment of Negroes at the Crosley Corporation plant." Ross answered, "I will state again that we present the voice of the people. The voice of the people is that they will not work with niggers." Despite the FEPC's best efforts, only three of the participants in the hearing (Cambridge Tile, Kirk and Blum, and Schaible) changed their discriminatory employment policies during the war.[89]

After the Cincinnati hearings, in the spring of 1945, McKnight turned his attention back to the northern part of Ohio where he and his staff had the most success. In May 1945 the committee held its final Ohio hearing in Akron. It was an unusual hearing in that it centered on the complaint of one person, Herman Poole, a black machinist. Poole's family moved to Akron in the late 1920s when Herman was twelve years old. His talent for working with tools and metal blossomed about this time. In 1928, while in grammar school, he took a job in a tool shop doing light machine work on racing cars. He also began attending training courses in pattern drawing, blueprint reading, radio, and electricity. At fifteen he assembled a motor scooter out of scrap parts. The scooter, the top speed of which was thirty miles per hour and which could go a hundred miles per gallon, earned Poole some local acclaim. Yet because Poole was black he was barred from the journeyman system and the American Federation of Labor locals, which in Akron were lily-white. New Deal training programs in the Work Projects Administration allowed Poole to pursue further his interests in electricity and metal manufacturing. After completing a final government training course in November 1942, he reported to the Akron United States Employment Service office. Unlike the experience of Fred Mance in Cleveland, the manager of this USES gave Poole, despite his lack of apprenticeship training, a Machinist II designation, which meant that he qualified as an all-around machinist.[90]

On 7 November 1942, with referral card in hand, Poole applied to a local defense contractor, the Goodyear Aircraft Corporation, for a job as a machinist. The company employment manager refused to offer the posted position and instead asked Poole to work as a plant janitor. Poole declined and went to the office of George W. Thompson, the assistant executive secretary of the Akron Association for Colored Community Work, an organization that assisted black workers in job placement. The next day Thompson and Poole returned to Goodyear and he received a job as production assemblyman with the promise to be promoted to machinist work within two weeks. The days passed and no promotion came. It was well known that Poole was "tops in his department," but his requests for a machinist's job went unanswered.[91] After many months of negotiating with Goodyear's management by himself, in February 1944 he filed a grievance with his union, UAW-CIO Local 856. Like Poole, however, the UAW local had no success.[92]

In May 1944 Harold W. McCoy, the president of UAW-CIO Local 856, filed a formal complaint of discrimination with the FEPC on behalf of Herman Poole. After a few conferences between Goodyear officials and representatives of the FEPC, the committee's chairman decided to hold a public hearing in Akron to air Poole's grievance. The FEPC's hope was that the hearing would bring unwanted public attention to Goodyear's discriminatory employment policies and force the company to rectify past violations of the executive order and avoid future ones. The all-day hearing was held on 14 May 1945 in the State Court of Appeals courtroom in Akron. The committee's lawyer, Frank D. Reeves, an African American who had worked with the NAACP, argued that Goodyear refused to promote Poole because of his race. Goodyear's attorney, Walter B. De Bruin, did not deny the accusation but asserted that the managers' hands were tied because the plant's International Association of Machinists (AFL) union would strike if blacks were put in its departments. The FEPC did not accept this excuse and in its decision told Goodyear to upgrade Poole and stop discriminating against workers. To its credit, Goodyear did promote Poole, although the AFL union continued to object.[93]

Owing much to the Poole case and its successes in Cleveland, FEPC officials believed that they made substantial advances in Ohio. Although the committee had been stymied in some important cities such as Cincinnati and Columbus, the FEPC and its local allies had successfully fought discrimination against black men and women in other places, including Akron, Cleveland, and Zanesville. In general the FEPC had more success in the northern parts of Ohio than in the southern, again reflecting the midwestern pattern. Despite the regional variations, by the end of the war the FEPC had earned the respect of many, including members of the Columbus FEP Council who had initially refused to work with the committee. This respect was earned in the field, adjusting complaints such as Herman Poole's and challenging employment discrimination in receptive and hostile environments. The FEPC did not radically change employment patterns in Ohio, but it demonstrated that governmental pressure could at least alter them, creating opportunities where there had formerly been none.[94]

7. The FEPC and the Motor City

DETROIT HOLDS a special place in the history of the American home front during the Second World War, as the Motor City was at the heart of major wartime transformations. The conversion to war production resuscitated the city's industries, and Detroit became a main production center for the arsenal of democracy. The city was also a microcosm for the nationwide social changes wrought by the war. As many scholars have shown, Detroit presents an illustrative case study not only of the strained relations between whites and blacks but also of the new relationship between minority workers and the federal government.[1]

This chapter carries that analysis a step further by investigating the quest to create equal job opportunities in the defense industries through the struggles, triumphs, and failures of the FEPC. Although the committee did not come close to eradicating discrimination, it had a more beneficial influence than historians have previously recognized. This chapter maintains that African-American and other minority workers made advances in industrial employment during the war both because of tight labor markets and because of the combined activities of the FEPC, civil rights organizations, and some labor unions. There were limits on this advancement, however. In general, despite the FEPC's efforts on behalf of African-American women (which came late in the war), black male workers fared better than black female workers. Minority job gains were also curtailed because many union officials and rank-and-file members actively opposed equal employment opportunity. These unionists often maintained the color line by using hate strikes, which the FEPC sought to prevent and quickly end. Despite the limitations and setbacks for minority workers during the Second World War, local and federal activism helped to open unprecedented opportunities for employment and justice in the tight labor markets of the American home front.[2]

This chapter relies heavily on the FEPC's records and draws on the work of several historians. What makes it novel is the recognition that the FEPC was an important ally in the fight for equal employment opportunities for both minority men and women. In other words, the federal government established the ground rules and added legitimacy to the struggles to create equal job opportunities. Yet the Fair Employment Practice Committee did not act unilaterally; it had the assistance of local labor and civil rights groups. The history of the FEPC in wartime Detroit highlights the interactions between local organizations and national agencies.[3]

Only a few decades before it became an arsenal for democracy, Detroit was "a quiet tree-shaded city, unobtrusively going about its business of brewing beer and making carriages and stoves."[4] "And then," as the historian Charles Merz wrote, "came Ford." The rise of Ford and other automobile manufacturers changed the urban environment forever. Detroit quickly became a polyglot industrial center. Before the First World War and restrictive immigration laws, thousands of Poles, Germans, Bulgarians, and Ukrainians came to the city. During the 1920s southern whites and blacks flocked to Detroit to fill the insatiable demand for automotive workers. From 1910 to 1930 the African-American community dramatically increased in size. In 1910, 5,741 blacks accounted for 1 percent of the population of the city. In 1920 there were 40,838 African Americans, who now made up 4 percent of the population (a 600 percent rise). The 1930 census enumerated 1,568,662 people in Detroit, 8 percent (120,066) of whom were black.[5]

From the beginning the mix of whites and blacks produced tensions. In the 1920s the most significant fights were over housing. Blacks were segregated into two areas. On Detroit's west side there were two African-American neighborhoods, and downtown there was Paradise Valley, which got its name from migrant workers who during the First World War were "Goin' to Paradise" to claim five-dollar-a-day jobs.[6] Conditions there were harsh and overcrowded. Frequently mob actions enforced Jim Crow living conditions. Perhaps the most famous episode came in 1925 when Dr. Ossian H. Sweet, a black physician, tried to break the residential pattern by purchasing a house in a white neighborhood, an act that produced a deadly confrontation with a white crowd.[7]

In addition to crowd actions, many whites funneled their anger and hostility into several right-wing organizations. In the early 1920s Detroit was a center for the Ku Klux Klan. The local branch, founded in 1921, was heavily involved in politics. In 1924 Charles S. Bowles ran as the Klan's mayoral candidate and lost a close election to Republican John W. Smith. This electoral

defeat marked the height of Klan influence in Detroit, which was supplanted in the late 1920s by a similar group known as the Black Legion, which ter-
rorized blacks, Catholics, Jews, and labor organizers. A few "ministers of
hate," most notably Father Charles E. Coughlin, Reverend J. Frank Norris,
and Reverend Gerald L. K. Smith, the former lieutenant to Huey Long, also
resided in the city.[8] According to Michigan's WPA guide, by the mid-1930s,
"Detroit had a representation of every kind of panacea, political nostrum,
and agitation."[9]

African Americans in Detroit defended their civil rights and expanded their
opportunities via numerous organizations, including the NAACP, the Urban
League, the National Negro Congress, and the Universal Negro Improvement
Association. Blacks also forged alliances with Detroit's Jewish organizations,
such as the Jewish Community Center, and relied on some white benefactors
like Henry Ford. Although several automobile plants hired blacks during the
1920s, most kept them laboring as foundry workers or janitors. Ford was the
exception. After the First World War he established contacts within Detroit's
black community, particularly churches and the Urban League, which referred
"reliable" workers to him.[10] Ford hired thousands of skilled and unskilled
blacks, who by 1941 made up over 12 percent of Ford's ninety-one thousand
workers.[11] The United Automobile Workers (UAW) often charged that Ford
employed blacks to discourage unionization by exploiting the racial hostility of his white workers. Although he had no qualms about using blacks to
stop the UAW, Ford's actions may have also originated from another source.
"In Ford's view," August Meier and Elliott Rudwick have concluded, "Negroes, like other disadvantaged groups, were social outcasts who needed and
would appreciate his help." Detroit blacks were indeed thankful for the assistance and held Ford in the highest esteem until the 1940s.[12]

Detroit's African Americans developed another ally during the New Deal.
In the 1930s and 1940s the leadership, especially the left radicals, of the United Automobile Workers sought to gain the support and confidence of black
activists and workers. Aside from an ideological commitment to interracial
unionism, there were important practical reasons for wanting blacks in the
UAW. The only way to organize Ford and the other large automobile manufacturers was to switch black workers' loyalty away from the automakers and
to the union. This was no easy task. Despite the assistance of Gloster B. Current, a locally popular black musician and the militant head of the Detroit
NAACP Labor Committee, Louis E. Martin, the editor of Michigan's largest
black newspaper, *The Michigan Chronicle,* and Shelton Tappes, an experienced, left-leaning black organizer, the UAW struggled to earn the respect of
black workers and leaders. The turning point came during the 1941 strike to
organize Ford, when the union received the backing of the national leadership of the Urban League and the NAACP. At a crucial moment in the strike

Walter White of the NAACP flew to Detroit to show support for the UAW, which afterward successfully organized Ford. Although Detroit's black leaders had forged a new alliance with the UAW, many black workers remained skeptical about the union's commitment to them. There were good reasons to be wary of the UAW. During the late 1930s and early 1940s the union did little to help black workers, whose biggest problem was unemployment.[13]

Joblessness in Detroit knew no racial bounds. In 1937 the UAW estimated that out of 516,000 automotive workers, no fewer than 320,000 (62 percent) were out of work.[14] Many of the rest were only employed part-time. When Detroit's manufacturers began accepting defense contracts, however, mostly whites and not blacks were hired in the automotive factories.[15] In October 1940 the Michigan State Employment Service investigated black Detroit's employment problems and discovered that although African Americans were 7 percent of the city's population, they were over 10 percent of those seeking work.[16] "Every major census and survey since 1930," the federal investigators found, "indicated that more unemployment exists among Negro workers than among white workers, and also, that the duration of unemployment is longer among Negroes."[17]

Although the UAW organized and assisted unemployed white auto workers, it was inconsistent in fighting to get jobs for out-of-work blacks. The problem was with the rank and file of certain locals. At Packard, for example, UAW Local 190, which was allegedly organized by the local KKK, resisted the employment of African Americans in anything but unskilled positions. Not all UAW locals behaved in this fashion. Ford's Local 600 at River Rouge, which had a strong Communist contingent, welcomed blacks as workers, members, and leaders. Still the UAW leadership often looked the other way when locals discriminated, and thus blacks looked elsewhere for support in fighting job bias and unemployment.

In the early 1940s, when mobilization and conversion began, black workers in Detroit as in other midwestern cities were not allowed to participate in the defense effort. White employers generally only hired white workers. As a result, despite the huge upswing in government orders for war materials, thousands of African Americans remained unemployed. Out of the seventy thousand African Americans in the Detroit labor force in early 1941, only thirty thousand (42 percent) were employed. Over half of that number were in manufacturing. Ten thousand worked at Ford; 150 at Buick; one hundred at Cadillac; fifty at Pontiac; and six at Oldsmobile. Most labored in low-paying unskilled and semiskilled jobs. Few black women worked in factories; most made their living as personal servants.[18]

Civil rights organizations first called on the state and city governments for help. Both Democratic Governor Murray D. Van Wagoner and Democratic Mayor Edward J. Jeffries initially seemed sympathetic to the plight of black workers. In spring 1941 Governor Van Wagoner sent letters to Michigan's major manufacturers pleading for an end to job discrimination. "I strongly urge both employer and worker," he wrote, "to extend to every loyal citizen, regardless of race or color, the right to participate in our industrial efforts of production for national defense."[19] While Van Wagoner failed to follow up his statement with any practical actions, Mayor Jeffries created the Detroit Interracial Committee in early 1941 to investigate the problems of African-American workers and help ease them into wartime employment. The committee met several times and issued a largely unnoticed report on its observations.[20]

Aside from these actions, the state and city governments did little to aid minority workers. Perhaps Van Wagoner and Jeffries thought that not much action was needed as the job situation for African Americans had begun to improve by the summer of 1941. In June 1941 Buick hired six hundred more blacks, and Pontiac took on an additional four hundred. Many of these employment gains were a direct result of the efforts of a short-lived federal wartime agency, the Office of Production Management. The OPM's Negro Employment and Training Branch, headed by the black New Dealer Robert C. Weaver, had a job akin to the one the FEPC later took over. Weaver was to create employment opportunities for blacks in the war industries. To do that in Detroit, he hired an assistant, J. Lawrence Duncan, an African American who was a longtime resident of the Motor City and who had numerous contacts within the automotive industry and used them to negotiate job openings for blacks. Consequently, during the summer of 1941 optimism was high among the city's black leaders.[21] The head of the Detroit Urban League (DUL), John C. Dancy, wrote in 1941 that "this upward trend is expected to jump by leaps and bounds within the next twelve months due to anticipated shortages of qualified white workers, increased production, and the realization of the value of utilizing local labor reserves before resorting to the use of migratory workers."[22]

Despite their early success, Weaver and Duncan quickly ran into two problems. First, the factory jobs that they secured for blacks were generally the hottest, dirtiest, and most dangerous. Few blacks could find well-paid, skilled work. The second problem was in some ways more serious. White workers within Detroit's industries objected to any job advancements by minority workers. For instance, in September 1941 Weaver negotiated a verbal agreement between the management of the Packard Motor Company and UAW-CIO Local 190 that "there would be no discrimination against Negro workers in transferring from non-defense to defense production, and further that Negro skilled workmen would be given an equal chance to ply their trade."[23] A few days later two black workers were promoted to the metal polishing department. Two hundred fifty white workers at Packard immediately staged a forty-minute sit-down strike in protest. C. E. Weiss, the head industrial relations manager at Packard, promptly demoted the two black polishers and work resumed. At Weaver's insistence, the UAW president, R. J. Thomas, investigated the situation by having Curt Murdock, the president of Local 190, meet with Weiss. Weiss told Murdock that he would reinstate the two workers. Although Weiss did contact the black men and offered them the upgraded jobs, he also told them that by working at Packard they would "subject themselves to physical danger from white workers." The two never returned. Soon after, Murdock again met with Weiss, who this time stated that "Packard would not be turned into an arena" and that the resolution to union problems was up to Thomas and not the company.[24] Not wanting to upset Packard's rank and file, which composed an important faction in his political base, Thomas responded indecisively, merely sending an innocuous note to Local 190's executive board admonishing it to abide by the OPM agreement to avoid discrimination in the transfer of employees.[25]

The incident at Packard was not an isolated case in Detroit or in the Midwest, and blacks, frustrated with the lack of results obtained by Weaver and Duncan, began to send their complaints of discrimination to the newly formed FEPC. In late summer 1941, for example, Albert J. Lucas wrote the FEPC that he had received a job referral card notifying him to report to Briggs Manufacturing. "Upon my arrival there," he wrote, "I found several men in the employment office who had also received cards like mine, all Caucasians." The personnel manager refused to interview Lucas and told him that the card had been sent "by mistake."[26] Although it docketed Lucas's complaint and the dozens that followed, the FEPC was tied up in other places such as Chicago and Milwaukee. Detroit's civil rights groups therefore initially took the lead in fighting for fair employment in the war industries.[27]

After conferring with civil rights leaders in other midwestern cities, Detroit's activists joined a national trend and formed a new organization to fight wartime employment discrimination and aid the FEPC in its work. On 16 January 1942 community leaders assembled at the Lucy Thurman YWCA to discuss ways of aiding minority workers in Detroit. Among the African Americans present were John Dancy of the Detroit Urban League; Gloster Current of the Detroit NAACP; Reverend Charles Hill of the Hartford Avenue Baptist Church; Geraldine Bledsoe of the United States Employment Service in Detroit; Walter Hardin, a UAW organizer; and Louis Martin of the *Michigan Chronicle*. Several whites also attended, including Zaio Woodford, a leading Detroit attorney, feminist, and vice president of the Detroit Federation of Women's Clubs; John W. Gibson, the president of the Michigan CIO Council; Frank Winn of the UAW-CIO's War Policy Division; Albert Cohen, the executive director of the Detroit Jewish Vocational Services; and Jack Raskin, the executive secretary of the Michigan Civil Rights

Federation. That night they formed the Metropolitan Detroit Council on Fair Employment Practices (Detroit FEP Council) as a vehicle to break down job barriers. The executive secretary of the Detroit FEP Council was Clarence W. Anderson, a black sociology instructor at Wayne State University. The organization's first chairman was Edward L. Cushman, the white state director of the Michigan Employment Service and later the state director of the War Manpower Commission. The council's purpose, akin to that of the FEPC and other midwestern FEP councils, was to "eliminate discrimination in government, and in employment and training for defense industries against individuals because of their race, creed, color, sex, or national origin."[28] The interdenominational and interracial makeup of the group also resembled that of other midwestern FEP councils. The main difference was the inclusion of "sex" in the Detroit council's constitution. No document remains to indicate at whose behest this word was inserted. Perhaps the UAW's representatives requested it, or maybe it was Woodford the feminist. In any event, it was a clear indication that the Detroit FEP Council would take the complaints of black women workers seriously.[29]

The Detroit FEP Council concentrated on attacking job bias at the Ford Motor Company. The choice was an obvious one. Since the 1920s Ford had had fairer employment practices than the other major automobile manufacturers, and during the war it employed thousands of blacks at its Highland Park, River Rouge, and Willow Run plants.[30] Yet the majority of these laborers were male. In this respect Ford was much like other employers in the city and across the Midwest. Regardless of the need for war production workers, black women in Detroit generally remained concentrated in nonessential services. Only 74 of 280 war plants in Detroit that hired female labor used African-American women.[31] The leaders of the Detroit FEP Council, wanting to change this pattern and increase job opportunities for black women, must have reasoned that their chances for success were higher at Ford, which was one of the city's major employers of black men.

On 29 May 1942 representatives of the Detroit FEP Council, led by Zaio Woodford, met with Harry H. Bennett, the infamous head of the union-busting Ford Service Department, to discuss the employment of black women. According to Woodford, Bennett leaned back in his chair with his feet up on his desk and his arms folded and listened to the complaints. When Woodford was finished, Bennett sat forward and stated that "first there were no discriminations [sic]." He went on to say that "there was no reason why this committee, or any other, should come to them and tell them what to do." Bennett insisted that "Mr. Ford has been very kind and generous to the colored people" and that he "couldn't see any reason why the Ford Motor Company should be made a guinea pig of." Finally, sensing that the Detroit FEP Council was informally carrying out the work of the FEPC, he told the group

that "he did not need any executive order, and did not see why this administration, and everybody else and committees like this, should continue to cause
Henry Ford trouble."[32]

The failure at Ford meant that the Detroit FEP Council needed to devise
another strategy. It had to forge stronger community alliances to bring the
pressure necessary to break down the well-entrenched genderized color employment barriers. Council members chose not to ask Mayor Edward Jeffries
for help. Up to 1942 the mayor had treated black concerns seriously and had
challenged discrimination. But after the 1942 Sojourner Truth Housing controversy, when whites fought to prevent blacks from moving into new public housing, Jeffries gradually abandoned his commitment to African Americans, siding instead with white reactionary forces in Detroit. The Detroit FEP
Council began to work closely with other powerful organizations, particularly the FEPC and the UAW-CIO Local 600 at Ford.[33]

At Ford's River Rouge plant, African Americans accounted for 20 percent
of Local 600, whose black leaders, such as Shelton Tappes and Horace Sheffield,
pushed hard to stop employment discrimination and counter white opposition to equal job opportunities. In addition to issuing several strong resolu-
tions calling for an end to job bias and pledging support for the FEPC, Local
600's black activists tried to negotiate with Ford to increase the number of black
women working in the plant. In February 1942 Sheffield and Oscar Noble of
Local 600 met with several Ford managers and asked that 7 percent of all wom-
en hired at Willow Run be African-American. The proposal was flatly rejected. As one Ford personnel director explained, the company "feared that the
employment of Negro women would create a disturbance in the plant due to
the refusal of the white women already working there to work with Negro
women."[34] By late summer 1942 the leaders of Local 600 had also concluded
that wide-scale, community-based direct action was needed against Ford.[35]

On 20 August 1942 the Detroit FEP Council, the DUL, the NAACP, and Local
600 staged a four-hour demonstration at the employment office at Willow Run.
The rally's handbill, stating clearly that "this is not a strike," declared:

> This demonstration is an irresistible, spontaneous mass movement on the part
> of all Ford workers and many civic organizations who desire full participation
> of *All the People* in carrying out the war against Hitler. *We want the whole world
> to know that the Ford Motor Company is flagrantly violating the executive order
> of President Roosevelt, No. 8802, which declares that "there shall be no discrimi-
> nation against Race, Creed, or Color in hiring in Defense Industries."* We feel that
> this is every man's war regardless of race. We are fighting for Democracy abroad.
> We want Democracy at home as well. *Mr. Ford, Negro women and men will and
> must play their rightful part in helping win this war.*[36]

In addition to staging public protests, civil rights and labor leaders cooperated with the FEPC, which had begun to focus on employment discrimi-

nation against Detroit's minority male and female workers. Together the FEPC, the NAACP, the Detroit FEP Council, and the UAW-CIO won a small victory on 25 September 1942 when Ford hired twenty-seven black women at Willow Run. Similar pressure three months later prompted Ford to hire four African-American women for production-line jobs at River Rouge. Despite a brief work stoppage staged by white workers, they were able to hold on to their positions. Civil rights and union leaders also called on the FEPC to investigate discrimination complaints from other Detroit war plants, including Hudson Naval Ordnance Arsenal, Continental Motors, and U.S. Rubber. On 27 November 1942 the committee announced that it had set tentative dates for public hearings in Detroit for February 1943, and in early January 1943 the FEPC opened a Detroit office headed by G. James Fleming, an African American who had managed the *Philadelphia Tribune* before the war. He was assisted by J. Lawrence Duncan, who had recently joined the War Manpower Commission. Fleming also employed three white FEPC field workers: Jack B. Burke, Daniel R. Donovan, and Ernest Trimble. The primary goal of these officials was to prepare the hearings against the violators of Executive Order 8802. The proceedings were designed to publicly expose employment discrimination and its deleterious effects on war production, thereby pressuring defense employers into accepting their wartime duty to hire regardless of race, creed, color, or national origin.[37]

Undoubtedly the organizations fighting for fair employment in Detroit were pleased by the FEPC's new presence there. At the same time, however, some were upset that the committee had scheduled the hearings for 1943. Victor Reuther, the head of the UAW's War Policy Division, wired the FEPC complaining that February was too late. "Decision by FEPC to delay discrimination hearing in Detroit to February shocks those of us who take seriously the Government's policy regarding discrimination. Dangerous employment policy involving segregation and discriminatory practices is in the making," he warned, "and if continued will result in labor strife and turmoil."[38] Reuther requested that the Detroit hearings be held in December. As it turned out, they were delayed further. On 11 January 1943 the head of the War Manpower Commission, Paul McNutt, who had administrative jurisdiction over the FEPC, quashed the Detroit hearings, along with the others that the committee had planned for the Midwest, in order to rein in the FEPC.[39]

The cancellation of the proposed FEPC hearings had a damaging effect on black morale in Detroit and the nation generally. Even before McNutt's action federal officials and civil rights leaders believed that African-American morale was at a nadir. Blacks were particularly upset about their economic situation. In January 1943 one-fifth of the black labor force, roughly sixteen thousand workers, in Wayne County were unemployed.[40] At the same time three-fifths of the people on Detroit's WPA rolls were African-American. As

Reverend Charles Hill explained to the FEPC in the spring of 1943, "many of the Negro youth are embittered. They go to factories with boys with whom they have been graduated from high school; the white boy is employed immediately and this [black] boy is told the company does not employ Negroes."[41] Horace Sheffield wrote President Roosevelt in 1943 that "the Negro populace [in Detroit] is seething under" these discriminatory economic conditions.[42] FBI investigations confirmed Hill's and Sheffield's assessments. In its 1943 survey of racial conditions, the bureau's Detroit agents concluded that dissatisfaction over job opportunities was a contributing factor to racial problems in the city. When the FEPC, the only agency of the federal government that seemed capable of dealing with job bias, was prevented from taking action in Detroit, blacks were angered further. In response, Reverend Hill of the Detroit FEP Council led a delegation, consisting of Horace Sheffield and Frank Winn of the UAW, Louis Martin of the *Michigan Chronicle,* and Gloster Current of the Detriot NAACP, to Washington, D.C., to meet with McNutt. Hill's group may have made an impression on McNutt. In any event he did not prevent the return of the FEPC to Detroit to continue preparations for a series of hearings.[43]

On 6 April 1943 Jack Burke, an FEPC investigator, met with sixteen civil rights leaders from various organizations, including the Detroit FEP Council, the Civil Rights Federation, the National Negro Congress, and the Detroit NAACP. They told Burke of the desperate need for FEPC action. Trained black workers, many of whom had amassed five to six hundred hours of classroom experience, were denied opportunities to work. Charles Hill alleged that just to get an interview sometimes required bribes. Even so, the situation was not hopeless. As Geraldine Bledsoe of the Detroit FEP Council explained at the meeting, the percentage of black men in Detroit's war industries had jumped from 5.6 percent in May 1942 to 8.4 percent in April 1943. Employers were not, however, employing African-American women. Although their opportunities had improved since 1942, black women comprised only 3.3 percent of war workers in Detroit, and roughly twenty-eight thousand were waiting for wartime jobs. Although most of those with jobs were employed by Ford, they represented only a small fraction of its total workforce. The assembled group was convinced that the FEPC, led by "responsible men of the type of Jack Burke," could solve the employment problems of Detroit's minority workers, and they requested that the FEPC reschedule hearings in the city.[44]

To demonstrate public support for the FEPC and to protest discrimination in war industries and housing, on Sunday, 11 April 1943, Gloster Current, the head of the NAACP's Labor Committee, sponsored a mass rally in Cadillac Square. Ten thousand whites and blacks jammed into the square to hear addresses by Reverend Charles Hill, James McClendon, the president of the Detroit NAACP, Walter Reuther of the UAW, and Col. George E. Strong of the U.S. Army, a white industrial relations expert who had worked with the leadership of the FEPC and the UAW to end many racially motivated wildcat strikes. After Strong finished his speech, the assembled group was presented with the Cadillac Charter, a document summarizing the UAW's demand that "all industry participating in the war effort treat all labor alike, regardless of race, color, creed, religion, or national origin, in hiring, upgrading, and training of men and women, fully observing Executive Order 8802."[45] Following the demonstration, Horace Sheffield, the newly appointed head of the UAW's Inter-racial Committee, sent a copy of the Cadillac Charter to President Roosevelt. General Edwin M. Watson, one of FDR's secretaries, responded by promising that the FEPC would "continue to carry on [its] efforts to reduce discrimination."[46]

A week after the Cadillac Square rally, the FEPC finally reset hearing dates for 24 and 25 May 1943. Fleming, the head of the FEPC's Detroit office, utilized local activists to build strong cases against violators of Executive Order 8802. The FEPC decided to pressure the Teamsters Union Local 299, the Detroit Post Office, and several automobile parts companies, including Nash-Kelvinator and Ray Day Piston, into adopting fair employment practices. The companies and the Teamsters had denied black workers jobs and promotions while the post office had refused to upgrade Jewish employees. Absent from the proposed list of hearing participants were the major automobile manufacturers. Ford still discriminated against black men and especially black women. Yet the company was Detroit's, as well as the nation's, largest employer of African Americans. Fleming concluded that although the FEPC had received "important grievances" involving all of Ford's plants, "the evidence at hand is not sufficient for a public hearing, at this time, against the Ford Motor Company."[47] The committee was sticking to its best cases, which it hoped would at least open some doors for minority workers.[48]

The FEPC needed strong cases because committee members knew that achieving fair employment practices in Detroit was a difficult task. As in many midwestern cities, the FEPC had support among civil rights and some labor activists. For example, C. Pat Quinn, the president of the Greater Detroit and Wayne County Industrial Union Council (CIO), wrote the FEPC that his organization pledged its "full support and cooperation to the Committee."[49] John F. Shepherd, the president of the Michigan Civil Rights Federation, promised to aid the FEPC with the hearings. Other groups in Detroit, however, were equally pledged to oppose the FEPC's actions. In early 1943 G. James Fleming met with John L. Lovett, the head of the Michigan Manufacturers' Association, who told him that his organization, which was composed of the city's major companies, was prepared to answer any allegations brought by the FEPC. "Mr. Lovett," Fleming later commented, had "all the tools of toughness, sarcasm and eloquence on his side."[50] Several union locals also resisted fair employment in Detroit, demonstrating their opposition by staging numerous hate strikes during the spring and early summer of 1943 at Chrysler, Chicago Pneumatic Tool, and Ford.[51]

Major wildcat strikes in the months preceding the proposed FEPC hearings indicated not only the difficulty in breaking down racial employment barriers but also the widening gulf between whites and blacks. On 20 April 1943, for instance, Hudson's management hired a black man to be trained as a plant guard. Almost immediately the company's twenty-one white guards went on strike for three days and came back to work only when they realized that management was not backing down. In April and early May there were other strikes by white workers at Briggs, U.S. Rubber, and Packard. Black workers, frustrated by discrimination and the hostility of whites, also went on wildcat strikes. On 29 April 1943 three thousand black foundry workers at Ford's River Rouge plant struck after three black workers were assaulted by two plant guards. In accordance with FEPC policy, Fleming helped to end that strike by sending the African-American workers a telegram stating that the FEPC "deplored" the work stoppage.[52] The committee shared the federal government's overall goal of uninterrupted industrial production. FEPC officials also believed that these wildcat strikes heightened racial tensions and made fair employment untenable. Hence Fleming urged the workers to return to their jobs and settle their grievances through their union (UAW-CIO Local 600) and through the FEPC. Although the workers returned to work, tension at Ford as well as Chrysler and Packard remained high.[53]

In part because it did not want to exacerbate industrial tensions, the FEPC again delayed the hearings, rescheduling them for 28 and 29 June 1943. This action drew many letters of protest, including one from J. Lawrence Duncan of the War Manpower Commission, who complained to the committee that if the hearings were not held soon, "confidence in FEPC will be lost."[54] Despite the new hearing dates industrial and racial tensions continued. On 24 May twenty-five thousand white Packard workers went on strike to protest the hiring of four black women and the upgrading of three black men. G. James Fleming, R. J. Thomas of the UAW, and Col. George Strong tried to end the walkout by meeting with the white workers. Thomas was heckled by the crowd gathered outside the plant. One voice, reportedly belonging to a white southerner, shouted "I'd rather see Hitler and Hirohito win than work beside a nigger on the assembly line."[55] The striking workers had the tacit approval of Packard's personnel managers and the leaders of Local 190. C. E. Weiss, the chief personnel manager, urged the white workers as they left the plant to "hold out in their demand that Negroes not be hired or upgraded."[56] Colonel Strong then issued a public statement that all striking workers would be fired, making them available for the draft. Whites returned to Packard, although they continued to oppose fair employment. Evidence collected by the NAACP suggested that the Ku Klux Klan faction within the UAW led the opposition to fair employment at Packard as well as at Hudson and Ford.[57]

The racial animosity demonstrated by wildcat strikes and by the 1942 Sojourner Truth Housing Project controversy reached a climax in the Detroit race riot of June 1943. The riot, the worst during the war, began at Detroit's main recreational area, Belle Isle Park, where on the hot Sunday evening of 20 June fights broke out between white and black men. As news of the fights and rumors of murder and rape spread so did the fighting, which lasted four days. By the time federal troops restored order on 24 June, twenty-five African Americans and nine whites were dead, nearly seven hundred were injured, and $2 million worth of property had been destroyed. Naturally the FEPC hearings scheduled for 28 June were canceled.[58]

Although shocking, the riot surprised few close observers. Louis Martin, the editor of the *Michigan Chronicle,* wrote that "Detroit [had been] a racial haystack, just waiting for a match."[59] In his analysis of the conflict, Walter White of the NAACP judged that its causes were rooted in part in the massive migration of southern whites and blacks to Detroit. In the year preceding the race riot, 250,000 to 300,000 southerners came to Detroit, just under fifty thousand of them black.[60] There was intense competition for adequate jobs, housing, and public facilities, all of which created seething social tensions.[61] Other contributing factors were the failure of Detroit's government and business leaders to address the needs of either African-American or white newcomers, the refusal of local law enforcement to check the activities of the KKK and other hate groups, and, as White put it, the "vacillation of the Fair Employment Practice Committee."[62]

What was astonishing about the Detroit riot was the relative calm displayed by factory workers. Walter White and United States Attorney General Francis Biddle both credited the UAW leadership, whose educational programs and strong stand against discrimination had lessened some of the tensions on the shop floor. The Fair Employment Practice Committee's chairman viewed the relative industrial peace during the riot as a sign of the "decency and patriotism of the overwhelming majority" of workers.[63] Fleming of the FEPC was also encouraged, and believed that "this behavior in the plants may well be credited to the fact, when all is said and done, that these workers know each other better, have mutual interests and recognize their interdependence."[64] In other words, the FEPC believed that further job gains in Detroit were possible.

Although there were no FEPC hearings during the summer of 1943, Fleming and his assistants continued to work on complaints concerning several automakers, the Detroit Post Office, and the Teamsters Local 299. They made some progress at a few auto plants. Continental Motors and GM hired more African-American men and women during July and August 1943. Fleming found Ford to be a more formidable challenge. In September 1943 he and two white FEPC investigators met with Harry Bennett to discuss dozens of cases of discrimination. Bennett kept the three waiting in the outer office for three hours. Bennett's secretary told them confidentially that Bennett only wanted to meet with the two white FEPC representatives and wanted Fleming, a black man, to leave. Fleming refused to go and wrested from Bennett a verbal agreement to stop discriminating against black men and women and to stop recruiting white workers from the South as long as African Americans were available in Detroit. Despite this success, Fleming was generally displeased with the accomplishments of the FEPC at Detroit's automobile plants.[65] As he wrote at the time, "it is fair and safe to say that all these automotive companies have areas of employment where Negroes may move a few steps above the lowest unskilled brackets; at the same time there are skills and sections to which Negroes are not upgraded or placed, and there are certain types of work which, even if Negroes perform, they are not given equal payment with white workers."[66]

Progress with the postal cases was similarly difficult. President Roosevelt's postmaster general, Frank C. Walker, had answered the FEPC's charge that the Detroit office discriminated against Jewish workers by refusing to upgrade them. Walker wrote the FEPC that "this matter was made the subject of a complete and extensive investigation and from the facts presented the conclusion has been reached that there has been no discrimination."[67] As of August 1943 there were still no Jews in supervisory positions at the Detroit Post Office. Fleming was equally unsuccessful in resolving the cases of discrimination against the Teamsters Union Local 299, which was run by Jimmy Hoffa. All these cases and more were left for Edward M. Swan, who became head of the Detroit office when Fleming was reassigned to the Philadelphia FEPC office in September 1943.[68]

Swan, an African American and native of Michigan, was well prepared to run the Detroit FEPC office. During the Great Depression he had served as the Michigan Director of Negro Affairs of the National Youth Administration, where he investigated and fought discrimination with J. Lawrence Duncan, who held a similar post with the Michigan Employment Service. To assist Swan, the FEPC allowed Daniel Donovan and J. Lawrence Duncan to continue working in the Detriot office. Swan later gained two other black investigators, George W. Crockett, a UAW organizer, and Lethia W. Clore from the Cleveland FEPC office.[69] At the time that Swan took charge, the Detroit office had the largest caseload of any FEPC facility in the Midwest. There were over two hundred open cases in late summer 1943, and most concerned racial discrimination.[70]

Because of his limited resources and because Detroit race relations were, in the words of Louis Martin, "still dynamite," Swan attacked employment discrimination cautiously and had no immediate plans for public hearings.[71] He focused his energies initially on large manufacturers, particularly Ford and Bohn Aluminum, which were the source of half of the complaints docketed by the Detroit office. Although Swan helped to resolve some cases, the gigantic demand for war workers in Detroit was more effective, causing a dramatic increase in the number of black employees at defense plants by December 1943. Detroit was one of three cities in the Midwest that the War Manpower Commission labeled as having "acute" labor shortages, meaning that demand outstripped supply. By 1944 seventy thousand African Americans (roughly 18 percent of whom were women) worked in Detroit's war industries, comprising about 9 percent of the total number employed in those plants.[72] Blacks also filled the demand for other types of workers. The local transit industry, for example, employed over two thousand African Americans. No other transit system in the Midwest or the nation was so integrated.[73]

Although market forces often seemed to prompt the hiring of minority workers in Detroit, the FEPC was not irrelevant. In addition to its continuing efforts to adjust complaints of employment discrimination, it strove to create peaceful and harmonious working conditions in the city's factories. Like other FEPC officials in midwestern cities such as Cincinnati, Edward Swan was a key player in ending wildcat strikes over racial issues that continued—albeit less frequently—after the 1943 race riot. Several stoppages involved black workers. On 28 October 1943 the management at the Dodge Truck Plant dismissed two black workers who refused job transfers. Dozens of black employees went on strike in retaliation. Swan, Duncan, and Colonel Strong settled the strike and again urged African Americans to use union grievance machinery or the FEPC if they had complaints. A larger strike came in November 1944 when six thousand black metal polishers at Packard walked out for two days to protest alleged unfair treatment in their department. The strike paralyzed Packard, which sent all its thirty thousand workers home until the FEPC and UAW negotiated their return. Whites also went on strike, sometimes over the hiring of black workers, as happened at the Taylor-Gaskin Company, and other times over the employment of Japanese Americans, as occurred at the Palmer-Bee Company. Swan also helped resolve these industrial disputes by meeting with managers and union leaders to end the strikes while maintaining the job gains of minority workers.[74]

By late summer 1944 strikes over racial issues were less frequent, yet industrial race relations often remained quite hostile. In July 1944 at the Chrysler Tank Arsenal a noose was hung from the plant rafters as a message to a black production worker after he allegedly put his arm around a white female coworker. At the Detroit Diesel Engine plant white Christian workers harassed Bernard Kiel, calling him a "dirty Jew" and putting a sign that read "pawn broker" above his work station.[75] The FEPC tried to combat white worker prejudice with an educational campaign, the highlight of which was a public speech on 8 October 1944 by the FEPC chairman, Malcolm Ross. He had come to the city on an invitation from the Detroit FEP Council, which waged its own intense educational crusade against job bias. With posters, pamphlets, and public appearances, FEPC officials sought to unite employers, union and nonunion workers, community activists, and local government officials behind the federal government's program for fair employment.[76]

In addition to trying to improve race relations and settle wildcat strikes, the FEPC continued to fight unfair employment practices. Following the examples set by FEPC officials in Chicago and Cleveland, Swan tried to overcome the limitations set by a small staff of no more than five full-time workers and annual budget of roughly ten thousand dollars by unifying the struggle against employment discrimination under the FEPC's banner. In late 1943 he arranged for the Detroit FEP Council to refer cases of discrimination directly to the city's FEPC office. After making a formal agreement with the UAW, Swan also worked with the union's Fair Practices Department, which had been set up in October 1944 and was headed by George Crockett, a former FEPC investigator. Finally, Swan cooperated closely with J. Lawrence Duncan of the WMC. When a discrimination complaint reached the WMC office first, Duncan tried to adjust it himself. If he failed, he would send the case to Swan. Using this tag-team method, the two federal officials broke color barriers at Republic Aircraft, Briggs, and Central Boiler, a factory that made steel parts for Chrysler, GM, and Packard.[77]

A particularly close but less successful FEPC-WMC collaboration was the struggle to break the color barriers of Detroit's trucking companies, which were essential for the delivery of army vehicles to coastal areas. This fair employment battle centered on Teamsters Local 299, which was run by Jimmy Hoffa, who prevented blacks from joining. Many African Americans drove trucks in the city, which had seven Teamsters locals, six of which allowed blacks as members and drivers. The jobs that blacks could get, however, were on intracity short-haul runs carrying garbage, coal, lumber, and factory rubbish. The better-paying interstate long-haul routes were controlled by Hoffa's lily-white local. The story of Oscar Purvey, a black trucker, typifies the problem. Purvey had twelve years of experience driving fruit trucks between Florida and Boston. After moving to Detroit, he applied at a local trucking company, which had a closed shop agreement with Local 299. Hoffa denied Purvey membership in the union, and eventually Purvey took a job hauling rubbish. At first the Detroit WMC tried singlehandedly to adjust Purvey's complaint and similar ones from other black truckers. When meetings with Hoffa failed to integrate his local, the WMC denied USES referrals to companies that had labor agreements with Hoffa. This had no effect on Local 299's discriminatory policies. In mid-1944 the WMC gave the Teamsters' cases to the FEPC for disposition. Swan and several other FEPC officials met numerous times with Hoffa, who was "belligerent throughout" the conferences. At one point Hoffa flatly told the FEPC, "we don't permit Negroes in 299 . . . what are you going to do about it?"[78] On 2 June 1945 the FEPC finally had a hearing in Detroit to settle dozens of complaints against the Teamsters. Although the Detroit WMC gave the committee support in making well-documented cases against Local 299, the hearing was a complete failure. Since the FEPC did not have the power of subpoena, neither Hoffa nor any other member of his local attended the proceedings, and only three of the nine trucking companies that were asked to appear did so. FEPC officials, led by chairman Malcolm Ross, merely scolded the company officials who were there and who the FEPC believed were equally culpable.[79]

Although the Teamsters hearing was not successful, Swan believed that it had improved the FEPC's stature in Detroit. "Many persons who heretofore have been lukewarm" towards the agency, he wrote, were now "in favor" of it.[80] After the hearing a few manufacturers contacted the FEPC about creating fair employment in their plants. But by the summer of 1945 Swan's efforts were not dramatically affecting employment patterns in Detroit. Although the city remained acutely short of labor throughout the war, Swan was unable to resolve the issue of discrimination in promotions or job bias against black women. He blamed the limits of federal activism on his tiny budget (which was about the same as that of the Detroit FEP Council) and small staff.[81]

By late in the war, integration in low-skill jobs was no longer a problem for black men and some women. African-American workers held nearly 21 percent (95,000) of the 459,500 manufacturing jobs in Detroit by 1945.[82] They represented 14 percent of the city's labor force, twice as much as in 1940.[83] In other words, over three times more blacks had defense jobs on V-J Day than on the eve of Pearl Harbor. These gains were among the largest in the Midwest and the nation.[84]

What caused this incredible change? Gloster Current of the Detroit NAACP attributed the advances to the manpower requirements of war industries in the Detroit area, which according to him had "eliminated" the problem of employment "for the time being."[85] Although there is no denying the importance of wartime labor shortages, the FEPC also helped blacks achieve a measure of economic justice during the war. As the black New Dealer Robert Weaver wrote after the war, although economic necessity was an essential factor in the job advancements of African Americans, the FEPC's efforts were also "extremely important."[86] The committee's office in Detroit handled over four hundred cases of discrimination. Fleming and Swan settled nearly 70 percent of these. This percentage was the best in the Midwest. The FEPC offices in Chicago, Cleveland, Cincinnati, and St. Louis not only handled fewer complaints but failed to match the success rate of the Detroit office.[87] What was different about the Motor City? The level of cooperation from local civil rights activists and especially labor activists like George Crockett, Shelton Tappes, and Horace Sheffield enabled Fleming and Swan to act effectively.[88]

Because of the FEPC's partial successes in Detroit and because of the more important role of market forces in creating job opportunities, some historians have been extremely critical of the committee. In his study of Michigan during the war, Alan Clive writes that the committee's efforts "boiled down to a 'legalized nuisance,' a monotonous pestering that merely forced employers to seek more subtle means of preserving the color bar." In some respects Clive is correct. There were definite limits to what the FEPC was able to accomplish. It never completely eradicated the genderized racial employment barriers that prevented Detroit's African-American community from participating fully in the war industries.[89]

Yet knowledgeable contemporary observers in the Motor City believed that the FEPC's presence had been beneficial. The *Detroit Free Press* editorialized in 1944 that the committee had "done excellent work." The *Detroit Tribune* later commented that the FEPC "was a great achievement," without which, several civil rights leaders believed, many job barriers would not have been removed. Indeed one can wonder whether Ford would have ever hired black women had the committee not intervened. FEPC officials in Detroit handled hundreds of discrimination cases, settling nearly seven out of ten of them. In addition Swan and his small staff mobilized and encouraged local activism against employment discrimination, in essence giving federal endorsement to community efforts to end job bias. They also tried to improve racial relations through quiet persuasion and public education, including conferences and lectures. As Clarence Anderson of the Detroit FEP Council told a congressional committee in 1944, Swan, Fleming, and the other FEPC officials not only opened job opportunities but also fostered racial harmony in industry and in the city generally after the race riots. Thus the FEPC in Detroit was more than a "nuisance." With the cooperation of local civil rights and labor organizations, it made modest—yet solid—strides against employment discrimination and eased racial tensions during the war.[90]

8. Stretching the Social Pattern: The FEPC and St. Louis

In the Midwest the Fair Employment Practice Committee had some of its most difficult cases in cities near the South. St. Louis was no exception. Despite its best efforts late in the war, the committee did not dramatically affect job bias in St. Louis, although it established a suboffice and held two separate sets of hearings. Part of the problem derived from St. Louis's labor market, which did not experience severe shortages. Stringent conditions in other midwestern production centers, such as Cleveland and Detroit, spurred employment integration. The other problem was related to well-entrenched community traditions of discrimination and de facto segregation. As an FEPC official explained after the war, the St. Louis "social pattern" was not easily "stretched," and thus the barriers to black employment were not generally overcome.[1]

Akin to cities such as Cincinnati and East Alton, St. Louis adopted many of its racial mores from the South. To both blacks and whites it was just another "southern city."[2] Prejudice, discrimination, and segregation were common facets of daily life that remained largely unchanged in the 1940s. According to one historian, wartime St. Louis was "one of the most segregated cities in the nation."[3] In 1916 the city council had passed an ordinance making it illegal for blacks to move into residential areas that were 75 percent white. Although the United States Supreme Court's *Buchanan v. Warley* (1917) decision made such laws unconstitutional, the St. Louis Real Estate Exchange used other methods to maintain residential segregation. Schools, including the private St. Louis and Washington Universities, hotels, movie theaters, barber shops, the Major League baseball stadium, and restaurants were also segregated. Most African Americans, who worked in the city's downtown, had to bring their lunches since no cafeteria, except for the one at Union Station, would serve them.[4]

Racial prejudice filtered into other areas of city life. In 1944 the Swedish sociologist Gunnar Myrdal noted that "Negroes in Border cities" such as Washington, D.C., and St. Louis met with "relatively more prejudice both from the police and from the courts" than in cities farther north. Economically, African Americans in St. Louis had been severely handicapped by discrimination. Most worked in low-paying jobs as domestic servants, janitors, and common laborers in steel and iron mills.[5]

According to FEPC chairman Malcolm Ross, what differentiated St. Louis from the "Deep South" was that discrimination as well as segregation were "challenged [and] considered debatable."[6] Between the First and Second World Wars, the organization that most aided African Americans in fighting Jim Crow in St. Louis was the local Urban League. Founded in 1917, the St. Louis Urban League (SLUL) was dedicated to "equalizing life chances for all people," especially southern black migrants.[7] From 1910 to 1920 the black population in St. Louis rose from 43,960 to 69,854. Black St. Louisans, who accounted for 9 percent of the urban population in 1920, struggled in overcrowded and unsanitary living conditions. They had little access to decent health care and well-paying jobs. The SLUL tried to ameliorate the situation by creating a nursery in 1917 and a dental clinic in 1920. It also successfully pressured the local Tuberculosis and Health Society to hire its first black social worker to deal with disease in the black neighborhoods. In addition, under the direction of executive secretary John T. Clark, the league helped African Americans find jobs. The SLUL's employment service grew dramatically during the 1920s, serving thousands per year. Most of the positions available were domestic service and low-skill work in factories such as Scullin Steel.[8]

Many of these jobs were lost during the Great Depression. In 1931 National Urban League officials made a survey of 106 American cities and discovered that the percentage of unemployed blacks in the labor force was anywhere from 30 to 60 percent greater than that of whites.[9] In 1933 70 percent of African Americans in St. Louis were jobless and 20 percent had only part-time work.[10] To mitigate the effects of the depression, the St. Louis Urban League organized self-help projects such as the Federation of Block Units, which was composed of neighborhood civic organizations engaged in beautification, voter registration drives, and gardening projects to supplement the diets of needy families and the unemployed. The units also lobbied the city government for new zoning and sanitation ordinances.[11]

During the lean years of the 1930s the SLUL continued to assist black workers. Although the league interviewed tens of thousands of job applicants, it could only place a small fraction of them. In 1936, for example, the SLUL found jobs for twenty-two hundred, only 10 percent of those who filed that year.[12] In an attempt to open more employment opportunities the SLUL negotiated with the New Deal relief officials, who too frequently discriminated against black women and men. Such pressure sometimes worked, as several

WPA projects were opened to blacks on a segregated basis. Nevertheless some New Deal programs, such as the WPA Household Training Centers, remained off-limits to African Americans. In addition to federal administrators, the Urban League battled St. Louis's lily-white trade unions, which hampered efforts to find work for unemployed blacks on city and federal construction projects. For instance, in 1932 construction began on the federally funded Homer G. Phillips Hospital for Negroes. Because the building contract included a closed shop labor agreement, black craftsmen, who were not allowed in any AFL building unions, were denied employment.[13] As Charles A. Collier, the industrial secretary of the SLUL, wrote at the time, "it is a sorry comment that Negroes should be denied the right [to work], as skilled workers on [a hospital] for them."[14]

SLUL officials decided that the best way to fight union discrimination was to form black unions, taking advantage of Section 7(a) of the National Industrial Recovery Act. One direct result was the creation in 1934 of the International Laborers and Builders Corporation (ILBC), an organization of bricklayers, carpenters, cement finishers, electricians, hod carriers, painters, and paperhangers. The ILBC won a momentary victory when it negotiated the employment of black workers on the Phillips Hospital project. White AFL workers went on strike for two months until all blacks were fired. Continued frustration with white unions encouraged blacks to create another independent umbrella labor organization. With the assistance of the St. Louis Urban League, African-American hotel workers, janitors, motion picture operators, and construction workers formed the St. Louis Urban League's Negro Workers' Council. In the late 1930s black workers also collaborated with newly formed CIO unions in St. Louis in order to ease racial barriers to industrial employment. Although organizing black workers was a significant achievement, the CIO, the Negro Workers' Council, and the ILBC failed to substantially improve economic conditions for African Americans. Nevertheless, these Depression-era experiences laid the groundwork for black wartime activism in St. Louis, which generally followed an all-black organizational structure, while keeping ties with some CIO unions and the federal government.[15]

When the defense mobilization began in 1940, 109,000 African Americans lived in St. Louis, comprising 13 percent of its population. Of the nearly fifty thousand in the labor force, 20 percent were seeking work and 11 percent were on WPA projects.[16] The St. Louis Urban League relied on private meetings and formal requests to improve the situation. In July 1940, for example, Sidney R. Williams of the SLUL sent letters to "fellow white citizens of Saint Louis" arguing that "National Unity and Democracy . . . can know no color-line." Williams urged the St. Louis Chamber of Commerce to request that its members and affiliates drop the color barriers to employment, that trade unions discontinue rituals that barred blacks, and that all employers "give Negro young people the same opportunity accorded to all other young people." The plea fell on deaf ears, and the SLUL was able to find defense work for only a few blacks in 1940 and early 1941.[17]

By the middle of 1941 there was no shortage of war-related jobs, particularly on the federally funded construction projects building new defense plants. As Richard R. Jefferson of the St. Louis Urban League wrote, however, "against this backdrop of expanding industrial production . . . an examination of the experiences of Negro workers reveals an amazing set of contradictions and discriminatory employment policies." The federal government spent hundreds of thousands of dollars in the St. Louis area on new production facilities, hiring over twenty thousand construction workers, many of them recruits from southern cities. Yet fewer than three thousand were black. Save for three union painters in a "colored" local of the Brotherhood of Painters, Decorators, and Paperhangers, all African Americans were employed as common laborers and hod carriers. Despite the increasing difficulty of finding experienced skilled and semiskilled workers, no blacks were allowed to help build the vast powder factory just outside St. Louis or the massive United States Cartridge plant. Furthermore, as E. J. Bradley, the vice president of the St. Louis Brotherhood of Sleeping Car Porters, told Frank S. Horne, a race relations assistant in the United States Housing Authority, "it is absolutely impossible to get Negro mechanics [hired] on any . . . USHA projects in the St. Louis area due to discrimination solely in the white unions." This discrimination persisted, Jefferson noted, "in spite of vigorous efforts of government agencies, the Urban League and other interested organizations."[18]

One of the first federal government officials to visit St. Louis to assist black workers was Robert C. Weaver of the Negro Employment and Training Branch of the Office of Production Management. In June 1941 Lewis W. Clymer, a native of St. Louis and a Howard University graduate, joined the OPM staff in Kansas City. Clymer, the only black in the office, worked with the St. Louis Urban League to relax racial barriers to jobs and training. He was somewhat successful in creating educational opportunities. After meetings with several managers of iron and steel works in the area, classes in gas and electric welding, air-hammer chipping, and related crafts were set up for black workers. Although this was an important accomplishment, training was not the central problem. In fact it was readily available for both whites and blacks. The Carver School of Aeronautics, for example, trained black and white men and women in various phases of aircraft production, including inspection, blueprint reading, drafting, and engine mechanics.[19] But as Delores de Leery, the placement supervisor at Carver, later complained to President Roosevelt, "the doors are definitely barred by a strong feeling of discrimination against qualified Negro workers." Despite the backing of the St. Louis Urban League,

Clymer was unable to change the "brazen acts of race discrimination" displayed by St. Louis's war contractors.[20]

Like the Negro Employment and Training Branch of the OPM, the Fair Employment Practice Committee's initial forays in St. Louis made little impact. Although the first committee's tiny staff was preoccupied with its publicity campaign and with preparation for its first round of hearings, the executive secretary of the FEPC, Lawrence Cramer, sent white investigator Daniel R. Donovan to St. Louis in late December 1941 to meet with SLUL officials and local industrialists. From John Clark of the Urban League Donovan learned the details of the employment problems facing black workers, and from the employers he learned what manufacturers planned to do about the situation. Shortly before Donovan's visit, the managers of the major defense firms, such as U.S. Cartridge, had met and decided, with the full support of the St. Louis Chamber of Commerce, to hire enough blacks to comprise about 10 percent of their work forces and thus forestall any FEPC investigation.[21] The FEPC officially opposed this plan, stating that it would hamper the war effort. "A plant with its 10 percent Negro quota filled cannot hire Negro workers, even if they are at the gates and badly needed." Committee members also disliked the St. Louis quota plan because it was "unfair to Negroes," as it limited "their opportunities . . . to only a few industries willing to admit them." As FEPC officials explained, "an employer able and willing to hire Negroes to man a third of his jobs cannot do so because of the quota."[22]

Although the FEPC disapproved of the employment quota in St. Louis, it did little to prevent its implementation. The committee was intensely busy with other matters. Moreover the federal government, in particular the OPM and the FEPC, had no explicit policies prohibiting such employment patterns, and in fact Robert Weaver had promoted them. No matter how opposed the FEPC was to quotas, the plan meant defense jobs for blacks, which until that point were almost nonexistent. By the spring of 1942 two major factories, which had just been built, began hiring African-American workers. The Curtiss-Wright Corporation, which nationally had instituted fair employment policies, and the United States Cartridge Company, hired several hundred black workers in skilled and unskilled jobs, including welders, riveters, assemblers, and inspectors. Both plants still limited employment opportunities by segregating black workers into separate buildings, which to most white business and civic leaders was an acceptable method of overcoming white resistance to the opening of new jobs for blacks.[23]

Civil rights activists in St. Louis were initially ambivalent about the new job opportunities. On the one hand, as Richard Jefferson of the Urban League pointed out, "this form of segregation in industry can be looked upon with favor [because] these firms made a reasonable effort to use the available Negro labor supply." On the other hand, many questioned whether the firms were complying with the letter and spirit of Executive Order 8802. The job quotas and segregation seemed to limit not only future employment but also upgrading. In addition, Jefferson and others were also wary of the quota plan because while Curtiss-Wright and U.S. Cartridge were trying to follow it, most other defense employers were not. "At least 100 important war production plants," he pointed out, had "no Negro workers."[24]

Black leaders became more suspicious of white industrialists in St. Louis when, on 16 May 1942, U.S. Cartridge laid off several hundred black workers because of mounting opposition from white employees. A new all-black organization, the St. Louis Unit of the March on Washington Movement (St. Louis MOWM), led the fight to reinstate the workers. The St. Louis MOWM was more radical than other local black organizations and was one of the most active branches of Randolph's organization, with a membership of four thousand by 1945. It had been formed three days before U.S. Cartridge's layoff. Its leaders were David M. Grant, a black attorney and a patronage dispenser for the local Democratic Party, and Theodore D. McNeal, an international field organizer for the Brotherhood of Sleeping Car Porters who in 1960 became the first black state senator in Missouri. Grant and McNeal, along with representatives of the local branches of the Urban League and NAACP, met with managers at U.S. Cartridge soon after the firings. They demanded the rehiring of the black workers, immediate compliance with Executive Order 8802, the immediate employment of black women in production, equal opportunity for in-plant training, and equal opportunity for upgrading of African Americans. According to St. Louis MOWM leaders, company officials remained "committed to a policy of discrimination and separation of its Negro employees."[25] The St. Louis MOWM initially planned to contact the FEPC to challenge this policy. But because, as Elizabeth Grant, a member of the MOWM unit and the wife of David Grant, later wrote, the first committee "was not effectively functioning" in St. Louis, the group reconsidered and decided instead to "go to the streets."[26] On 20 June 1942 the St. Louis MOWM staged a demonstration at the gates of U.S. Cartridge. Dozens of African Americans marched, carrying signs saying, "Is this democracy?" "Fight the Axis, don't fight us," "We are loyal Americans, too," and "Fellow Americans, where is your conscience?"[27]

After the protest, white managers at U.S. Cartridge rehired three hundred blacks and pledged to hire seventy-five "Negro women matrons" who were "to clean the lavatories of the white women production workers."[28] In July 1942 plant officials announced that the company would train an additional two hundred black men for production-line jobs. The march also had another effect. It brought the St. Louis MOWM into close contact with the leadership of the local United Electrical Radio and Machine Operators of America (UE-CIO). In William Sentner, the Communist leader of the UE at U.S. Cartridge, Grant and McNeal found a valuable ally.[29] Nevertheless, as had been the case in the 1930s, there were limits to what these activists could do. A month later U.S. Cartridge had not employed all the black men that it had trained and hired only twenty black matrons. In addition, there were no African-American women among its 23,500 production workers.[30]

U.S. Cartridge was not the sole violator of Executive Order 8802 in St. Louis. Most large war plants, including Amertorp, Bussman, Carter Carburetor, McQuay-Norris, and Wagner Electric, employed even fewer blacks and none in skilled positions. Blacks who had production jobs worked on segregated lines. Local United States Employment Service officials contributed to this employment pattern. The USES had two offices in St. Louis, one for whites and one for African Americans. St. Louis industrialists relied on the white office to find their skilled and semiskilled workers. Generally it did not matter what ethnicity or religion these USES referrals were.[31] As G. B. Pearson, the head of the white office, remarked in the July 1942 issue of *Employment Security Review*, "Jews . . . aliens and naturalized citizens—emigres from friendly and enemy countries . . . have been put to work." The few blacks who used the "colored" office, however, were referred to low-skill jobs only after they passed a series of examinations, including venereal disease tests. The local USES officials had no qualms about limiting employment opportunities or sending blacks to segregated work areas. In fact they supported the idea that segregation eliminated, as Pearson explained, "any possible friction which might result from prejudices of white fellow workers."[32]

To draw federal attention to unfair employment practices in the city, the leaders of the St. Louis MOWM sent a ten-page letter to FEPC chairman Malcolm MacLean on 24 July 1942, describing the employment problems of black St. Louisans. The discriminatory employment policies of ten war factories were detailed as well as the practices of local unions that "consistently block[ed] Negroes from defense employment."[33] The problems were worse than the letter revealed. Over 75 percent of St. Louis defense factories had no black workers. Unemployment among blacks remained astonishingly high. According to one historian, as late as the fall of 1942 for every black hired for a war job five still remained unemployed. Even at the plants that hired African Americans discrimination was rampant. For example, at McQuay-Norris, an ordnance manufacturer, black machine cleaners received fifty-seven cents an hour while white cleaners earned more than sixty.[34] The St. Louis MOWM urged the FEPC to hold public hearings to redress the grievances of black workers denied war jobs, promotions, and equal pay for equal work.[35]

In anticipation of FEPC hearings the St. Louis MOWM tried to create a supportive atmosphere. On 14 August 1942 it held a fair employment rally at Kiel Municipal Auditorium. David Grant of the St. Louis MOWM, Walter White of the NAACP, A. Philip Randolph of the MOWM, and Milton P. Web-

ster of the FEPC were the principle speakers. Webster gave a particularly stir-
ring oration, causing at least one member of the audience to write him afterward and offer his services as "an investigator in your organization."[36] The St.
Louis MOWM also demonstrated against local war plants. In early September it picketed Carter Carburetor, a factory with over $1 million in war con-
tracts that had no blacks among its 2,660 workers. Before arriving at Carter's
gates, the demonstrators, carrying placards with such slogans as "President
Roosevelt says 'no discrimination,' St. Louis war industries reply, 'says you!'"
walked through white neighborhoods, meeting no opposition and sometimes
applause from residents.[37] Unlike the first St. Louis MOWM march, this one
yielded no new jobs.[38]

Public protests and rallies, it seemed, had no effect on such well-entrenched
job bias. Hence on 27 November 1942 the FEPC announced that it would
conduct public hearings in St. Louis in order to "bring many of the largest
holders of war contracts into line with the national policy of full utilization
of manpower and of fair employment."[39] Two months later the head of the
War Manpower Commission, Paul McNutt, canceled these hearings in an
attempt to curtail the FEPC's activities.

The St. Louis MOWM protested the cancellation of the FEPC hearings by
sending President Roosevelt a giant postcard signed by its membership that
called on FDR to allow the committee to continue its activities. Yet even without the FEPC economic opportunities for blacks expanded dramatically
during early 1943. As one journalist reported, "the employment problem has
eased a good deal [and] most of the Negroes who wanted war work have been
absorbed in good jobs."[40] There were approximately eighteen thousand African Americans employed in St. Louis's war industries, a 225 percent increase
over 1942. Several manufacturers, such as Curtiss-Wright, were training and
employing black women. These gains can be attributed to a general—but
momentary—labor shortage and the activities of the St. Louis MOWM and
its allies, such as William Sentner and the UE, who organized black workers
and fought to increase their numbers in unskilled and skilled jobs.[41]

During early 1943, while economic conditions continued to improve for
blacks and some social barriers fell (including the integration of the main
post office's cafeteria), job bias remained in many industries. Large and small
factories alike maintained discriminatory policies. The General Chemical
Company, for example, had no African Americans among its 250 employees.
Even at the plants that hired blacks, unfair employment practices continued.
As a St. Louis Urban League official later commented, only where one found
"disagreeable odors, fumes, dust and extremes of temperatures" did one find
"Negroes . . . in the production of industrial chemicals."[42] U.S. Cartridge,
which became St. Louis's largest defense employer, hired African Americans
but kept them in a segregated building, number 103, and denied them job

upgrades. When management tried to place "Negro move-men" in its lily-white building number 202, twenty white women walked off their jobs. U.S. Cartridge's industrial relations director pleaded with the women, arguing that "Negroes constituted the only available labor of this type."[43] Although the strikers promised to take that under consideration, they only returned to work when management withdrew the black workers. David Grant of the St. Louis MOWM then negotiated an agreement with U.S. Cartridge to hire and train more blacks in skilled positions. Two weeks later all thirty-six hundred African Americans in building number 103 walked out, believing that U.S. Cartridge was not living up to the bargain. With the assistance of the St. Louis MOWM and the UE, the strikers finally returned to work after management promised to train a few black foremen in building number 103. Up to that point all supervisors were white. Although this was a significant concession, it did not alter the nature of employment segregation that kept blacks from jobs for which they were qualified.[44]

During 1943 the St. Louis MOWM kept the pressure on defense plants. Along with the St. Louis NAACP, the MOWM unit began to send complaints of discrimination that the local organizations failed to settle to the FEPC. By mid-1944 the committee had docketed over one hundred such grievances. The St. Louis MOWM also began a campaign in May 1943 to integrate other firms, particularly Southwestern Bell Telephone Company, which was advertising positions but refusing to hire black women. On 12 June 1943 David Grant and 342 members of his organization marched in front of the Southwestern Bell offices carrying signs that read "$4000 spent daily by Negroes in St. Louis for phones! Yet not one decent job for us," and "How can we die freely for democracy abroad if we can't work equally for democracy at home?"[45] The MOWM also tried to change Southwestern Bell's employment policy by urging black customers to pay their bills in pennies. When that did not work the MOWM handed out stickers that read "Discrimination in employment is undemocratic—I protest it! Hire Negroes Now!!" to be affixed (in lieu of payment) on telephone bills.[46] By September Southwestern Bell had opened an office in a black neighborhood and hired black employees.[47]

According to FBI agents in St. Louis, the MOWM unit's continuing efforts to fight job segregation and discrimination angered white St. Louisans, particularly recent migrants "from Southern states [who were] endeavoring to discipline local Negroes." During the war there were no major racial incidents. Whites tended to channel their hostilities into peaceful actions. For example, in 1943 Reverend Gerald L. K. Smith of Detroit visited St. Louis and held a rally at Kiel Auditorium that drew a large crowd. Despite the relative calm, in late 1943 the FBI concluded that it was conceivable that "a spontaneous racial outbreak" might occur.[48] To combat the rising racial tensions and encourage unity, the St. Louis MOWM held its second rally at Kiel Auditorium in May 1943, which again featured David Grant and A. Philip Randolph. More effective in reducing anxieties were the activities of the Mayor's Race Relations Committee, appointed by Mayor Aloys P. Kaufmann in August 1943. Edwin B. Meissner, the president of the St. Louis Car Company, led the committee, which was composed of seventy-three members, twenty-four of whom were black. The Mayor's Committee tried to relieve tensions by becoming a force for change, working to integrate public accommodations, schools, and factories.[49] Although the Race Relations Committee helped guard against riots, it did not improve job opportunities for blacks and as a result it added its voice to the chorus calling for FEPC action in St. Louis.[50]

In early 1944 Father Francis J. Haas, the chairman of the FEPC, sent Theodore E. Brown, an African-American FEPC investigator, to St. Louis to establish a suboffice in order to facilitate a series of public hearings against the largest defense contractors. Brown had a master's degree in labor economics from Northwestern University and had served as a BSCP field agent in Chicago. Despite his sound credentials, Brown made several strategic errors in preparing the hearings. In particular, he relied too heavily on the St. Louis MOWM. Turning to the MOWM unit, the city's most active civil rights organization, for assistance was perhaps a logical move. But unlike other groups, such as the Chicago, Cleveland, or Detroit FEP Councils, which aided the FEPC, the St. Louis MOWM's methods were less dependable. For example, during 1942 and 1943 Grant and McNeal sent several MOWM members to defense plants that refused blacks in order to generate complaints. Once the grievances were forwarded to the FEPC, the St. Louis MOWM leaders sent its members to other plants. The result was that the same persons filed dozens of complaints. Although there was no denying the presence of discrimination, these cases gave the appearance of disingenuousness if not conspiracy. Since FEPC officials relied on moral suasion, they needed to build the strongest cases possible. In St. Louis this did not happen.[51]

The FEPC's chances for success were also hampered by economic conditions in St. Louis. By December 1943 production had slowed and wartime employers were laying off workers. Shortly before Christmas both Curtiss-Wright and U.S. Cartridge released several thousand employees. By May 1944, the *Chicago Defender* estimated, seventeen thousand black women in St. Louis were jobless, partly because of discrimination and partly because war plants were no longer hiring. From late 1944 until the end of the war St. Louis remained, according to the War Manpower Commission, an area of "substantial labor reserve," a condition that limited the FEPC's ability to open job opportunities. As jobs became more scarce, organized white resistance to fair employment increased. On 17 March 1944 several hundred white workers at the General Cable Corporation staged a day-long wildcat strike to protest the hiring of a few blacks. Two months later, white workers struck at the St. Louis

Car Company when the local UAW-CIO proposed a nondiscrimination contract clause. This strike was particularly discouraging since the company's
president, Edward Meissner, was also the chairman of the Mayor's Race Relations Committee.[52]

Theodore Brown and the FEPC were not intimidated by white resistance
or deterred by the difficult labor market. On 13 June 1944 the committee
scheduled hearings in St. Louis for 1 and 2 August 1944. The companies involved were Amertorp, Bussman, Carter Carburetor, McDonald Aircraft,
McQuay-Norris, St. Louis Shipbuilding and Steel, U.S. Cartridge, and Wagner Electric. The first day of hearings was devoted to plants that refused to
hire African Americans, particularly women. Although during its first four
years the FEPC did not focus much national or local attention on the complaints of discrimination from black women, in its last year it strove to redress the more than twelve hundred complaints submitted by African-American women workers before December 1944.[53]

At the hearings, the representatives from Amertorp, Bussman, Carter Carburetor, McDonald Aircraft, U.S. Cartridge, and Wagner Electric defended
their refusal to employ black women, arguing that white women would strike.
The companies' lawyers reasoned that if white employees opposed job integration then the lack of black employees was not the company's fault. George
B. Logan, Bussman's attorney, pleaded "not guilty" to the charge of discrimination. "It is not *our* discrimination," he claimed, "it is community discrimination, the result of a community attitude. This attitude is more than city-
wide. It is state-wide. It is probably half nation-wide, and is a heritage from
the blood of the first settlers. It is beyond our power to change it or affect it."[54]
FEPC officials encountered the same rationales for job discrimination the next
day during the hearings against McQuay-Norris, St. Louis Shipbuilding and
Steel, and U.S. Cartridge. Managers at all three refused to upgrade black men
and women.[55] Perhaps A. J. Mummert, the vice president of McQuay-Norris,
explained the companies' positions best when he told the committee, "in our
experience in operations in different communities we have come to know that
each community has its own customs or practices and we have learned that
it is well to conform to them. We have also learned that the tolerance level is
different in different communities and that fact must be recognized. These
customs and practices begin at the bottom with the rank and file and cannot
be changed over night by management or any other agency."[56] In short, company officials denied responsibility, hiding behind community patterns of
social and economic segregation.

The FEPC rejected these rationalizations of job discrimination, insisting
that the companies were not to "take refuge" in community customs and that
they must abide by Executive Order 9346 and hire black men and women.
In its decisions after the hearings, the committee ordered the manufactur-

ers to cease and desist their discriminatory policies and "take the following affirmative action": 1) hire the black women and men who had filed complaints, 2) educate white workers about FEPC regulations, 3) devise and announce publicly a nondiscrimination employment and promotion policy, and 4) submit monthly reports to the FEPC. Owing to the weak nature of the complaints, some of which were dismissed at the hearings, and the intense opposition by white workers to job integration, none of the eight companies immediately changed their employment practices. Nevertheless the hearings had a very important, if unintentional, result: the beginning of the marriage between the idea of fair employment and the phrase "affirmative action," which up to that point had been mainly used, without reference to gender, in labor disputes settled by the National Labor Relations Board.[57]

Reaction in St. Louis to the hearings was mixed. Although most black activists were glad that the FEPC conducted the proceedings, they were discouraged by the results. An editorialist in the black newspaper, the *St. Louis Argus*, wrote shortly after the hearings that "it is to be regretted that so few white people can see, that so long as they fight to maintain the same old way of doing things just so long will we all be a backward people in the eyes of the world." Whites did not criticize the FEPC in the city's mainstream newspapers, which seemed to support the hearings by covering closely the events and by publishing no negative editorial comments. Nevertheless white outrage against the FEPC hearings reached the committee members. Several people wrote letters to President Roosevelt in mid-August 1944 asking him to stop the FEPC. Henry Knickmeyer, a white resident of St. Louis, told FDR that "your committee on Fair Employment Practice is being used by some to bring to print alleged discriminations that will not help unity but will stir up trouble."[58] Another white St. Louisan wrote that "it is my patriotic duty to tell you what the FEPC is doing." According to this person, the FEPC was a part of a secret "Negro movement" to ease "White People [*sic*] out of their jobs by forging false circumstantial evidence against" them, which was just a part of a larger plan to "tak[e] over the South."[59]

After the St. Louis hearings FEPC chairman Malcolm Ross maintained the suboffice in the city to keep pressure on employers to practice fair employment. Theodore Brown remained in charge of local FEPC activities and continued to rely on the MOWM for support. Brown and his allies were generally unable to convince most of the participants in the hearing to hire and upgrade black women and men. The managers of Carter Carburetor, McQuay-Norris, and Wagner Electric, for example, kept insisting that their hands were tied by "established customs." The industrialists also feared complying with the FEPC because of fierce union resistance. On 19 October 1944 management at McQuay-Norris attempted to comply with the FEPC's directives and place black core handlers in a plant with fifty white women UE members, who struck until the African-American workers were removed. Brown, who had negotiated a cooperation agreement with William Sentner of the UE, appealed to the union's leadership for assistance that never came.[60]

The UE's leadership in St. Louis was unable to sway its rank and file to support fair employment. On 17 December 1944 UE Local 825 at McQuay-Norris held a meeting to discuss compliance with FEPC directives. The local's leaders, Otto Maschoff and Betty Raab, tried to pass a resolution to "reaffirm our beliefs in the policies of our union, the CIO and the nation to prevent and eliminate discrimination in employment because of race, creed, or color," and to allow "the executive board of Local 825 [the] authority to effectuate the policies set forth in this resolution." The resolution passed initially but was later defeated after strong protest from white workers.[61] Dejected by the results, Maschoff and Raab resigned their posts, and McQuay-Norris continued to violate Executive Orders 8802 and 9346. In any event, by 1944 the UE's leadership seemed to have soured on the idea of helping the FEPC and its local supporters such as the MOWM. Wildcat strikes by black workers in 1944 angered pro-Soviet UE leaders, who blamed the FEPC and the MOWM for encouraging African Americans to challenge the authority of the union and thereby threaten the war effort against fascism.[62]

Brown's efforts were not entirely in vain, and during the spring of 1945 a few more St. Louis war plants opened their gates to blacks. Emerson Electric began hiring black women and men, as did National Carbon, Chevrolet, and Century Electric. Perhaps Brown's most impressive accomplishment was the integration of black workers into formerly white-only buildings at U.S. Cartridge. Plant managers finally broke the employment barriers for blacks after continuous pressure from the FEPC and the St. Louis MOWM and after realizing that, as David Grant put it, "preconceived notions about the Negro worker [were] absolutely untrue." Blacks in U.S. Cartridge's building number 103 were among the company's most productive employees and had better attendance records than the workers in any other building.[63]

Another major success in St. Louis was the integration of the General Cable Company. This was more a result of the efforts of the company's president, Dwight R. G. Palmer, who was born and raised in St. Louis and who would later serve on President Dwight D. Eisenhower's Committee on Contract Compliance, than of the FEPC. General Cable employed black men on integrated production lines. Plant officials, however, were afraid to hire black women, believing that white women workers would strike. They were correct. In January 1945 General Cable's employment manager decided to train several black women for production jobs. As soon as white women workers, who were members of the International Brotherhood of Electrical Workers (IBEW-AFL), learned of the plan, over one thousand went on a wildcat strike. After the strike plant managers refused to train or employ black women or promote black men. In early spring 1945 Theodore Brown of the FEPC contacted General Cable to discuss some two dozen complaints of discrimination collected by the St. Louis MOWM. When negotiation failed the FEPC held a closed-door hearing on 9 March 1945 in the Civic Courts Building in downtown St. Louis. General Cable's lawyer, A. L. Fergenson, promised to "employ, train, and upgrade without regard to race, color, creed or national origin."[64] By April, however, nothing had been done. FEPC chairman Malcolm Ross planned to take further action but reconsidered after two army generals convinced him that job integration would result in work stoppages, hindering production schedules. The generals also wanted Ross to speak with Palmer, the company president, who had reportedly "threatened to take matters into his own hands and personally see to it that Negro girls were put on the machinery, white girl opposition or not."[65] The generals, however, were too late. On Easter Sunday 1945, Dwight R. G. Palmer flew from New York to St. Louis to convince his white workers to accept black women. He called a mass meeting of his employees and made a passionate, eloquent plea for unity, patriotism, and fair employment. "If this Easter period and this war mean anything," he told them, "then let's realize that what we are fighting for is the very thing that is right up under our nose at the present time—tolerance."[66] Palmer's words had a tremendous effect. Within a few days black women and men were working on integrated production lines and no one struck or protested publicly.[67]

Malcolm Ross saw the General Cable case as "one bright spot" in the committee's final activities.[68] As the FEPC's *Final Report* stated, committee members were generally disappointed with the results in St. Louis. Few companies, especially those involved with the hearings, adopted fair employment policies. According to committee members, the FEPC's failures "might have stood for the limit to which the St. Louis 'social pattern' could be stretched were it not for notable examples," such as General Cable and U.S. Cartridge. FEPC officials, however, wished that these accomplishments, particularly the integration of U.S. Cartridge, had come earlier in the war. As Charles Houston wrote in late 1944, "it was unfortunate that the pattern of segregation should have been fastened on the Negro workers because I am convinced that if at the outset [of the war] . . . Negroes had been employed and assigned without segregation . . . there would have been no serious or prolonged labor troubles." Perhaps if the FEPC had been more active before 1943 more gains could have been made. Yet it was not so much a lack of will as a lack of resources that prevented the committee from overcoming employment and social patterns such as union discrimination that were already well established in the 1930s. The FEPC's experiences in St. Louis were similar to those in Cincinnati, but much better than those in East Alton, Illinois, only twenty miles north.[69]

9. A "Vicious and Destructive Attack": Congress and the End of the FEPC

DESPITE THE FEPC's activities and accomplishments in the Midwest and elsewhere—or perhaps more accurately because of them—its days were numbered. Since its creation in June 1941, conservative politicians and some of FDR's political advisors had tried to derail and destroy the FEPC. The committee weathered these attacks for four years. Although the FEPC did not eliminate employment discrimination, it made some advances and significantly raised awareness of the problem. Yet the more the committee attempted, the angrier its opponents became. In December 1943 conservative Republicans and most southern Democrats in Congress launched what A. Philip Randolph called a "vicious and destructive attack" on the committee.[1] Anti–New Deal, antigovernment, and anticommunist rhetoric helped to glue this political alliance together, which despite the efforts of liberal Republicans and Democrats from the Midwest and Northeast eventually dismantled the FEPC in June 1946.[2]

As noted earlier, Congress virtually ignored the committee during its first two years. Congressional attacks followed the reorganization of the FEPC in 1943. As southern and other racially conservative legislators realized that FDR would not scuttle his agency, and as they learned the extent of the new committee's powers and intent, they began to voice their opposition.[3] On 3 December 1943—three months after the opening of twelve FEPC regional offices—Representative John Rankin (D, Miss.) asserted in the House that "those bunch of crackpots down here in what they call the 'Fair Employment Practice Committee' seem to be doing everything they possibly can to . . . force [whites] to accept Negroes on terms of social equality." Rankin predicted that if the FEPC succeeded in making employers hire blacks it would "bring race trouble, just as it did in Detroit, Michigan and Harlem, New York." He also felt that the committee was committing "one of the most dangerous acts of communistic nonsense [that he had] ever seen attempted by anybody on the Federal payroll." Labeling the FEPC a "rump organization," Rankin demanded the immediate abolition of the "so-called Fair Employment Practice Committee."[4]

To convince other congressmen that the FEPC ought to be eliminated, Representative Howard W. Smith (D, Va.) launched an investigation of the committee in late December 1943. Earlier in 1943 Smith and other anti–New Deal congressmen had created a House committee to investigate the scope and authority of a select number of executive agencies. The Smith Committee targeted Roosevelt's wartime agencies, including the Office of Price Administration, the National War Labor Board, the War Food Administration, and the Fair Employment Practice Committee. The Smith Committee provided conservative congressmen with a forum to attack the Roosevelt administration. According to Smith's biographer, the Virginia representative was more than a conservative; he was a "reactionary," disturbed by any expansion of the federal government to help certain social groups.[5] In racial matters Smith adhered to a personal code of hatred, especially against African Americans. Nothing infuriated him more than the creation of the FEPC, a federal agency that in his mind stirred up strife and that in reality assisted people whom he despised. Thus the Smith Committee's investigations of the FEPC were more than a political mechanism to guard against government oversight. They were a political vendetta against Roosevelt and the New Deal.[6]

The Smith Committee held three separate hearings concerning the FEPC. The proceedings focused on the committee's actions to integrate the Philadelphia Rapid Transit Company, the Seafarers International Union of North America (AFL), and sixteen southern railroads. The goal of the hearings was to show that the FEPC had exceeded its legal bounds by issuing directives and to demonstrate that the committee members were communist sympathizers, bent on economic as well as social equality for African Americans.[7]

The Smith Committee never issued preliminary or final reports, although it published the transcripts of its hearings. The investigations did not directly impact the FEPC's operations. The importance of Representative Smith's activities lay instead in their relation to the 1944 congressional battles over the FEPC. Smith gave his anti-FEPC colleagues in the House and Senate rhetorical ammunition to shoot at the Fair Employment Practice Committee. In the subsequent debates over the FEPC many senators and representatives drew upon the transcripts of the Smith Committee hearings to support their actions to destroy the committee.

Conservative congressmen sought to eliminate the FEPC by denying it operating funds. The fight to deprive the committee of resources began on 23 February 1944, three days after the Smith Committee's hearing about the

FEPC's actions against the Seafarers International Union of North America. Senator Richard B. Russell (D, Ga.) introduced an amendment to the Independent Offices Appropriation Bill (H.R. 4070) for the fiscal year ending in June 1945. Russell's amendment aimed to eliminate all government offices, bureaus, and agencies that were in existence for more than twelve months without congressional funding. As of February 1944 there were several federal agencies in that category, including the FEPC, which had been operating for twenty-two months. Up to that point the President's Emergency Fund had paid the FEPC's bills. If H.R. 4070 passed with the Russell amendment (which it did in June 1944 without much debate) and there was no specific FEPC allotment in that year's War Agencies Appropriation Bill (H.R. 4879), the agency would die, which was what Senator Russell wanted.[8] As he told reporters, "I hope [the amendment] wipes out the Fair Employment Practice Committee."[9]

President Roosevelt, who had become a strong supporter of the FEPC since its reorganization, took swift action to protect the committee from the Russell amendment. Believing that the Russell amendment would pass, on 9 March 1945 FDR sent the Senate Committee on Appropriations a request that the 1945 War Agencies Appropriation Bill provide the FEPC with $585,000 for 1945 operating expenses.[10] The committee's congressional friends also rallied to its aid. On 24 March 1944 Senator Clayton D. Buck (R, Del.) introduced an amendment that proposed to insert an exception into the Russell amendment to the Independent Offices Appropriations bill so that it would not apply to the FEPC. By a vote of thirty-six yeas to twenty-two nays (thirty-eight not voting) the Buck amendment passed.[11] It carried on the strength of a political alliance of northeastern Democrats and midwestern and western Republicans, of which Buck ironically was neither. Outraged by this, Russell criticized the "distorted" appropriations bill and vowed to vote against it. Implied was the threat that unless he and his conservative colleagues were allowed to kill the FEPC they would hold up the funding for the war effort. After echoing the claims of the Smith Committee, which lambasted the FEPC as a tool of the American Communist Party, Russell called for another vote. Several western Republicans and western Democrats deserted the original voting alliance.[12] Although most liberal northeastern and midwestern senators voted yea, the Buck amendment was defeated twenty-six to thirty-three (thirty-seven not voting).[13] For the first time, Russell forged an anti-FEPC coalition of southern Democrats and western Republicans, what Joseph F. Guffey (D, Pa.) called an "unholy alliance," that in the end overpowered congressional backing for the FEPC and led to its destruction in 1946.[14]

With the probable passage of the Independent Offices Appropriations Bill, liberal supporters of the FEPC tried to restore the FEPC's funding via the 1945 War Agencies Appropriations Bill. On 25 May 1944 the House Committee on

Appropriations reported out the war agencies bill with a five-hundred-thousand-dollar allotment for the FEPC, which sparked intense debate in the Senate and House. On 26 May 1944 Representative Malcolm C. Tarver (D, Ga.) introduced an amendment to the Appropriations Bill to "strike . . . the proposed appropriation for the Fair Employment Practice Committee." Tarver used testimony from the Smith Committee to justify his initiative, recounting the Smith Committee's versions of the FEPC's problems with the Seafarers International Union and the Philadelphia Transit Company. In addition, he asserted that the FEPC was attempting to upset the racial status quo. Tarver professed his belief that blacks should be accorded "the fullest measure of economic opportunity which they are capable of using advantageously." And yet he also believed that he knew "the real enemies of the Negro" who "falsely pose as his friends and seek to stir up dissatisfaction in his heart and mind." Despite Tarver's passionate speech, his amendment did not pass a teller vote, although it had some bipartisan support.[15]

Twenty-six May was more than a day for amendments; it was a day for rallying anti-FEPC congressmen. Congressional debating ran long as southern representatives spoke late into the evening about the evils of the FEPC. Jamie L. Whitten, a Democrat from Mississippi, stated that the president's committee employed too many blacks, that it was "following the Communists' lead," and that it was going against "God's law" by attempting to change the status of southern blacks. Tampering with "God's law," Whitten claimed, would result in the creation of a "mongrel race." "We from the South will have no part of it," he stated categorically. Fellow southerner Asa L. Allen (D, La.) agreed and derided those "Communists and other radical groups" who were "taking advantage of the war to push to the front their own economic and social theories." Rankin echoed Allen by calling the FEPC a "Communist bunch" who discriminated against whites "who are in [a] hopeless minority on that conglomerate committee." He also went through the FEPC's list of employees, pointing out their alleged connections to "subversive," "un-American," and "Communist" groups. For example, he linked Will Maslow, the FEPC's director of operations, to a publication called *Health and Hygiene,* "which was founded as an extension of the Communist *Daily Worker.*"[16]

Representative Hugh Peterson of Georgia—a member of the Smith Committee—agreed with Rankin's accusations and threatened to vote against the 1945 War Agencies Appropriations Bill if the funding for the FEPC were not removed. He vehemently opposed the committee, stating that "Negro domination of its nature [was] both unfair and intolerable." To support his claim he summarized the Smith Committee hearings. Finally he warned his fellow congressmen that "we are fast slipping into a communistic state, and if this progress is not halted, we shall soon be totally swallowed up by the damnable philosophy of communism." Others used the rhetoric of anticommunism.

Representatives Richard M. Kleberg (D, Tex.), Ovie C. Fisher (D, Tex.), and John S. Gibson (D, Ga.) all rose to denounce the FEPC in similar fashion.[17]

The FEPC did have its supporters in Congress. Liberal senators such as Robert M. La Follette Jr. (R, Wisc.), Scott Lucas (D, Ill.), and Robert F. Wagner (D, N.Y.) backed the agency. In the House, Mary T. Norton (D, N.J.) and Vito Marcantonio (ALP, N.Y.), who in 1941 had introduced the first bill to create a permanent FEPC, defended the committee. During the extended session of 26 May, Marcantonio charged that those who wanted to kill the FEPC were attempting "to perpetuate a Hitlerite concept of race supremacy in this country." He declared the FEPC "a continuation of the Emancipation Proclamation." He saw the committee as "democracy in action, the democracy for which men are fighting and dying everywhere in this world." Midwestern Representative George G. Sadowski (D, Mich.) shared Marcantonio's view and asked, "in losing the best of a generation to the Nazi brute, are we attacking discrimination with boldness and righteous scorn befitting our soldier-liberators?" Answering his own question he said, "in honest truth, we can say that in these days the Bill of Rights and the 'four freedoms' are being excoriated by some in America, who have never caught the real meaning of democracy." Although less eloquent, Harry P. Jeffery (R, Ohio), Arthur G. Klein (D, N.Y.), and Mary Norton also voiced their support for fair employment practices. Norton, the chair of the House Labor Committee, promised to give a fair hearing to the bills to make the FEPC a permanent government commission.[18]

The debates about the War Agencies Appropriations Bill for 1945 raged until June 1944. Anti-FEPC congressmen continued to use the Smith Committee hearings as evidence of the FEPC's maleficence and to assert that the FEPC was a communist-front organization. On 20 June 1944 Senator Russell proposed an amendment to the bill to delete the FEPC appropriation. This movement failed by a vote of thirty-nine to twenty-one (thirty-six not voting).[19] Few northeastern and no midwestern senators voted for the amendment. Oddly, this time the western Republicans also opposed Russell, who countered with a series of additional amendments providing for an appeal process that would enable employers to challenge FEPC directives, forbid plant seizures as a result of noncompliance with the FEPC, and prohibit FEPC rulings that were contrary to laws enacted by Congress. These amendments passed, paving the way to final passage of the Appropriations Bill on 20 June. The bill contained five hundred thousand dollars for the FEPC, sustaining it for 1945. Yet for the friends of the FEPC this was an incomplete victory. Although the concerted efforts of FDR and midwestern and northeastern legislators saved the committee from death at the hands of Representative Tarver and Senator Russell, the committee had only a one-year lease on life, at the end of which the funding battle would resume.[20]

After the War Agencies Appropriations Bill was enacted, congressional interest in the FEPC waned for a few months. It was not until the time came to pass the 1946 War Agencies Appropriations Bill (H.R. 3368) that the FEPC again became an issue. This struggle to appropriate money for the FEPC was the last congressional battle over the wartime committee. As in 1944, southern congressmen with some Republican assistance attempted to strike all funds earmarked for the FEPC. On 21 March 1945 President Roosevelt requested that the House pass a war agencies appropriations bill that provided the FEPC with an operating budget of $599,000. The House Appropriations Committee, led by Clarence Cannon (D, Mo.), denied the president's request and reported out the 1946 Appropriations Bill without an allocation for the FEPC. Friends of the FEPC in the House tried to put an allotment back into the bill. On 8 June 1945 Representative Adolph J. Sabath (D, Ill.) spoke at length about the importance of continuing the FEPC into the postwar period. He quoted from a 5 June 1945 letter from the newly installed President Harry S. Truman, who stated that "to abandon at this time . . . the Fair Employment Practice Committee" was "unthinkable." Sabath also evoked the ghost of Franklin D. Roosevelt. "May I in conclusion say this? Not only is President Truman in favor of the legislation, but the very last request made by our late President Roosevelt on the day he died was that the Fair Employment Practice Commission [*sic*] be continued." Sabath claimed that FDR's secretary "called on me at 3 o'clock in the afternoon on that day conveying the President's request that I do everything in my power to endeavor to bring about the adoption of a rule for this legislation."[21]

Other liberal representatives, including Andrew J. Biemiller (D, Wisc.) and John J. Rooney (D, N.Y.), supported Sabath's attempt to give the FEPC funding. Ellis E. Patterson (D, Calif.) called on his colleagues to "repair the damage" done to the Appropriations Bill. Another California representative, Helen Gahagan Douglas (D), spoke persuasively about the harm that would be done if the FEPC did not receive funds. "Failure at this time to provide for the Fair Employment Practice Commission [*sic*] does more than dirty the hem of our democracy," she argued. "It casts doubt in the minds of all the colored peoples of the earth who are, incidentally, in the great majority, as to the quality of our democracy. It raises the question among the colonial peoples of the earth, most of whom are colored, as to whether or not we are really their friends, whether or not we will ever understand their longing and right for self-determination." Despite Douglas's forceful words, the House passed the 1946 War Agencies Appropriations Bill without funding for the FEPC by a vote of 252 to 2 with 178 not voting. As Marcantonio put it that same day, it was in the hands of the senators to uphold "the best democratic traditions of this country and restore the FEPC's appropriation."[22]

Senator Dennis Chavez (D, N.Mex.) introduced an amendment to the Senate version of the Appropriations Bill giving the FEPC a 1946 operating budget of $446,000. In support of his own proposal, Chavez referred to the Declaration of Independence and the Gettysburg Address. Predicting red-baiting rhetoric against his amendment by southern senators, he also declared that he was "not defending communism at all; I could not do so; but this is what happens: once in a while, when someone dares to take sides with a class of people who might need help under the law, when he undertakes to work for the little fellow, and to help the man who is hungry and who is trying to support his family on $15 a month, he is accused of being a communist. If such a person is a communist, then I must be one."[23]

Chavez's amendment met with stiff opposition from southern Democrats. Majority Leader and moderate Kentucky Democrat Alben Barkley offered a compromise by substituting a reduced appropriation of $250,000. By a vote of forty-three to twenty-five (twenty-seven not voting), the amendment was added to the 1946 War Agencies Appropriations Bill.[24] Barkley's proposal received overwhelming support from Republicans of all regions as well as strong Democratic support from the Northeast and West. Only southern Democrats were unified against it. Some of the FEPC's friends also cast negative votes. Senator Wayne Morse (R, Ore.) voted against the measure not because he opposed the FEPC but because he thought the allotment was inadequate. As Morse told his fellow senators, "I think the FEPC was dealt a mortal blow." Senator Theodore G. Bilbo (D, Miss.) tended to agree, but felt that the Senate had not gone far enough. If it had been up to Bilbo, he would have not "voted for 1 cent for a temporary or a permanent FEPC." Still he thought that the Senate's battle over the wartime FEPC's funding had not been in vain. "We have saved the taxpayers of the country $196,000," he declared with his characteristic wit, "for my 2 days' work, that means $98,000 a day. I am satisfied with that rate of compensation."[25]

The adoption of the Barkley amendment was only the beginning of the fight. The 1946 War Agencies Appropriation Bill remained to be passed. Southern senators were determined to prevent the passage of the bill with funding for the FEPC. The final struggle over the wartime committee took place on 12 July 1945, three days before the 1945 War Agencies Appropriation Act expired. Leading the attack on the FEPC was Senator Bilbo. For hours he derided the FEPC, which by his erroneous count employed "66 Negroes, so many Jews, so many Japanese." Bilbo predicated his opposition on his fear that the FEPC would destroy segregation, which would in turn lead to "miscegenation and mongrelization of both the white race and the black race."[26]

During the breaks between Bilbo's long harangues, southern support began to shift in favor of the War Agencies Appropriation Bill. Senator Cannon (D, Mo.) offered an amendment to the Barkley compromise so that the funds provided to the FEPC would be for the purpose of "completely terminating the functions and duties of the Committee on Fair Employment

Practices." In other words, the money was to facilitate the liquidation of the committee. Throughout the day of 12 July opponents of the FEPC began to support the War Agencies Appropriation Bill with the Cannon amendment. Bilbo, with Rankin's help, continued to argue against the FEPC, but for them it was too late. Cannon's amendment attracted enough support so that on 16 July the 1946 War Agencies Appropriation Bill became law with widespread bipartisan support.[27]

As Senator Morse predicted, the enactment of the appropriation bill was a mortal blow to the wartime FEPC. Without proper operating funds, the committee had to reduce its staff from 128 to 31 and close all field offices except for three in the Midwest—Chicago, Detroit, and St. Louis. In a final effort to change unfair employment patterns, the committee toyed with the idea of one last midwestern hearing that would seek to settle many of the remaining discrimination cases that the Cincinnati, Chicago, Cleveland, Detroit, and St. Louis offices had collected. The committee believed that further gains in the region could be made. In its judgement, "although there were conspicuous failures [in the Midwest], many large and small companies, through the effects of . . . the FEPC, brought their practices into line with the Executive Order." Experience had shown that, with the exception of a few places, job discrimination in the Midwest was not "dyed-in-the-wool."[28] Without adequate funding and without staff, however, this proposed last round of hearings was shelved.[29]

In addition to a reduced staff and budget the FEPC had another major problem. President Truman, who had appeared to back the FEPC during the congressional debates, prevented the committee from working effectively. On 23 November 1945 Truman ordered the FEPC not to issue a directive against the Capital Transit Company of Washington, D.C., which discriminated against African Americans. Truman did not believe that the FEPC had jurisdiction over the transportation industries. The committee, of course, thought otherwise, and the following day Charles H. Houston wrote a letter to Truman requesting a conference on the issue. President Truman refused and Houston resigned from the FEPC for a second time, telling the president that "the failure of the Government to enforce democratic practices and to protect minorities in its own capital makes its expressed concern for national minorities abroad somewhat specious, and its interference in the domestic affairs of other countries very premature."[30]

Blocking the FEPC's directives to the Capital Transit Company foreshadowed Truman's next action against the committee. To clarify the FEPC's role in postwar America, on 18 December 1945 Truman issued Executive Order 9664 directing the committee to continue its operations for the period allotted by the 1946 War Agencies Appropriation Act. The FEPC's duties, as outlined by Truman, were to "investigate, make findings and recommendations, and report to the President, with respect to discrimination in industries engaged in work contributing to the production of military supplies or to the effective transition to a peaceful economy."[31] In essence Truman made the FEPC a mere fact-finding agency. The meaning of the executive order was not lost on some civil rights groups, who summarily denounced Truman's action. On 30 June 1946 FEPC chairman Malcolm Ross presented the president with the committee members' resignations along with the fruits of the last fact-finding mission, the FEPC's *Final Report*.[32]

Unlike the FEPC's *First Report*, which contained many charts and statistics, the committee's terminal report was basically a narrative outlining what it had done and what remained to do. The impact and importance of the FEPC on the Midwest was made relatively clear. In the Midwest the committee had developed procedures for attacking discrimination in employment. It came to rely on the case method system of adjusting individual complaints and issuing cease and desist orders, eschewing the job quotas created by other New Deal and wartime agencies. At times this approach was successful, especially in the northern parts of the Midwest and in areas with tight labor markets. The key was not the condition of the labor market, however, but the support of local labor and civil rights activists, liberal businessmen, and government officials. Working together, fair employment was tenable. Without that backing, especially in areas with high racial tensions or balanced labor markets, the limits to the FEPC's abilities were considerable. Still, for an agency with less than twenty workers in the Midwest, it had tackled an enormous task.

Detailed statistical analyses of the committee's work since 1943 were not possible without proper funding and staff. The lack of accurate data makes it difficult to render a final judgement on the effectiveness of the FEPC. The general numbers available show that the committee was extremely active. From June 1941 to June 1946, fewer than 120 FEPC officials processed over twelve thousand cases, settling nearly five thousand (42 percent) satisfactorily.[33] Over the five years, nearly 80 percent of the committee's cases involved African Americans and Mexican Americans; almost 10 percent were based on creed, involving mainly Jews; and 10 percent concerned issues of national origin. From August 1944 to August 1945 alone, the committee held fifteen public hearings, docketed 3,485 complaints, and settled 1,191 (34 percent) of them to its satisfaction. The FEPC conducted thirty hearings in all, concerning 132 companies, 38 unions, and 5 government agencies. It also helped eliminate discrimination through the operation of eight agreements with other federal agencies and with two labor unions, the UAW and UE.[34]

What precisely this activism yielded remains an unanswered, and perhaps unanswerable, question. It is clear that job opportunities for minority workers expanded dramatically during the war. A million and a half minority workers found places in prime war industries and another three hundred thousand were in federal service on V-J Day. Certain social groups fared better than others. As the committee's experiences in Chicago, Detroit, and the Twin Cities indicate, most employment barriers for American Jews fell significantly during the war.[35] Seventy percent of the FEPC's religious cases concerned Jews and 30 percent dealt with the complaints of Catholics, Jehovah's Witnesses, and Seventh-Day Adventists. Many of the complaints involved discriminatory job advertisements specifying "Gentiles only." FEPC officials, cooperating with local Jewish employment services, were successful in removing most such phrases from want ads.[36] Over a million African Americans entered civilian jobs, mostly after 1942. The percentage of blacks in war industries increased from 2.5 percent in 1942 to 8.3 percent in late 1944. Black men fared better than black women: 13 percent of all black male war workers were in semiskilled jobs in 1940. By late 1944 the percentage had increased to 22 percent. Black women also made great strides in semiskilled work. In 1940, 5 percent of all black female war workers were in that category; by 1944 over 8 percent were.[37]

What drove these changes? According to the economist and black New Dealer Robert C. Weaver, economic necessity was an essential factor. "Negro males were not considered for employment," he wrote, "until great progress

The OWI-supplied caption from July 1942 reads: "A young Negro stands ready to wash or 'degrease' this airplane motor prior to its shipment. He's an employe of a large midwest airplane plant." (Franklin D. Roosevelt Library, Records of the Office of War Information, Record Group 20; photograph by Ann Rosener, #PX 66-116[29])

had been made in tapping the reserve of available white women." "And Negro women," he added, "were not considered seriously as a source of labor supply until there was a shortage of colored men." Many historians have adopted this as the primary reason for an increase in minority employment during the war.[38]

Unlike many more recent scholars, Robert Weaver, while acknowledging the importance of market forces, also argued that the FEPC's efforts to end job discrimination were "extremely important." This was particularly true in the Midwest. Although the committee did not even come close to eradicating job bias, it nevertheless made some advancements. In the Midwest, from 30 June 1941 to 30 June 1944, the FEPC handled over fourteen hundred complaints of discrimination. Through innumerable private meetings and nine series of public hearings, the committee was able to close over 60 percent and settle satisfactorily about 35 percent of its midwestern cases, which was comparable to the national averages for that time period. In the Midwest the FEPC's pressure tactics worked best in places where manpower shortages existed. For example, in Cleveland and Detroit committee officials satisfactorily settled almost 40 percent of their cases. Such results were not

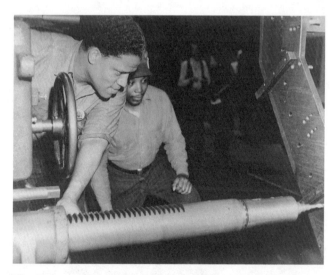

The OWI-supplied caption from September 1942 reads: "Being of different racial strain from Hitler or Hirohito, Guy L. Miles wouldn't stand much chance of survival in an Axis-controlled America. A skilled machine operator, who makes parts for medium tanks in a large midwest factory, he's fighting the fascist fanatics as grimly and intensely as America's men on the fighting fronts." (Franklin D. Roosevelt Library, Records of the Office of War Information, Record Group 208; photograph by Ann Rosener, #PX 65-702[19])

duplicated in St. Louis or Columbus, Ohio, which had more balanced labor markets. Thus the FEPC used tight labor markets to push industrial gates further open for minority workers.[39]

In addition to adjusting complaints of discrimination the FEPC also helped to end job bias through various activities. It organized and rallied the support of local civil rights and labor activists. Without this concerted action many of the advances in the Midwest as well as the nation, such as those at U.S. Cartridge in St. Louis or Buick Aviation in Chicago, might not have been possible. FEPC officials influenced employment patterns in other ways as well. They helped employers create equal opportunity by fighting white worker resistance. The FEPC was instrumental in settling several dozen racially motivated wildcat strikes. Knowing that one could count on the committee in such industrial disputes made adopting fair employment practices easier. The FEPC also changed unfair employment practices by assisting and coordinating educational efforts against job bias.

Educational campaigns had an indirect impact on employment practices. These efforts, which included public demonstrations and conferences in which FEPC officials participated, often created an atmosphere that fostered change. Perhaps the best example of this indirect influence was the case of General Cable's president, Dwight R. G. Palmer, who ended discrimination in his company because he agreed with the main message of civil rights organizations during the Second World War, which was that America could not fight for democracy abroad and not practice it at home. As FEPC chairman Malcolm Ross wrote, because of these indirect influences, "no exact measure of [the] FEPC's effectiveness is possible." By the same token, there is no denying that the FEPC acted as a catalyst motivating employers, workers, and activists to fight and adopt fair employment practices in the Midwest.[40]

This is not to state that there were not problems and failures. Generally the FEPC's efforts were frustrated in places where labor supply met demand, where Jim Crow was firmly entrenched, and where opposition to the FEPC overwhelmed support. In East Alton, Cincinnati, and St. Louis, the committee was generally unable to change unfair practices for these reasons. The FEPC also failed in places where it could not mount intensive campaigns, as in Indiana. Given more resources, the committee might have accomplished more in Indiana as well as in Minnesota. Even where it was largely ineffective the FEPC still made an impact, especially in the minds of the people it helped. For example, despite the failures in Cincinnati, in 1945 a black resident described the FEPC "as a quiet but effective key, opening the shackles of shameful, undemocratic, anti-American race prejudice, and freeing the Negro to earn his living on equal terms with all other people." Although during and after the Second World War minority workers in the Midwest continued to struggle with employment discrimination, they had witnessed one means to change their situation, a means that they valued and sought to recreate during the 1950s and 1960s.[41]

The end of the Fair Employment Practice Committee came during a critical period when many workers, particularly blacks and Jews, who had experienced the breaking of job barriers during the war witnessed a resurgence of employment discrimination. Soon after V-J Day, thousands of blacks and Jews were laid off and not rehired. Although some Christian whites were also fired, they did not encounter the same difficulty in getting new jobs. Seniority rules that favored white workers, promises that employers made to white soldiers, and a general return to prewar discriminatory hiring practices contributed to the employment problems of blacks and Jews. As early as the fall of 1944, FEPC officials had predicted the hardships of minority workers in the transition to a peacetime economy, but they were largely unable to help them.[42]

The postwar job situation for African-American and Jewish workers was generally grim in the Midwest. There were some exceptions. As FEPC officials wrote in the committee's *Final Report,* "of all the communities about which information was received for the purpose of this report . . . Chicago showed the least severe post-VJ-day losses for Negro workers." In Milwaukee and Columbus the employment picture was also encouraging. Yet problems remained. In Chicago many blacks who were laid off by war plants were rehired, but in less-skilled and lower-paid positions. The same happened in Milwaukee. Furthermore, as the Chicago Urban League reported in 1946, 60 percent of the ten thousand manufacturing industries in the city did not hire blacks. Also in 1946, as United States Employment Service officials noted, an increasing number of Chicago employers placed discriminatory job orders. For example, from 1 to 15 February 1946, 35 percent of all employers requesting workers from the USES specified racial and religious restrictions.[43] Discriminatory specifications against Jews also reappeared in Chicago newspapers. By spring 1946 it was clear that Jews, like African Americans, were having a hard time finding work. In March 1946 the Chicago Bureau of Jewish Employment Problems conducted an employment survey and found that over 50 percent of Jewish job applicants were required to state their religion and 15 percent of the applicants heard phrases akin to "we do not employ Jews."[44]

Many employers in other midwestern cities renewed unfair employment practices. For example, in Detroit during the first two weeks of February 1946 the USES received 541 discriminatory job orders. Although the Detroit USES office did not fill these orders, USES officials in other cities, such as Cleveland, did. The most pressing problem for minority workers in the Midwest was unemployment. In Cleveland, Cincinnati, Detroit, Minneapolis, St. Louis, and St. Paul, many major war plants, including Scullin Steel, U.S. Cartridge, and Wright Aeronautical, that had employed thousands of African Americans shut down following V-J Day. Some companies, such as Minnesota Mining and

Manufacturing and Minneapolis Honeywell, remained open but fired their black employees. Except in Chicago and Milwaukee, unemployment among midwestern African Americans was high. In St. Louis, for instance, 12 percent of all black workers were jobless; among whites the unemployment rate was 5 percent. For midwestern Jewish workers job discrimination was less of a problem than for other minority groups. Nevertheless, as the National Community Relations Advisory Council reported in 1947, "the end of war has seen a marked increase in reported instances of discrimination and in other symptoms of unfair employment practices" against Jews. The council based its conclusion on a survey of fifteen cities, including Cincinnati, Chicago, Cleveland, Detroit, Milwaukee, Minneapolis, and St. Louis.[45]

In the last few months of its existence the FEPC tried to fight discrimination practices by arranging for local organizations to take its place in the Midwest. For example, Lethia Clore, a black woman who had worked in the Detroit suboffice and later replaced Harold James as the head of the Cincinnati office in 1945, called on the Mayor's Friendly Relations Committee (MFRC), an agency created in November 1943 to improve race relations, to continue the committee's work. Although Clore and the members of the MFRC knew that the municipal committee could only act as a "clearing house for complaints" and would have "no authority to enforce or investigate findings," they were confident that the group could build upon the FEPC's accomplishments.[46] In Detroit FEPC officials turned the reins over to a private organization, the Detroit Metropolitan Fair Employment Practice Council, which according to Edward Swan, the head of the Detroit FEPC office, had "done an outstanding job" in assisting the FEPC.[47] These plans to substitute the FEPC with local institutions failed. In January 1946 the Detroit War Chest, which had funded the Detroit FEP Council, reduced its appropriation from twelve thousand dollars to two thousand dollars per year, effectively ending the council's ability to handle grievances.[48] In Cincinnati the MFRC lived through the reconversion period but, without any authority, was unable to adjust complaints that it proved valid.

Frustrated by their local, independent attempts to challenge discrimination, many civil rights and labor activists in the Midwest joined a national trend in calling for permanent fair employment practice commissions at all levels of government. The movement for a permanent, federal FEPC started in 1943 when A. Philip Randolph organized the National Council for a Permanent Fair Employment Practice Commission. Despite well-organized lobbying efforts that eventually included a march on Washington for jobs and freedom, those pushing for another federal agency were thwarted for twenty-one years. Conservative congressmen from both parties allied time and time again to stop permanent FEPC bills, often using techniques and rhetoric that mimicked the debates over the wartime committee. In the meantime civil rights organizations worked to enact municipal and state FEPC laws. By 1964 some three dozen states (including Illinois, Indiana, Michigan, Minnesota, Ohio, and Wisconsin) and two hundred cities (including Cincinnati, Chicago, Cleveland, Detroit, Gary, and St. Louis) had fair employment statutes and commissions.[49]

In general these state and municipal commissions were timid, weak, and ineffectual. According to Herbert Hill of the NAACP, over the twenty years during which these agencies operated, "state FEP enactments proved unable to cope with the problem of changing the Negro occupation patterns" because the "FEP commissions [did] not provide a solution to structural unemployment problems." Because of the almost complete failure of state and local FEP commissions, by the 1960s hopes rode on the enactment of the 1964 Civil Rights Act, Title VII of which established a statutory Equal Employment Opportunity Commission (EEOC). At first the EEOC, in essence the administrative grandchild of the FEPC, had few powers to enforce nondiscrimination against "race, color, religion, sex, or national origin." In 1972, however, it gained the legal capabilities to fight employment discrimination. Although its methods often differ from the original FEPC, the EEOC is the culmination of the struggle that began in the 1940s to have the federal government fight employment discrimination. Although many of the job barriers that the FEPC broke down during the Second World War were rebuilt after the war, the idea of federal involvement in fair employment lived past the 1940s and continues today, which is yet another legacy of Franklin D. Roosevelt.[50]

Compliance Data from Companies Attending the 19–20 January 1942 Chicago Hearings

Company	Date	Total Employees	Nonwhite Employees (%)	
Allis-Chalmers	Jan. 1942	17,022	110	(0.64)
	July 1942	20,632	129	(0.62)
	Oct. 1942	22,597	196	(0.86)
	Dec. 1943	24,862	434	(1.74)
	Aug. 1945	17,686	693	(3.91)
A. O. Smith	Jan. 1942	6,484	0	
	July 1942	8,594	237	(2.76)
	Oct. 1942	10,372	470	(4.53)
	Dec. 1943	14,790	802	(5.42)
Bearce Manufacturing	May 1942	11	2	(18.18)
	June 1942	15	5	(33.33)
	June 1945	174	15	(8.62)
Buick Aviation (Melrose Park)	Jan. 1942	2,300	0	
	Feb. 1942	4,600	52	(1.13)
	July 1942	8,015	350	(4.37)
	Oct. 1942	8,952	a	
	Dec. 1943	15,233	a	
Harnischfeger	Jan. 1942	3,200	0	
	July 1942	3,495	5	(0.14)
	Oct. 1942	3,490	10	(0.28)
	Dec. 1943	3,309	18	(0.54)
Heil	Jan. 1942	2,400	2	(0.08)
	July 1942	2,485	140	(5.63)
	Oct. 1942	3,130	135	(4.31)
	Dec. 1943	2,958	115	(3.89)
	May 1945	3,070	122	(3.98)
Majestic Radio and Television	Jan. 1942	385	0	
	Dec. 1943	496	17	(3.43)
Norberg	Jan. 1942	2,290	35	(1.52)
	July 1942	3,225	8	(0.25)
	Oct. 1942	3,250	15	(0.46)
	Dec. 1943	3,759	40	(1.06)
Stewart-Warner	Jan. 1942	8,254	0	
	July 1942	8,884	44	(0.49)
	Oct. 1942	9,700	210	(2.17)
	Dec. 1943	10,144	500	(4.92)

(cont.)

Company	Date	Total Employees	Nonwhite Employees (%)
Studebaker	Jan. 1942	12,410	45 (0.36)
	July 1942	13,745	313 (2.27)
	Oct. 1942	16,425	351 (2.13)
	Dec. 1943	25,638	1,380 (5.38)

Sources: Allis-Chalmers compliance report, December 1943, FEPC microfilm, reel 76, and Allis-Chalmers compliance report, 1 August 1945, FEPC microfilm, reel 62; Bearce compliance report, June 1942, FEPC microfilm, reel 49, and Bearce compliance report, 9 June 1945, FEPC microfilm, reel 62; Buick Aviation compliance report, December 1943, FEPC microfilm, reel 76, and War Production Board, "Status of Minority Group Employment in Firms Summoned by the President's Committee to the Hearings Held in Chicago, Illinois, in January, 1942," FEPC microfilm, reel 37; Harnischfeger compliance report, December 1943, FEPC microfilm, reel 76; Heil compliance report, December 1943, FEPC microfilm, reel 76, and Heil compliance report, 26 May 1945, FEPC microfilm, reel 62; Majestic Radio and Television compliance report, December 1943, FEPC microfilm, reel 76; Norberg compliance report, December 1943, FEPC microfilm, reel 76; Stewart-Warner compliance report, December 1943, FEPC microfilm, reel 76; A. O. Smith compliance report, December 1943, FEPC microfilm, reel 76; and Studebaker compliance report, December 1943, FEPC microfilm, reel 76.

a. Figures were not available.

Wartime Hate Strike Data

Table 1. Midwestern Work Stoppages in Which the FEPC Aided in the Settlement, June 1943–December 1944

Company	Employment Data	Strike Dates	Man-Days Idle	Reason for Strike
Allied Steel Casting Co. (Harvey, Ill.)	365 total 155 nonwhite	23 Mar. 1944	177	Management removed partition between black and white toilets
American Steel Foundries Co. (East St. Louis, Ill.)	1,634 total 815 nonwhite	30 June 1944	a	Management placed blacks as crane operators
Bohn Aluminum & Brass Co., Plant #1 (Detroit, Mich.)	2,420 total 202 nonwhite	22 Jan. 1943	< 1	Upgrading of blacks
Chicago Pneumatic Tool Co. (Detroit, Mich.)	961 total 21 nonwhite	29 Apr. 1943	<1	Demotion of black foreman
Chrysler Highland Park Plant (Highland Park, Mich.)	11,520 total 610 nonwhite	16 Mar. 1943	388	Working conditions
Chrysler Tank Arsenal (Detroit, Mich.)	a	Apr. 1944	1,652	Discriminatory transfer
Detroit Aluminum & Brass Co. (Detroit, Mich.)	942 total 156 nonwhite	1 Feb. 1943	<1	Resistance to black women as operators
Dodge Truck Plant (Detroit, Mich.)	4,399 total 617 nonwhite	28 Oct. 1943	200	Dismissal of black women
Duplex Printing Press Co. (Battle Creek, Mich.)	1,508 total 4 nonwhite	27 Jan. 1943	250	Whites resist training of black welders
Eastern Malleable Iron Co., Eberhard Mfg. Division (Cleveland, Ohio)	598 total 103 nonwhite	8 Dec. 1943	420	Conditions of employment
Ford Motor Co., Lincoln Plant (Detroit, Mich.)	5,408 total 440 nonwhite	30 Apr. 1943	<1	Protests against dismissals
General Cable Co. (St. Louis, Mo.)	3,688 total 283 nonwhite	17 Mar. 1944	<1	Whites protest hiring of blacks
General Aircraft Co. (Akron, Ohio)	22,519 total 944 nonwhite	18 Apr. 1944	1,297	Discriminatory transfers
Harsch Bronze & Foundry Co. (Cleveland, Ohio)	540 total 200 nonwhite	28 Sept. 1943	373	Wage differential
Hudson Motor Co., Jefferson Plant (Detroit, Mich.)	10,654 total 316 nonwhite	21 Apr. 1943	168	Whites resist training of black workers
Illinois Ordnance Co. (Carbondale, Ill.)	4,480 total 136 nonwhite	7 Jan. 1944	4,089	Whites resist promotion of black inspector
Inland Mfg. Co. (Dayton, Ohio)	5,923 total a	Apr. 1944	316	Whites protest upgrading of black women

Table 1. (cont.)

Company	Employment Data	Strike Dates	Man-Days Idle	Reason for Strike
Monsanto Chemical Co. (East St. Louis, Ill.)	1,615 total 375 nonwhite	13 May 1944	2,814	Working conditions
Packard Motor Car Co. (Detroit, Mich.)	30,502 total 2,557 nonwhite	4 June 1943	89,685	Whites resist promotion of blacks to production lines
Pressed Metals of America (Port Huron, Mich.)	479 total a	17 July 1944	428	250 whites protest assigning black woman to the day shift
St. Louis Car Co. (St. Louis, Mo.)	1,197 total 120 nonwhite	23 May 1944	<1	Requisition of nondiscriminatory clause in contract
U.S. Rubber Co. (Detroit, Mich.)	7,850 total 600 nonwhite	19 Mar. 1943	3,955	Whites resist upgrading of black workers
Vickers Inc., Oakman Plant (Detroit, Mich.)	a	25 Mar. 1944	800	Whites resist black trainee in lab. dept.
Wright Aeronautical Co. (Lockland, Ohio)	33,587 total 5,927 nonwhite	5 June 1944	32,300	Whites protest transfer of blacks
Youngstown Sheet & Tube Co. (Indiana Harbor, Ind.)	6,922 total 1,153 nonwhite	10 Jan. 1943	4,089	Whites resist promotion of black inspector

Sources: "Data on Work Stoppages in which FEPC Aided in the Settlement," FEPC Micro, reels 4 and 69; U.S. Census Bureau, *Statistical Abstract of the United States, 1943,* 224–25, and U.S. Census Bureau, *Statistical Abstract of the United States, 1948,* 156–57.

a. Data not provided.

Table 2. Racially Motivated Strikes, June 1943–December 1944

	Work Stoppages	Man-Days Idle
Midwest	25	143,407
United States	48	310,393

Sources: "Data on Work Stoppages in which FEPC Aided in the Settlement," FEPC microfilm, reels 4 and 69; U.S. Census Bureau, *Statistical Abstract of the United States, 1943,* 224–25, and U.S.Census Bureau, *Statistical Abstract of the United States, 1948,* 156–57.

Table 3. Work Stoppages in the United States during World War II, January 1941–December 1945

	Strikes	Workers Involved	Man-Days Idle
1943–44	8,708	4,096,916	22,221,608
1941–45	20,714	7,299,497	87,476,721

Sources: "Data on Work Stoppages in which FEPC Aided in the Settlement," FEPC microfilm, reels 4 and 69; U.S. Census Bureau, *Statistical Abstract of the United States, 1943,* 224–25, and U.S. Census Bureau, *Statistical Abstract of the United States, 1948,* 156–57.

Notes

Introduction

1. Jeffries, *Wartime America;* Daniels, "Bad News from the Good War"; and *Cincinnati Post,* 3 March 1942.

2. Fair Employment Practice Committee (FEPC), *First Report,* 114–15; FEPC, *Final Report,* vii–ix; Ross, "Equal Job Opportunity," 93; and Sitkoff, *A New Deal for Blacks,* 334.

3. Kilar, "The Great Lakes Industrial Region."

4. Ayers, Limerick, Nissenbaum, and Onuf, *All Over the Map;* Nelson, *Farm and Factory;* and FEPC, *First Report,* 114–15.

5. Dalfiume, "The 'Forgotten Years' of the Negro Revolution"; and Goings and Mohl, "Toward a New African-American Urban History," 288.

6. FEPC, *First Report,* 114–15; and FEPC, *Final Report,* 19, 37.

7. Polenberg, *War and Society,* 123; Polenberg, *One Nation Divisible,* 34; Chafe, *The Unfinished Journey,* 18; and Brinkley, *American History,* 753. Many of these writers seem to take their cue from Bernstein's essay "America in War and Peace," 297–99.

8. See Ross, *All Manner of Men;* Kesselman, *The Social Politics of FEPC;* Ruchames, *Race, Jobs, and Politics;* and Garfinkel, *When Negroes March.* The most recent books on the FEPC, Reed's *Seedtime for the Modern Civil Rights Movement* and Daniel's *Chicano Workers and the Politics of Fairness,* have also examined the FEPC at the local level. Daniel argues that the FEPC was ineffectual in the Southwest. Reed's assessment of the FEPC is much more positive. He argues that despite the committee's setbacks it made advances against employment discrimination in many areas of the nation.

9. Arnesen, "Up from Exclusion"; Hill, "The Problem of Race in American Labor History"; and Stein, "Race and Class Consciousness Revisited."

10. Ambrose, *D-Day, June 6, 1944,* 487; Lichtenstein, *The Most Dangerous Man in Detroit,* 194–219; and Boyle, *The UAW and the Heyday of American Liberalism,* 46–48.

11. Brinkley, *The End of Reform,* 3; Leuchtenberg, *In the Shadow of FDR;* and Daniel, *Chicano Workers and the Politics of Fairness,* 188–89.

12. Evans, Rueschmeyer, and Skocpol, *Bringing the State Back In,* 3–37; Dubofsky, *The State and Labor in Modern America,* xi–xviii; Lieberman, *Shifting the Color Line;* and Arnesen, "Up from Exclusion," 156.

Chapter 1: "A Refreshing Shower in a Thirsty Land"

1. Goodwin, *No Ordinary Time*, 43; and Brinkley, *The End of Reform*, 3.

2. "The President Accepts the Nomination for a Third Term," in Rosenman, *The Public Papers and Addresses of Franklin D. Roosevelt*, 296–97.

3. *World Almanac and Book of Facts*, 849; and Cardozier, *The Mobilization of the United States in World War II*, 131–58.

4. Civilian Production Administration (CPA), *Industrial Mobilization for War*, 18; and Winkler, *Home Front U.S.A.*, 1–11.

5. U.S. Census Bureau, *Historical Statistics of the United States*, 98, 446, 466; and CPA, *Industrial Mobilization for War*, 14–15.

6. Haynes, *The Negro at Work during the World War and during Reconstruction*, 21; and FEPC, *First Report*, 87–88.

7. Weiss, *Farewell to the Party of Lincoln*, 209–35.

8. Federal Security Agency, *Workers and the National Defense Program*, 7.

9. Ibid., 7, 19–20.

10. "Out in the Cold," 209; Finkle, *Forum for Protest*, 58–62; and *Cleveland Call and Post*, 15 June 1940.

11. White, "It's Our Country, Too," 66.

12. CPA, *Industrial Mobilization for War*, 22–23, 81–85; and NDAC press release, 23 October 1940, quoted in CPA, *Labor Policies of the National Defense Advisory Commission and the Office of Production Management*, 4, 104, 190.

13. Letter, Thurgood Marshall to Robert C. Weaver, 24 July 1940, NAACP microfilm, 13-C-7; Watson, *Lion in the Lobby*, 126; and Drake and Cayton, *Black Metropolis*, 218–20.

14. NDAC press release, 23 October 1940, NAACP microfilm, 13-A-18; "Address by Sidney Hillman Associate Director General, OPM, to the First Annual Conference on the Negro in Business, April 18, 1941," NAACP microfilm, 13-A-18; and "National Defense Labor Problems," 319, 322.

15. Weaver, "The Defense Program and the Negro," 324.

16. See Garfinkel, *When Negroes March*.

17. Northrup, *Organized Labor and the Negro*, 11–12; Pfeffer, *A. Philip Randolph*; and Bracey and Meier, "Allies or Adversaries?"

18. O'Reilly and Gallen, *Black Americans*, 307–39; Janken, *Rayford W. Logan*, 127–29; Pfeffer, *A. Philip Randolph*, 69; and letter, Walter White to A. Philip Randolph, 28 May 1941, NAACP microfilm, 13-B-23.

19. FEPC, *Minorities in Defense*, 9; and letter, Sidney Hillman to All Defense Contractors, 11 April 1941, NAACP microfilm, 13-B-11.

20. *Amsterdam News*, 19 April 1941, quoted in Garfinkel, *When Negroes March*, 56; Dalfiume, "The 'Forgotten Years' of the Negro Revolution," 93; *Chicago Defender*, 26 April 1941; and *Cleveland Call and Post*, 10 May 1941.

21. CPA, *Labor Policies of the National Defense Advisory Commission and the Office of Production Management*, 190–99.

22. *Congressional Record* 87, pt. 2 (13 March 1941): 2259; *Congressional Record* 87, pt. 3 (29 April 1941): 3374; letter, A. Philip Randolph to Franklin D. Roosevelt, 29 May 1941, FDR Papers, OF 93, box 4; letter, Scott W. Lucas to Preston Bradley, 11 September 1945, Scott W. Lucas Papers, box 27; and Pfeffer, *A. Philip Randolph*, 57–58, 69–70.

23. Kessner, *Fiorello H. LaGuardia and the Making of Modern New York*, 526–27.

24. White, *A Man Called White*, 191–93; and "Employment in Defense Industries: Address Delivered by A. Philip Randolph before the Thirty-second Annual Conference of the National Association for the Advancement of Colored People, Houston, Texas, June 25, 1941," NAACP microfilm, 1-C-10.

25. Terkel, *The Good War,* 337–38.

26. "Executive Order 8802," *Federal Register* 6, no. 125 (27 June 1941): 4544. Noticeably, the executive order does not mention sex discrimination. There is no clue to this omission in the Joseph Rauh papers, the FEPC's records, or the records of the Bureau of the Budget, which generally kept files on all executive orders. Randolph's organizing principle was racial discrimination and the executive order addressed that point. Perhaps fighting sex discrimination was not a top priority for Randolph and federal officials. In addition to any gender bias, Rauh may have left "sex" out so that the order would not upset labor unions that in general did not support anti–sex discrimination legislation. There is perhaps another reason gleaned from the years following the 1964 Civil Rights Act. After the passage of the act, states like Wisconsin had to rewrite protective legislation for women that was invalidated by Title VII. Not wishing to step on the thorny issue of protective legislation, Rauh may have expediently omitted "sex" from this list of protected classes. See Graham, *The Civil Rights Era,* 136–39.

27. Memo, Mary McLeod Bethune to FDR, 26 June 1941, FDR Papers, OF 93, box 4; *Chicago Defender,* 5 July 1941; "Defense Jobs," 247; and Earl B. Dickerson press release, 9 January 1942, Brotherhood of Sleeping Car Porters (BSCP) Papers, box 6.

28. *Cleveland Gazette,* 19 July 1941; *Philadelphia Tribune,* 3 July 1941; *Baltimore Afro-American,* 28 June 1941; James, *Fighting Racism in World War II,* 118; Rustin, *Down the Line,* 10; Garfinkel, *When Negroes March,* 67; and Pfeffer, *A. Philip Randolph,* 50.

29. Ruchames, *Race, Jobs, and Politics,* 73–99; Garfinkel, *When Negroes March,* 63; *Cleveland Gazette,* 19 July 1941; *Congressional Record* 87, pt. 7 (11 September 1941): 7395; *Congressional Record* 87, pt. 3 (24 July 1941): A 3574; *New York Times,* 26 June 1941; and *PM,* 26 June 1941.

30. Reed, *Seedtime for the Modern Civil Rights Movement,* 21–26.

31. FEPC, *FEPC: How It Operates,* 7–14; FEPC, *Final Report,* viii; Ruchames, *Race, Jobs, and Politics,* 21–30; and Ross, *All Manner of Men,* 50.

Chapter 2: The Publicity Campaign and the Chicago Precedents

1. FEPC press release, 15 December 1941, NAACP microfilm, 13-B-10.

2. *Chicago Defender,* 20 December 1941.

3. Finkle, *Forum for Protest,* 96–98; and *Chicago Defender,* 31 January 1942.

4. A proposed hearing in El Paso, Texas, was canceled at Assistant Secretary of State Sumner Welles's request. Welles feared that an El Paso FEPC hearing would disrupt the *bracero* program that supplied Mexican workers to American factories. See Daniel, *Chicano Workers and the Politics of Fairness,* 41–54, 75–76.

5. *Chicago Defender,* 25 October and 1 November 1941; and Reed, *Seedtime for the Modern Civil Rights Movement,* 38–39.

6. Reed, *The Chicago NAACP and the Rise of Black Professional Leadership,* 118; Bates, "A New Crowd Challenges the Agenda of the Old Guard in the NAACP"; and Halpern, *Down on the Killing Floor,* 167–200, 215–17.

7. Grossman, *Land of Hope,* 181–207; Drake and Cayton, *Black Metropolis,* 228–29; and Scott, *Negro Migration during the War,* 102–18.

8. Barnett, "We Win a Place in Industry"; Chicago Commission on Race Relations, *The Negro in Chicago,* 393–94; Tuttle, *Race Riot,* 108–56.

9. Drake and Cayton, *Black Metropolis,* 26; and Kruman, "Quotas for Blacks," 50–51.

10. Letter, Theophilus M. Mann to Walter White, 16 March 1933, NAACP microfilm, 12-C-1; copy of Illinois House Bill 237, 58th General Assembly, 31 January 1933, NAACP microfilm, 12-C-1; and telegram, Walter White to Governor Henry Horner, 6 July 1933, NAACP microfilm, 12-C-1.

11. Weiss, *Farewell to the Party of Lincoln*, 206, 214.

12. Verbatim transcripts of the proceedings of the Commission on the Condition of the Urban Colored Population, 3–4 January 1941, FEPC microfilm, reels 1, 17; letter, Elmer Henderson to Edwin R. Embree, 22 September 1942, FEPC microfilm, reel 44; and Watters, *Illinois in the Second World War*, vol. 2, 263. The Horner Commission disbanded in March 1941 when the Illinois attorney general challenged the constitutionality of the commission and denied it operating funds.

13. Drake and Cayton, *Black Metropolis*, 218–32.

14. Dickerson, "The Participation of Negro Labor in Our War Effort," 30; *Chicago Defender*, 1 February and 10 October 1941; and letter, Walter White to Frances Biddle, 10 October 1941, NAACP microfilm, 13-A-14.

15. *Chicago Defender*, 15 March, 11 and 18 October 1941; NAACP file memo, 10 September 1941, NAACP microfilm, 13-B-11; and letter, J. Edgar Hodges to Milton P. Webster, 21 July 1941, BSCP Papers, box 129.

16. *Chicago Defender*, 15 February 1941; Roy Wilkins's summary of the Chicago MOWM July 1943 meeting, NAACP microfilm, 13-B-23; and Hill, *The FBI's RACON*, 463, 494.

17. Letter, Frank W. McCulloch to Milton P. Webster, 28 July 1941, Frank W. McCulloch Papers, box 9; and "Defense Jobs," 247.

18. *Laws of Illinois, 1941*, 557; letter, Frank W. McCulloch to Francis P. Murphy, 19 December 1941, Frank W. McCulloch Papers, box 9; McCulloch's notes from 29 May 1942 telephone conversation with Francis P. Murphy, Frank W. McCulloch Papers, box 9; and letter, McCulloch to Murphy, 30 July 1942, Frank W. McCulloch Papers, box 9.

19. Letter, Earl B. Dickerson to Frank W. McCulloch, 20 December 1941, Frank W. McCulloch Papers, box 9; G. James Fleming's supplementary report on Chicago, December 1941, FEPC microfilm, reel 6; and *Chicago Defender*, 12 May 1941.

20. FEPC file memo, 7 December 1941, FEPC microfilm, reel 47.

21. Letter, Annetta M. Dieckmann to Frank W. McCulloch, 5 August 1941, Frank W. McCulloch Papers, box 9.

22. Summary of the Chicago hearings, 19–20 January 1942, 1, FEPC microfilm, reel 37; and *Chicago Defender*, 24 January 1942.

23. Summary of the Chicago hearings, 19–20 January 1942, 2, 8–9, FEPC microfilm, reel 37.

24. Summary of the Chicago hearings, 19–20 January 1942, 7–8, FEPC microfilm, reel 37; *Chicago Defender*, 24 January 1942; and letter, Lawrence Cramer to Malcolm S. MacLean, 5 March 1942, BSCP Papers, box 129.

25. Letter, H. I. Barron to Robert C. Weaver, 29 August 1941, FEPC microfilm, reel 37; letter, H. H. Curtice to Will W. Alexander, 18 September 1941, BSCP Papers, box 129; letter, H. I. Barron to Earl B. Dickerson, 4 November 1941, FEPC microfilm, reel 37; and summary of the Chicago hearings, 19–20 January 1942, 3–5, FEPC microfilm, reel 37.

26. Summary of the Chicago hearings, 19–20 January 1942, 5–7, FEPC microfilm, reel 37.

27. Letter, Rose Meister to FDR, 6 October 1942, FEPC microfilm, reel 44; summary of the Chicago hearings, 19–20 January 1942, 9–13, FEPC microfilm, reel 37; *Milwaukee Journal*, 20 and 21 January 1942; and Meyer, *"Stalin over Wisconsin,"* 90–104, 124–26. Milwaukee is discussed in greater detail in chapter 5.

28. Summary of the Chicago hearings, 19–20 January 1942, 13, FEPC microfilm, reel 37. See appendix A for statistical summary of reports.

29. Letter, Walter White to Malcolm MacLean, 14 April 1942, FEPC microfilm, reel 37; *Cleveland Call and Post*, 7 February 1942; *Chicago Tribune*, 21 January 1942; Ruchames, *Race, Jobs, and Politics*, 42–43.

30. Reed, *Seedtime for the Modern Civil Rights Movement*, 40–41, 48–49.

31. FEPC press release, 17 October 1941, NAACP microfilm, 13-B-10; *Chicago Defender*, 11 November 1941.

32. "Discrimination against Negro Workers"; "AFL Slams the Door Again," 343; and Ethridge, "Jobs for Everybody," 24.

33. *Chicago Defender,* 12 May 1941; White House cross reference file, 23 April 1942, letter, Walter White to FDR, FDR Papers, OF 2538, box 2; and "Roundtable: Which Union is Fairer to the Negro: AFL or CIO?"

34. White House cross reference file, 23 April 1942, FDR Papers, OF 2538, box 2; letter, Walter White to Francis Biddle, 10 October 1941, NAACP microfilm, 13-A-14; letter, William Green to Roy Wilkins, 10 December 1941, NAACP microfilm, 13-A-15; "AFL Slams the Door Again," 343; and Seidman, *American Labor from Defense to Reconversion,* 29.

35. Telegram, American Consolidated Trades Council to Earl Dickerson, 15 February 1942, FEPC microfilm, reel 36; memorandum Elmer Henderson to George M. Johnson, n.d., FEPC microfilm, reel 37; and Watters, *Illinois in the Second World War,* vol. 1, 128.

36. Verbatim transcript of Chicago Journeymen Plumbers' Union Local 130 hearing, 4 April 1942, 1–25, FEPC microfilm, reel 18; statement to the Pipe Trades Council of Cook County, 29 August 1941, BSCP Papers, box 129; and Northrup, *Organized Labor and the Negro,* 23–25.

37. Verbatim transcript of Chicago Journeymen Plumbers' Union Local 130 hearing, 4 April 1942, 66–67, 139–89, FEPC microfilm, reel 18.

38. Verbatim transcript of Chicago Journeymen Plumbers' Union Local 130 hearing, 4 April 1942, 85, 107, FEPC microfilm, reel 18.

39. Summary of hearing concerning Steamfitters' Protective Association Local 597, 4 April 1942, 4, FEPC microfilm, reel 18; summary of hearing concerning Chicago Journeymen Plumbers' Union Local 130, 4 April 1942, 4–5, FEPC microfilm, reel 18; and *Chicago Tribune,* 5 April 1942. In 1945 the Great Lakes Naval Training Station finally abandoned some of its Jim Crow employment policies. See *Chicago Defender,* 7 July 1945.

40. Moreno, *From Direct Action to Affirmative Action,* 30–83; and Reed, *Seedtime for the Modern Civil Rights Movement,* 38–44.

41. Letter, Lester Granger to FDR, 24 June 1942, FDR Papers, OF 4245 G, box 3; letter, Fullerton Fulton to FEPC, 24 June 1942, FDR Papers, OF 4245 G, box 4; "U.S.A. Needs Sharp Break with the Past," 151; and *Chicago Defender,* 7 February 1942.

Chapter 3: Ruin and Rebirth

1. "The Negro's War," 79.

2. "Employment of Negroes by Federal Government," 888–90; Granger, "Negroes and War Production"; Weaver, "Defense Industries and the Negro"; and Randolph, "Why Should We March," 489.

3. FEPC meeting minutes, 18 January 1942, FEPC microfilm, reel 38; telegram, Walter White to FDR, 24 June 1942, NAACP microfilm, 13-B-11; letter, Lester Granger to FDR, 24 June 1942, FDR Papers, OF 4245 G, box 3; and *Chicago Defender,* 7 February 1942.

4. Blake, *Paul V. McNutt,* 319; Flynn, *The Mess in Washington,* 149–63; and Reed, *Seedtime for the Modern Civil Rights Movement,* 74–76.

5. Newman, *Hugo Black,* 313; Reed, *Seedtime for the Modern Civil Rights Movement,* 74–76; Shapiro, *White Violence and Black Response,* 301–96; and Capeci, *Race Relations in Wartime Detroit.*

6. Telegram, A. Philip Randolph to Walter White, 5 August 1942, NAACP microfilm, 13-B-11; telegram, Walter White to FDR, 6 August 1942, NAACP microfilm, 13-B-11; letter, Ashby B. Carter to FDR, 12 August 1942, FEPC microfilm, reel 42; Roosevelt, *The Complete Roosevelt Presidential Press Conferences,* vol. 20, entry 47; *New York Times,* 18 August 1942; and *Cleveland Call and Post,* 19 September 1942.

7. Letter, Earl B. Dickerson to FDR, 1 March 1943, BSCP Papers, box 132; minutes of executive board meeting of Chicago Metropolitan Fair Employment Practices Council,

24 September 1942, Frank W. McCulloch Papers, box 9; letter, Malcolm S. MacLean to Marvin McIntyre, 3 August 1942, FDR Papers, OF 4245 G, box 3; and Beecher, "This Is the Picture," 16.

8. White House press release, 17 August 1942, FDR Papers, OF 4245 G, box 3.

9. *Chicago Defender,* 5 December 1942 and 23 January 1943; Terkel, *The Good War,* 341–42; FEPC meeting minutes, 23 November 1942, FEPC microfilm, reel 1; and Reed, *Seedtime for the Modern Civil Rights Movement,* 77–103.

10. Randolph quote from *Brotherhood Worker* clipping in St. Louis MOWM Scrapbook, vol. 1; telegram, Walter White to FDR, 11 January 1943, NAACP microfilm, 13-B-12; letter, Walter White to FDR, 15 January 1943, NAACP microfilm, 13-B-12; and Reed, *Seedtime for the Modern Civil Rights Movement,* 85.

11. Letter, FDR to Malcolm S. MacLean, 6 February 1943, BSCP Papers, box 13; and letter, Charles H. Houston to Malcolm S. MacLean, 16 January 1943, FDR Papers, OF 4245 G, box 4.

12. Garfinkel, *When Negroes March,* 133–39, 155; Wechsler, "Pigeonhole for Negro Equality," 121–22; Beecher, "8802 Blues," 248–50; and Kapur, *Raising Up a Prophet,* 101–23.

13. Memo, Francis Biddle to FDR, 29 January 1943, FDR Papers, OF 4245 G, box 4; White House press release, 3 February 1943, FDR Papers, OF 4905, box 2; verbatim transcript of proceedings of the Conference on Scope and Powers of Committee on Fair Employment Practice, 19 February 1943, NAACP microfilm, 13-B-12; "Along the N.A.A.C.P. Battlefront," 87; and Reed, *Seedtime for the Modern Civil Rights Movement,* 107–12.

14. "Executive Order 9346," *Federal Register* 8, no. 106 (29 May 1943): 7183–84; and cabinet meeting minutes, 6 May 1943, Francis Biddle Papers, box 1.

15. FBI report on Earl B. Dickerson, 9 February 1942, FDR Papers, OF 4245 G, box 3; letter, Earl B. Dickerson to FDR, 1 March 1943, BSCP Papers, box 132; and Blantz, *A Priest in Public Service,* 586.

16. Letter, Lawrence W. Cramer to Milton P. Webster, 22 June 1943, BSCP Papers, box 132; Ross, "Results Obtained by Fair Employment Practice Committee Warrant Legislation to Make it Permanent," 184; FEPC, *FEPC: How It Operates,* 7; Lewis, "An Evaluation of the Fair Employment Practice Committee"; "The New FEPC," 231; Raushenbush, "Green Light for the FEPC," 498–503, 514; *New York Times,* 29 May 1943.

17. The FEPC had offices in Atlanta, Chicago, Cleveland, Dallas, Kansas City, New Orleans, New York City, Philadelphia, San Antonio, San Francisco, and Washington, D.C., and suboffices in Cincinnati, Detroit, Los Angeles, Pittsburgh, and St. Louis.

18. WMC, "Adequacy of Labor Supply in Important Labor Market Areas, September 1, 1943," Frances P. Bolton Papers, box 72.

19. FEPC, "Major Instances of Under-Utilization of Negroes," FEPC microfilm, reel 4.

20. When the FEPC was transferred to the WMC in 1942 the committee had thirty-four staff members, including the appointed committee members. The second FEPC had about 120 workers, over half of whom were in the field. See FEPC, *FEPC: How it Operates,* 4.

21. FEPC, *FEPC: How it Operates,* 5; and "Discrimination," FEPC microfilm, reel 8.

22. FEPC, *FEPC: How it Operates,* 6.

23. Ibid., 7–10.

24. FEPC, *First Report,* 23–28.

25. Summary of 26 July 1943 FEPC meeting, FEPC microfilm, reel 1; and "Operations Bulletin Regarding Relationship with Metropolitan Councils on Fair Employment Practice," FEPC microfilm, reel 69.

26. Letter, Walter White to Roscoe Dunjee, 5 October 1943, NAACP microfilm, 13-B-12; *A Monthly Summary of Events and Trends in Race Relations,* October 1943, 27; Blantz, *A Priest in Public Service,* 199–227; McNeil, *Groundwork;* and Reed, *Seedtime for the Modern Civil Rights Movement,* 129–30.

27. Robertson, *Sly and Able,* 339–42.

Chapter 4: The Chicago Office

1. Henderson was in charge of two administrative areas, the FEPC's regions VI and VIII. Region VI included Illinois, Indiana, and Wisconsin; region VIII encompassed the Dakotas, Iowa, Minnesota, and Nebraska. The Chicago office docketed few complaints from the Dakotas, Iowa, and Nebraska. These states are not examined in this book. See FEPC, *First Report*, 31.

2. Johnson, "Negro Internal Migration, 1940–1943," 10–12.

3. OWI press release, 19 April 1944, FEPC microfilm, reel 68; "Population Figures as of November 1, 1943," FEPC microfilm, reel 5; "Estimates of Negro Population in War Production Centers," FEPC microfilm, reel 5; "Migration to War-Industry Areas," 58–61; and Funigiello, *The Challenge to Urban Liberalism*, 3–38.

4. Bureau on Jewish Employment Problems, *Manpower and Minorities*, 5–6; and Bureau on Jewish Employment Problems, *Employment Barriers in Wartime*, 11–12.

5. WMC, "Adequacy of Labor Supply in Important Labor Market Areas, September 1, 1943," Frances P. Bolton Papers, box 72; memo, George A. Scott to William H. Spencer, 14 April 1943, War Manpower Commission (WMC) Records, Region VI, Appeal Cases 1942–1945, series 278, box 3573; "Statement of Frank Paz, President, the Spanish-Speaking People's Council of Chicago," in U.S. Congress, Senate Committee on Education and Labor, *Fair Employment Practices Act*, 41–43; and Albert, "Japanese-American Communities in Chicago and the Twin Cities," 115–24.

6. Confidential report on Chicago race relations situation, 29 June 1943, Philleo Nash Papers, box 27; Turner Catledge, "Racial Employment Problems, August 6, 1943," FDR Papers, OF 4245 G, box 5; OWI press release, 27 July 1943, NAACP microfilm, 13-B-12; and Drake, "Profiles: Chicago," 261–64.

7. Hill, *FBI's RACON*, 90, 91–92.

8. Letter, Sol Goldin to Austin H. Scott, 26 April 1943, WMC Records, series 278, box 3578; Bureau on Jewish Employment Problems, *Manpower and Minorities*, 6; and Drake, "Profiles: Chicago," 265–70.

9. Letter, J. Edgar Hoover to Jonathan Daniels, 20 May 1944, FDR Papers, OF 4245 G, box 7; Strickgold, *Memorandum #1*, 1; and Sitkoff, "Racial Militancy and Interracial Violence in the Second World War," 671.

10. Confidential report on the Chicago race situation, 29 June 1943, Philleo Nash Papers, box 27; and War Department, "Racial Tension Areas in War Production Centers," 2, 8, FDR Papers, OF 4245 G, box 8.

11. Hill, *The FBI's RACON*, 95–96.

12. "Proposal of Action for Special Conference on Racial Problems Called by Chicago Industrial Union Council, CIO, 25 June 1943, Council Chambers, City Hall," Philleo Nash Papers, box 47.

13. Letter, Will Alexander to Jonathan Daniels, 16 July 1943, FDR Papers, OF 4245 G, box 5; Drake and Cayton, *Black Metropolis*, 90–96; Biles, *Big City Boss in Depression and War*, 127; and Hill, *The FBI's RACON*, 95–96.

14. *Chicago Defender*, 8 January 1944; letter, Will Alexander to Jonathan Daniels, 16 July 1943, FDR Papers, OF 4245 G, box 5; Mayor's Committee on Race Relations, *City Planning in Race Relations*, 39–40, 46–47; and Weaver, "Racial Tensions in Chicago," 1–8.

15. Mayor's Committee on Race Relations, *Race Relations in Chicago*, 9–10.

16. Letter, A. Leon Bailey to Franklin D. Roosevelt, 20 June 1944, FDR Papers, OF 4245 G, box 4; Strickgold, *Memorandum #1*, 1–2, 7–8; Watters, *Illinois in the Second World War*, vol. 2, 279–80; and Terkel, *Hard Times*, 395–96.

17. Letter, Francis J. Haas to Fair Employment Practices Council of Metropolitan Chicago, 21 August 1943, FEPC microfilm, reel 43.

18. Bureau on Jewish Employment Problems, *Manpower and Minorities*, 10–11.

19. Fair Employment Practices Council of Metropolitan Chicago press release, 14 January 1942, UAW War Policy Division Collection, box 6; and letter, James M. Yard to Lawrence W. Cramer, 30 June 1942, FEPC microfilm, reel 45.

20. Memo, St. Claire Bourne to Malcolm Ross, n.d., FEPC microfilm, reel 3.

21. Summary of conference between Mayor Edward J. Kelly and Elmer Henderson, 13 October 1943, FEPC microfilm, reel 51; and "Proclamation, June 14, 1944," FEPC microfilm, reel 43.

22. *Chicago Defender,* 7 February 1942.

23. Letter, Elmer Henderson to William H. Spencer, 25 May 1945, WMC Records, series 278, box 3573; and War Manpower Commission (WMC), *History of the Mobilization of Labor for War Production during World War II,* 1–49.

24. Letter, Edward L. Doty to Milton Webster, 2 July 1942, BSCP Papers, box 130.

25. Telegram, American Consolidated Trades Council to Lawrence Cramer, 21 July 1942, FEPC microfilm, reel 45; letter, Lawrence W. Cramer to Paul V. McNutt, 29 June 1942, FEPC microfilm, reel 4; memo, Elmer Henderson to George M. Johnson, 24 August 1944, FEPC microfilm, reel 40; FEPC meeting minutes, 8 February 1943, FEPC microfilm, reel 1; monthly report Elmer Henderson to Clarence Mitchell, 15 October, 15 November 1945, FEPC microfilm, reel 37; letter, Hugo Williams to Walter White, 23 January 1947, NAACP microfilm, 13-C-9; *Chicago Defender* clipping, ca. January 1947, NAACP microfilm, 13-C-9; and Edward L. Doty, interview by Herbert Hill, 2 November 1967. Much later Doty claimed that Quirk stole two hundred thousand dollars.

26. No data was apparently collected for Simpson Construction. On 12 August 1942 Elmer Hansen, Simpson's president, sent a letter to Lawrence Cramer stating that he agreed "with the principle on which your Committee was founded [and was] willing to cooperate in a campaign of education and admonishment to attain the racial tolerance we seek." However, he also told Cramer that "if it becomes a case of persecution and compulsion [that he believed] the result will be a greater intolerance between groups than ever existed before." See letter, Elmer Hansen to Lawrence W. Cramer, 12 August 1942, FEPC microfilm, reel 78 FR.

27. "One of Those Things?" 12; Schonberger, "Employer Changes Hiring Policy," 18; *Cleveland Call and Post,* 2 January 1943; letter, George A. Rud to Senator Scott Lucas, 16 September 1943, WMC Records, series 278, box 3578; letter, George A. Rud to William Spencer, 16 September 1943, WMC Records, series 278, box 3578; letter, C. E. Wooliever to William Spencer, 25 September 1943, WMC Records, series 278, box 3578; memo, Elmer Henderson to Harry H. C. Gibson, 22 October 1943, FEPC microfilm, reel 50; and biweekly report, Elmer Henderson to Will Maslow, 30 April 1945, FEPC microfilm, reel 51.

28. *Chicago Defender,* 19 December 1942.

29. Studebaker compliance report, December 1943, FEPC microfilm, reel 76. See appendix A.

30. Memo, John A. Davis to Malcolm Ross, 25 May 1944, FEPC microfilm, reel 1.

31. Memo, Stanley D. Metzger to Malcolm Ross, 17 May 1944, FEPC microfilm, reel 1; "Statement on Work Stoppages," FEPC microfilm, reel 4; memo, William Spencer to Lester Brown, 17 August 1943, WMC Records, series 278, box 3573; memo, Clarence Mitchell to Philleo Nash, 24 July 1944, Philleo Nash Papers, box 26; memo, Joy P. Davis to John A. Davis, 28 March 1944, FEPC microfilm, reel 69; weekly report Elmer Henderson to Will Maslow, 10 January 1944, FEPC microfilm, reel 51; chronology of Pullman strike, FEPC microfilm, reel 63; memo, Elmer Henderson to Will Maslow, 30 June 1945, FEPC microfilm, reel 63; FEPC *First Report,* 79–82; Weaver, *Negro Labor,* 223; and National War Labor Board, *Termination Report of the National War Labor Board,* 150–55. See appendix B.

32. FEPC file report on George L. Detterbeck Company, 11 July 1944, FEPC microfilm, reel 7.

33. Letter, William Spencer to Elmer Henderson, 23 March 1941, WMC Records, series

278, box 3573; letter, Elmer Henderson to William Spencer, 6 December 1944, WMC Records, series 278, box 3578; and *Rhindlander News,* 16 September 1943.

34. Letter, George A. Scott to Joseph E. Brooks, 6 December 1944, WMC Records, series 278, box 3573; verbatim transcripts of FEPC, the Baltimore and Ohio Chicago Terminal Railroad Company and the Brotherhood of Railway Carmen of America hearings, 15–18 September 1943, FEPC microfilm, reel 29; FEPC file memo, n.d., FEPC microfilm, 73; and telegram, Elmer Henderson to George M. Johnson, 28 July 1944, FEPC microfilm, reel 40.

35. *A Monthly Summary of Events and Trends in Race Relations,* October 1944, 62, and February 1945, 188; *Chicago Defender,* 11, 18, and 25 July 1942; Zieger, *The CIO,* 152–59; Lichtenstein, *The Most Dangerous Man in Detroit,* 208–10; Hope, *Equality of Opportunity;* and Horowitz, *"Negro and White, Unite and Fight!"*

36. Memo, Elmer Henderson to Clarence Mitchell, 5 January 1945, FEPC microfilm, reel 40; biweekly report Elmer Henderson to Will Maslow, 23 October 1943, 5 August and 20 November 1944, 7 July 1945, FEPC microfilm, reel 51; monthly report Elmer Henderson to Clarence Mitchell, 15 October 1945, FEPC microfilm, reel 51; memo, Elmer Henderson to Malcolm Ross, 31 March 1944, FEPC microfilm, reel 51; confidential report to FEPC on Negroes as platform operators, 12 January 1945, NAACP microfilm, 13-B-12; OWI press release, 6 March 1944, Philleo Nash Papers, box 41; memo, Joy Schultz to Elmer Henderson, 15 March 1945, FEPC microfilm, reel 50; *Chicago Defender,* 12 December 1942, 18 September, 30 October, 18 December 1943, and 15 April 1944; and Nelson, *Farm and Factory,* 141.

37. William M. Ashby, "Report of the Executive Secretary of the Springfield Urban League," January and April 1942, Springfield Urban League Papers, box 1; letter, Robert Weaver to Reverend D. E. Webster, 16 June 1942, FEPC microfilm, reel 51; and memo, L. Virgil Williams to Elmer W. Henderson, 21 June 1944, FEPC microfilm, reel 51.

38. Memo, L. Virgil Williams to Elmer Henderson, 21 June 1944, FEPC microfilm, reel 51; William M. Ashby, "Report of the Executive Secretary of the Springfield Urban League," March, October, and December 1942 and January 1944, Springfield Urban League Papers, box 1; William R. Stewart, "Report of the Executive Secretary of the Springfield Urban League, January 1945," Springfield Urban League Papers, box 1; and Northrup, *Organized Labor and the Negro,* 2.

39. Letter, J. Edgar Hoover to Jonathan Daniels, 10 April 1944, FDR Papers, OF 4245 G, box 6; racial tension abstract concerning East St. Louis, FDR Papers, OF 4245 G, box 5; and FBI report on East St. Louis, 20 October 1943 and 10 April 1944, FDR Papers, OF 4245 G, box 6; Rudwick, *Race Riot at East St. Louis;* and Rudwick, "Fifty Years of Race Relations in East St. Louis," 3–15.

40. "Abstracts Concerning Racial Tension: East St. Louis," FDR Papers, OF 4245 G, box 5; letter, J. Edgar Hoover to Jonathan Daniels, 10 April 1944, FDR Papers, OF 4245 G, box 6; "Data on Work Stoppages in which FEPC Aided in the Settlement," FEPC microfilm, reel 4; memo, Mrs. Bright to Philleo Nash, 22 July 1944, Philleo Nash Papers, box 18; memo, Clarence Mitchell to Philleo Nash, 24 July 1944, Philleo Nash Papers, box 18; weekly report Elmer Henderson to Will Maslow, 27 March 1944, FEPC microfilm, reel 51. See appendix B.

41. Weekly report Elmer Henderson to Will Maslow, 17 July 1944, FEPC microfilm, reel 51; memo, Harry H. C. Gibson to Elmer Henderson, 7 August 1944, FEPC microfilm, reel 51; and memo, Harry H. C. Gibson to Elmer Henderson, 5 October 1944, FEPC microfilm, reel 51.

42. Memo, Evelyn N. Cooper to George M. Johnson, 12 February 1945, FEPC microfilm, reel 4.

43. Emanuel Bloch, "Summary of Olin Industries (Western Cartridge Division) for *Final Report,"* FEPC microfilm, reel 2; *Chicago Defender,* 3 February 1945, 3; Ross, *All*

Manner of Men, 17; and U.S. Census Bureau, _Sixteenth Census of the United States,_ vol. 2, pt. 2, 590.

44. Statement of charges against Western Cartridge Company, Case No. 71, FEPC microfilm, reel 3; letter, William Spencer to Elmer Henderson, 17 November 1943, WMC Records, series 278, box 3573; War Manpower Commission report on Western Cartridge Company, 2 December 1943, Illinois Commission on Human Relations Papers, box 12; and Watters, _Illinois in the Second World War,_ vol. 2, 99–100.

45. War Manpower Commission report on Western Cartridge Company, 2 December 1943, Illinois Commission on Human Relations Papers, box 12; memo, William Spencer to Elmer Henderson, 17 December 1943, Illinois Commission on Human Relations Papers, box 12; and Watters, _Illinois in the Second World War,_ vol. 2, 347–51. Spencer's concerns were not completely unfounded. In 1942 there were two major strikes at Western Cartridge over union grievances.

46. Illinois Interracial Commission, Summary Report, 5 February 1944, Illinois Commission on Human Relations Papers, box 12; letter, Martin H. Bickham to Elmer Henderson, 27 January 1944, Illinois Commission on Human Relations Papers, box 12; letter, Martin H. Bickham to Dwight H. Green, 27 January 1944, Illinois Commission on Human Relations Papers, box 12; and weekly report Elmer Henderson to Will Maslow, 31 January 1944, FEPC microfilm, reel 51.

47. Ross, _All Manner of Men,_ 49.

48. Verbatim transcript of Western Cartridge hearing, FEPC microfilm, reel 20.

49. Verbatim transcript of Western Cartridge hearing, FEPC microfilm, reel 20; Ross, _All Manner of Men,_ 60–61; and Watters, _Illinois in the Second World War,_ vol. 2, 262, 170–71.

50. Proposed decision in case no. 71, Olin Industries, Inc. (Western Cartridge Division), September 1945, FEPC microfilm, reel 20; and Ross, _All Manner of Men,_ 66. The Stacy committee was a three-man body led by North Carolina's Chief Supreme Court Justice Walter P. Stacy. The other two members were Judge William H. Holly of the Federal District Court of Chicago and the mayor of Cleveland, Frank J. Lausche. The committee met for several months with representatives of the southern railways and unions and made no recommendations. See Reed, _Seedtime for the Modern Civil Rights Movement,_ 137–39.

51. Powell, "The Negro Worker in Chicago Industry," 22.

52. FEPC, _First Report,_ 114; Chicago Urban League, _Industrial Relations Bulletin,_ 1; U.S. Congress, Senate Committee on Education and Labor, _Fair Employment Practice Act, S. 2048,_ 65–72; and FEPC, _Final Report,_ 41–97. Statistics from 1945–46 are sketchy. The FEPC did not have ample staff or budget to collect and analyze its last two years as it had its first two. See chapter 9.

Chapter 5: The Limits of Activism

1. The financial aspects of the FEPC are detailed in chapter 9. See FEPC, _First Report,_ 33.

2. Madison, "Hoosiers at War"; McShane, "Boom!"; Ayer, "Hoosier Labor in the Second World War"; Cavnes, _The Hoosier Community at War;_ and Turner, "Indiana in World War II."

3. Indiana State Defense Council and Indiana State Chamber of Commerce, _The Story of House Bill No. 445,_ 5; and Indiana State Defense Council and Indiana State Chamber of Commerce, _The Action toward a Solution,_ 9.

4. Turner, _Indiana at War,_ 500–507; Cavnes, _The Hoosier Community at War,_ 111–20; Thornbrough, _Since Emancipation,_ 76–81. The local biracial committees were in Anderson, Bloomington, East Chicago, Elkhart, Evansville, Fort Wayne, Gary, Indianapolis, Jeffersonville, Kokomo, Logansport, Marion, Michigan City, Muncie, New Albany, Peru, Richmond, Shelbyville, South Bend, Terre Haute, and Vincennes. The records of these local committees apparently did not survive the war.

5. Letter, Indiana State Industrial Council to all Affiliates, 2 August 1941, Indiana War History Commission Collection, box 9; State Federation of Labor, Resolution No. 49, November 1941, Indiana War History Commission Collection, box 9; and Thornbrough, *Since Emancipation*, 76–77.

6. "Results of Bi-Racial Committee Survey, 14 August 1941," Indiana War History Commission Collection, box 9.

7. Indiana State Defense Council and Indiana State Chamber of Commerce, *The Action toward a Solution*, 13.

8. Indiana State Defense Council and Indiana State Chamber of Commerce, *Job Opportunities for Negroes*, 3, 4–8.

9. Cavnes, *The Hoosier Community at War*, 119.

10. Letter, J. Chester Allen to Clarence A. Jackson, 2 August 1941, Indiana War History Commission Collection, box 9.

11. Works Progress Administration, Federal Writers' Project, *The Calumet Region Historical Guide*, 51–55; and Mohl and Betten, *Steel City*, 49–50, 51–90.

12. Cavnes, *The Hoosier Community at War*, 162.

13. Mohl and Betten, *Steel City*, 73–75.

14. Memo, William H. Spencer to Lester Brown, 17 August 1943, WMC Records, series 278, box 3573; *Chicago Defender*, 17 July 1943; and Ayer, "Hoosier Labor in the Second World War," 100.

15. Mohl and Betten, *Steel City*, 76–77.

16. Kerns, *A Study of the Social and Economic Conditions of the Negro Population of Gary, Indiana*, 68; and memo, Joy Schultz to Elmer Henderson, 28 September 1945, FEPC microfilm, reel 37.

17. Mohl and Betten, *Steel City*, 76.

18. Boris, "'You Wouldn't Want One of 'Em Dancing with Your Wife'"; and Mohl and Betten, *Steel City*, 76.

19. Memo, Harry H. C. Gibson to Elmer W. Henderson, 2 September 1944, FEPC microfilm, reel 51.

20. Ibid.

21. Memo, Joy Schultz to Elmer W. Henderson, 28 September 1945, FEPC microfilm, reel 37; and monthly report, Elmer W. Henderson to Clarence M. Mitchell, 15 October 1945, FEPC microfilm, reel 51.

22. Winkler, "The Philadelphia Transit Strike of 1944"; Hamby, *Beyond the New Deal*, 61–64; and Reed, *Seedtime for the Modern Civil Rights Movement*, 333–37.

23. Kerns, *A Study of the Social and Economic Conditions of the Negro Population of Gary, Indiana*, 64; Cavnes, *The Hoosier Community at War*, 173; Odum, *Race and Rumors of Race*, 73–89, 113–31; and Sullivan, *Days of Hope*, 160.

24. "Major Instances of Under-Utilization of Negroes," n.d., FEPC microfilm, reel 4; memo, Hayes Beal to Will Maslow, 30 April 1945, FEPC microfilm, reel 15; and Mohl and Betten, *Steel City*, 79.

25. Memo, R. A. Hoyer to W. W. Boyer, 13 June 1944, FDR Papers, OF 4245 G, box 7.

26. "Confidential Report: Gary, Indiana, Report on Racial Situation," Indiana War History Commission Collection, box 9; "Gary, Indiana Tensions," FDR Papers, OF 4245 G, box 5; *Chicago Defender*, 9 March, 6 October, 3 and 10 November 1945, 23 February 1946; *A Monthly Summary of Events and Trends in Race Relations*, December 1945, 148–52; and Cavnes, *The Hoosier Community at War*, 169–79. School strikes over racial issues had occurred in Gary in the 1920s as well as the 1940s. See Works Progress Administration, Federal Writers' Project, *The Calumet Region Historical Guide*, 54.

27. "Abstracts Concerning Racial Tensions: Indianapolis, Indiana Tensions," FDR Papers, OF 4245 G, box 5; and National Housing Authority, "Tension area reports, Indianapolis," n.d., FEPC microfilm, reel 71. In 1940 Indianapolis had a population of 386,977,

of which 51,142 were black. See U.S. Census Bureau, *Sixteenth Census of the United States*, vol. 2, pt. 2, 813.

28. Turner Catledge, "Racial Employment Problems, August 6, 1943," FDR Papers, OF 4245 G, box 5.

29. "Employability of Persons on Relief in Marion County, Indiana," 1397–1401.

30. Hill, *The FBI's RACON*, 158–69; and Cavnes, *The Hoosier Community at War*, 120.

31. Memo, G. James Fleming to Lawrence W. Cramer, 18 December 1941, FEPC microfilm, reel 45.

32. Memo, G. James Fleming to Lawrence W. Cramer, 2 January 1942, FEPC microfilm, reel 77.

33. Memo, David Sarnoff to All RCA Companies, 31 January 1942, FDR Papers, OF 4245 G, box 3.

34. Memo, Elmer Henderson to Joy Schultz, 10 November 1944, FEPC microfilm, reel 51; and Cavnes, *The Hoosier Community at War*, 124.

35. Letter, Walter White to Fay E. DeFrantz, 19 August 1941, NAACP microfilm, 13-A-3; letter, Fay E. DeFrantz to Walter White, 5 September 1941, NAACP microfilm, 13-A-3; memo, Joy Schultz to Elmer Henderson, 2 November 1944, FEPC microfilm, reel 51; and Cavnes, *The Hoosier Community at War*, 120–24.

36. Letter, William H. Book to Paul V. McNutt, 31 December 1942, FEPC microfilm, reel 42.

37. Letter, Lawrence W. Cramer to William H. Book, 12 January 1943, FEPC microfilm, reel 42; and Cavnes, *The Hoosier Community at War*, 124.

38. Unidentified newspaper clipping, n.d., "Management Endorses the Work of FEPC," FEPC microfilm, reel 3.

39. Memos, Joy Schultz to Elmer Henderson, 2 and 10 November 1944, FEPC microfilm, reel 51; and WMC, "Adequacy of Labor Supply in Important Labor Markets, August 1, 1944," Uniroyal Inc. Papers, box 25.

40. Memo, Elmer W. Henderson to Clarence Mitchell, 25 April 1945, FEPC microfilm, reel 15.

41. Memo, Elmer Henderson to Clarence Mitchell, 25 April 1945, FEPC microfilm, reel 15; telegram, Walter Frisbie to Malcolm Ross, 2 May 1945, FEPC microfilm, reel 15; letter, Loweel M. Trice to Malcolm Ross, 19 May 1945, FEPC microfilm, reel 15; and letter, Emanuel Bloch to Maceo Hubbard, 17 May 1945, FEPC microfilm, reel 4.

42. Letter, William H. Book to Joy Schultz, 6 April 1945, FEPC microfilm, reel 15.

43. Memo, Emanuel H. Bloch to Maceo W. Hubbard, 17 May 1945, FEPC microfilm, reel 7; and monthly report Elmer W. Henderson to Clarence Mitchell, 15 November 1945, FEPC microfilm, reel 51.

44. Memo, Joy Schultz to Elmer W. Henderson, 13 March 1944, FEPC microfilm, reel 51; memo, John A. Davis to Clarence M. Mitchell, 25 April 1944, FEPC microfilm, reel 63; U.S. Census Bureau, *Sixteenth Census of the United States*, vol. 2, pt. 2, 784; Research Committee of Evansville Postwar Planning Council, *Postwar Employment*, 1; and Cavnes, *The Hoosier Community at War*, 126–29.

45. Memo, Joy Schultz to Elmer Henderson, 7 August 1945, FEPC microfilm, reel 51.

46. Cavnes, *The Hoosier Community at War*, 126.

47. Memo, John A. Davis to Clarence M. Mitchell, 25 April 1944, FEPC microfilm, reel 63.

48. National Housing Authority, "Tension Area Report, Evansville," FEPC microfilm, reel 71; memo, Joy Schultz to Elmer W. Henderson, 13 March 1944, FEPC microfilm, reel 51; FEPC, *Weekly News Digest*, vol. 1, 6 October 1944, FEPC microfilm, reel 86; Hill, *The FBI's RACON*, 160; and Bigham, *We Ask Only a Fair Trial*, 228–32.

49. Memo, Joy Schultz to Elmer W. Henderson, 13 March 1944, FEPC microfilm, reel 51.

50. Memo, Joy Schultz to Elmer W. Henderson, 13 March 1944, FEPC microfilm, reel 51.

51. Memo, Leo R. Werts to William Spencer, 28 May 1945, WMC Records, series 278, box 3578; memo, Elmer W. Henderson to Will Maslow, 4 March 1944, FEPC microfilm, reel 40; memo, Joy Schultz to Elmer W. Henderson, 7 June, 29 September 1944, FEPC microfilm, reel 51; memo, John A. Davis to Clarence M. Mitchell, 25 April 1944, FEPC microfilm, reel 63; Cavnes, *The Hoosier Community at War,* 127; and Bigham, *We Ask Only a Fair Trial,* 228–32.

52. Thompson, *The History of Wisconsin,* vol. 6, 93; and U.S. Census Bureau, *Sixteenth Census of the United States,* vol. 3, pt. 1, 1093.

53. WMC, "Adequacy of Labor Supply in Important Labor Market Areas, 1 September 1943," Frances P. Bolton Papers, box 72; and Pifer, "A Social History of the Home Front," 210–78.

54. U.S. Census Bureau, *Sixteenth Census of the United States,* vol. 2, pt. 2, 549; and Prucha, *Atlas of American Indian Affairs,* 143. In 1940 the population of Wisconsin was 3,137,587, including 12,265 American Indians living on reservations within the state.

55. Wallace, "Wisconsin Puts Minorities to Work," 15–16.

56. "Indians in War Industries"; Clark, "Indian Women Harness Old Talents to New War Jobs"; Trent, "The Use of Indian Manpower"; and Bieder, *Native American Communities in Wisconsin,* 206.

57. Trotter, *Black Milwaukee,* 14, 39–67; Fink, *Workingmen's Democracy,* 178–218; Imse, "The Negro Community in Milwaukee," 3–9, 41–49; and Slocum, *Milwaukee's Negro Community,* 1–67.

58. Imse, "The Negro Community in Milwaukee," 3.

59. Trotter, *Black Milwaukee,* 39–54, 160; letter, Walter White to James W. Dorsey, 22 May 1933, NAACP microfilm, 12-C-1; and FEPC, *First Report,* 31.

60. Trotter, *Black Milwaukee,* 152, 148–60; Imse, "The Negro Community in Milwaukee," 5–6, 41–42; and U.S. Census Bureau, *Sixteenth Census of the United States,* vol. 3, pt. 2, 852.

61. Thompson, *The History of Wisconsin,* vol. 6, 93–94.

62. Letter, William V. Kelley to Lawrence W. Cramer, 29 April 1942, FEPC microfilm, reel 43; and Trotter, *Black Milwaukee,* 165.

63. Letter, William V. Kelley to Carl F. Zeidler, 9 December 1940, Carl Zeidler Papers, box 19; letter, Meyer Adelman to Zeidler, 11 January 1941, Carl Zeidler Papers, box 19; letter, James Dorsey to Zeidler, 6 July 1941, Carl Zeidler Papers, box 19; letter, Kelley to Zeidler, 12 November 1941, Carl Zeidler Papers, box 19; letter, Rose Meister to FDR, 6 October 1942, FEPC microfilm, reel 44; letter, Luther McBride to Francis J. Haas, 4 June 1943, FEPC microfilm, reel 44; letter, James W. Dorsey to G. James Fleming, 28 June 1943, FEPC microfilm, reel 45; Hill, *The FBI's RACON,* 161; and Trotter, *Black Milwaukee,* 162–63.

64. Summary of the Chicago hearings, 19–20 January 1942, FEPC microfilm, reel 37.

65. *Milwaukee Journal,* 4 and 13 May 1942; Trotter, *Black Milwaukee,* 165–75; and Meyer, *"Stalin over Wisconsin,"* 124–26.

66. Letter, William V. Kelley to G. James Fleming, 8 July 1942, FEPC microfilm, reel 37.

67. Trotter, *Black Milwaukee,* 165–68; and *Pittsburgh Courier,* 9 May 1942.

68. Allis-Chalmers compliance report, December 1943, FEPC microfilm, reel 76; Allis-Chalmers compliance report, 1 August 1945, FEPC microfilm, reel 62; Harnischfeger compliance report, December 1943, FEPC microfilm, reel 76; Heil compliance report, December 1943, FEPC microfilm, reel 76; Heil compliance report, 26 May 1945, FEPC microfilm, reel 62; Nordberg compliance report, December 1943, FEPC microfilm, reel 76; and A. O. Smith compliance report, December 1943, FEPC microfilm, reel 76. See appendix A.

69. Letter, James W. Dorsey to G. James Fleming, 28 June 1943, FEPC microfilm, reel 45; *Pittsburgh Courier,* 9 May 1942; *Chicago Defender,* 1 February 1942; memo, G. James Fleming to Francis J. Haas, 8 July 1943, FEPC microfilm, reel 45; and Trotter, *Black Milwaukee,* 170, 172.

70. Memo, Elizabeth Lyman to Philleo Nash, 15 January 1945, FDR Papers, OF 4245 G, box 8; and *Milwaukee Journal,* 10 September 1944.

71. FEPC press release, 12 January 1945, FEPC microfilm, reel 47.

72. Hill, *The FBI's RACON,* 164.

73. Ibid., 166; "Abstracts Concerning Racial Tensions: Milwaukee, Wisconsin," FDR Papers, OF 4245 G, box 5; letter, J. Edgar Hoover to Jonathan Daniels, 24 May 1944, FDR Papers, OF 4245 G, box 6; *Chicago Defender,* 12 February 1944; and Slocum, "Milwaukee's Negro Community," 9.

74. Kelley, "Don't Be Touchy," 4–5.

75. Memo, Joy Schultz to Elmer W. Henderson, 5 May 1944, FEPC microfilm, reel 51; letter, William V. Kelley to Lawrence W. Cramer, 29 April 1942, FEPC microfilm, reel 43; and Trotter, *Black Milwaukee,* 171–75.

76. Jeffrey, "The Major Manufacturers," 239–42; FEPC, *First Report,* 149; *Minnesota Statutes, 1939,* ch. 441; and *Minnesota Statutes, 1941,* ch. 238.

77. McWilliams, "Minneapolis," 61–65.

78. Memo, Harry H. C. Gibson to Elmer W. Henderson, 21 September 1944, FEPC microfilm, reel 52; memo, Elmer W. Henderson to Clarence Mitchell, 15 October 1945, FEPC microfilm, reel 52; letter, Cecil E. Newman and Charles W. Washington to Malcolm MacLean, 8 May 1942, FEPC microfilm, reel 49; minutes of conference between Elmer W. Henderson and Charles W. Washington, 4 October 1943, FEPC microfilm, reel 51; *Minneapolis Tribune,* 30 April 1945; and Hill, *The FBI's RACON,* 367–69.

79. Letter, Vincent A. Day to Personnel Director, 12 October 1942, Urban League of Greater Cincinnati Papers, box 11; letter, Cecil E. Newman and Charles W. Washington to Malcolm MacLean, 8 May 1942, FEPC microfilm, reel 49; and letter, Cecil E. Newman to Milton Webster, 29 August 1941, BSCP Papers, box 129.

80. Sidney B. Levinson, "Organization of the Twin City Council on Fair Employment Practice," n.d., Urban League of Cincinnati Papers, box 11.

81. Letter, Sidney Hillman to Ivan C. Lawrence, 18 March 1942, FEPC microfilm, reel 3; letter, Ivan C. Lawrence to Sidney Hillman, 23 February 1942, FEPC microfilm, reel 3; letter, Cecil E. Newman and Charles W. Washington to Malcolm MacLean, 8 May 1942, FEPC microfilm, reel 49; letter, Leonard Lageman to FDR, 8 September 1942, FEPC microfilm, reel 44; letter, Charles W. Washington to Francis J. Haas, 1 July 1943, FEPC microfilm, reel 45; letter, Anne P. Graves to FDR, 5 July 1943, FDR Papers, OF 4245 G, box 4; letter, Francis J. Haas to Twin City Council on Fair Employment Practices, 21 August 1943, FEPC microfilm, reel 44; minutes of conference between Elmer W. Henderson and Charles W. Washington, 4 October 1943, FEPC microfilm, reel 51; National Urban League, "Performance of Negro Workers in 300 War Plants: A Summary Report of the Industrial Relations Laboratory of the Department of Industrial Relations, 1943," FEPC microfilm, reel 4; letter, Caroline Soderquist to FDR, 31 March 1944, FDR Papers, OF 4245 G, box 4; letter, Douglas Hall to George M. Johnson, 24 July 1944, FEPC microfilm, reel 43; memo, Joy Schultz to Elmer W. Henderson, 12 September 1944, FEPC microfilm, reel 52; memo, Harry H. C. Gibson to Elmer W. Henderson, 21 September 1944, FEPC microfilm, reel 52; weekly report, Elmer W. Henderson to Will Maslow, 26 March 1945, FEPC microfilm, reel 52; *Minneapolis Spokesman,* 24 March 1944; and *Minneapolis Star-Journal,* 13 March 1944.

82. FEPC, *FEPC: How it Operates,* 7–10; and FEPC, *First Report,* 114.

Chapter 6: The FEPC in the Buckeye State

1. Davies, *Defender of the Old Guard,* 53.

2. Ibid., 48–63.

3. Rodabaugh, "The Negro in Ohio," 25; and Giffin, "The Negro in Ohio."

4. Franklin, *George Washington Williams;* Patterson, *Mr. Republican;* Giffin, "The Negro in Ohio"; and Kirk and McClellan, *The Political Principles of Robert A. Taft,* 74.

5. *Cleveland Call and Post,* 8 February, 11 April, 9 and 11 November 1940, and 25 January 1941; and Chavous, "Industrial Education for Negroes in Ohio," 7–8.

6. Giffin, "The Negro in Ohio," 402–42; Davies, *Defender of the Old Guard,* 64–95; Davis, *Black Americans in Cleveland,* 484; and Weiss, *Farewell to the Party of Lincoln,* 209–35, 267–95.

7. *Cleveland Call and Post,* 1 November and 14 December 1940, 18 January 1941, and 2 May 1942.

8. *Cleveland Call and Post,* 26 July 1941.

9. *Cleveland Call and Post,* 17 October 1942.

10. *Cleveland Call and Post,* 26 January, 27 February, 6 March, and 4 September 1943; Giffin, "The Negro in Ohio," 309; Rodabaugh, "The Negro in Ohio," 26–29; and Ohio General Assembly, *Journal of the House of Representatives,* 58, 157.

11. Quillin, "The Negro in Cleveland, Ohio," 518.

12. Ibid., 519.

13. Kusmer, *A Ghetto Takes Shape,* 57; and Davis, *Black Americans in Cleveland,* 159–97.

14. Kusmer, *A Ghetto Takes Shape,* 10.

15. Ibid., 174–205.

16. Abdell, "The Negro in Industry in Cleveland," 17–20; and Davis, *Black Americans in Cleveland,* 224–69.

17. Chesnutt, "The Negro in Cleveland," 27.

18. Green, *Population Characteristics by Census Tracts,* 9.

19. Lowry and Drucker, *Vocational Opportunities for Negroes in Cleveland;* Loeb, *The Future is Yours,* 19; Moore, "Status of the Negro in Cleveland," 12–14; Wye, "Midwest Ghetto," 119–36; and Davis, *Black Americans in Cleveland,* 272–94.

20. Letter, Walter White to David H. Pierce, 22 March 1933, NAACP microfilm, 12-C-24; Loeb, *The Future is Yours,* 1–69; Davis, *Black Americans in Cleveland,* 272–94; Wye, "Midwest Ghetto," 136–40; and Kusmer, *A Ghetto Takes Shape,* 244–74.

21. "Negro in Industry," NAACP of Cleveland Papers, box 1.

22. Ibid.

23. *Cleveland Call and Post,* 5 October 1940; and see *Chicago Defender,* 19 February 1944.

24. *Chicago Defender,* 19 February 1944; Wye, "Midwest Ghetto," 142–46; letter, C. L. Graves and Stuart R. Smith to L. Pearl Mitchell, 2 December 1944, L. Pearl Mitchell Papers, box 1; *Cleveland Press* (ca. 1941) clipping from Russell H. Davis Papers, box 1; and *Cleveland Call and Post,* 14 September 1940.

25. *Cleveland Call and Post,* 9 August 1941; and *Cleveland Press,* 7 August 1941.

26. "Summary Report of the Executive Secretary of the Cleveland NAACP, September 1941," 5, NAACP of Cleveland Papers, box 1.

27. "Negro in Industry," NAACP of Cleveland Papers, box 1.

28. *Cleveland Call and Post,* 21 September, 28 September, and 5 October 1940 and 22 November 1941.

29. *Cleveland Union Leader,* 12 September 1941.

30. *Cleveland Call and Post,* 21 and 28 March 1942.

31. Letter, John L. Schmeller to Douglas L. Hatch, 3 July 1941, NAACP microfilm, 13-A-9; letter, George H. Bender to Sidney Hillman, 16 July 1941, NAACP microfilm, 13-A-9; letter, Walter White to R. C. MacPherson, 28 July 1941, NAACP microfilm, 13-A-9; letter, Harry E. Davis to Walter White, 11 August 1941, NAACP microfilm, 13-A-9; letter, Walter White to Sidney Hillman, 11 August 1941, NAACP microfilm, 13-A-9; letter, Harry E. Davis to Walter White, 13 August 1941, NAACP microfilm, 13-A-9; letter, John L. Schmeller to Walter White, 3 April 1944, NAACP microfilm, 13-A-9; *Cleveland Plain Dealer,* 1 October 1941; *New York Times,* 8 May 1943; *PM,* 16 April 1943. In 1944 Cleveland lost one of its stron-

gest proponents of fair employment when Schmeller, along with his two brothers, Frank, who was the plant manager, and Edward, who was an assistant plant manager and chief metallurgist, were sent to federal prison for ten years after being convicted of purposely manufacturing defective airplane engine parts. Schmeller maintained that he had been framed by those wishing to take control of the company.

32. *Cleveland Call and Post,* 21 June, 20 September, 3 and 15 November 1941; meeting minutes of the Cleveland Urban League Executive Committee, June 20, 1941, 1, Urban League of Greater Cleveland Papers, box 1; "Summary Report of the Executive Secretary of the Cleveland NAACP, September 1941," 5, NAACP of Cleveland Papers, box 1; and Davis, *Black Americans in Cleveland,* 313.

33. *Cleveland Call and Post,* 23 August 1941.

34. *Cleveland Call and Post,* 9 May 1942.

35. *Cleveland Call and Post,* 16 and 23 May, 6 June, and 10 and 17 October 1942; and Loeb, *The Future is Yours,* 95.

36. Letter, C. L. Graves and Stuart R. Smith to L. Pearl Mitchell, 2 December 1944, L. Pearl Mitchell Papers, box 72.

37. *Effie Mae Turner v. The Warner & Swasey Company, November 20, 1942* (Cuyahoga County Court of Common Pleas, 1942), NAACP microfilm, 13-C-3; Effie Mae Turner's industrial training record, FEPC microfilm, reel 43; and *Cleveland Call and Post,* 19 September, 17 and 31 October, 28 November 1942.

38. *Cleveland Call and Post,* 5 December 1942; and *Cleveland Press,* 24 November 1942.

39. *Cleveland Call and Post,* 19 September 1942.

40. *Cleveland Call and Post,* 12 December 1942.

41. *Cleveland Call and Post,* 26 December 1942.

42. *Cleveland Press,* 15 December 1942; *Cleveland Call and Post,* 19 December 1942, 27 November and 11 December 1943; *PM,* 16 December 1942; letter, Chester K. Gillespie to Walter White, 26 December 1942, NAACP microfilm, 13-C-3; James, *Fighting Racism in World War II,* 226–27; Loeb, *The Future is Yours,* 100–101; and Jirran, "Cleveland and the Negro following World War II," 82.

43. *Cleveland Call and Post,* 2 January, 20 March, 3 April, and 1 August 1943; *Chicago Defender,* 2 January 1943; report William T. McKnight to Will Maslow, 25 November 1943, FEPC microfilm, reel 50; memo, Olcott R. Abbott to William T. McKnight, 13 August 1945, FEPC microfilm, reel 57 FR; and Loeb, *The Future is Yours,* 101–4.

44. Letter, Daniel E. Morgan to FDR, 15 August 1942, FEPC microfilm, reel 45.

45. Meeting minutes of the Cleveland YWCA Board of Trustees, 17 March, 21 April, 19 May, and 16 June 1942, YWCA of Cleveland Papers, box 1; file memo, regarding the Parker Appliance Company, n.d., Consumers League of Ohio Papers, reel 48; meeting minutes of the Cleveland Metropolitan Council on Fair Employment Practice, 24 March 1942, Consumers League of Ohio Papers, reel 48; *Cleveland Call and Post,* 30 May 1942; and Jewish Bureau on Employment Problems, *Some Aspects of Employment Discrimination.*

46. Meeting minutes of the Cleveland Metropolitan Council on Fair Employment Practice, 14 April 1942, Consumers League of Ohio Papers, reel 48; minutes of special session of the Cleveland Metropolitan Council on Fair Employment Practice, 24 October 1942, FEPC microfilm, reel 47; and *Cleveland Call and Post,* 23 May 1942.

47. Memo, Daniel E. Donovan to Lawrence W. Cramer, 27 October 1942, FEPC microfilm, reel 49.

48. Telegram, Luther O. Baumgardner to Lawrence W. Cramer, 10 May 1942, FEPC microfilm, reel 36; telegram, John O. Holly to Lawrence W. Cramer, 11 May 1942, FEPC microfilm, reel 36; letter, Lawrence W. Cramer to Luther O. Baumgardner, 19 May 1942, FEPC microfilm, reel 36; memo, Ernest G. Trimble to Lawrence W. Cramer, 21 July 1942, FEPC microfilm, reel 36; FEPC Press Release, 27 November 1942, NAACP microfilm, 13-B-10; *Cleveland Call and Post,* 7 March, 16 and 23 May, 27 June, 18 July, and 5 December

1942; *Cleveland Press,* 23 May 1942; *Chicago Defender,* 23 January 1943; and Ruchames, *Race, Jobs, and Politics,* 50.

49. FEPC Press Release, 27 November 1942, NAACP microfilm, 13-B-10; minutes of special session of Cleveland Metropolitan Council on Fair Employment Practice, 24 October 1942, 1–6, FEPC microfilm, reel 47; memo, William T. McKnight to Will Maslow, 25 November 1943, FEPC microfilm, reel 50; *Cleveland Call and Post,* 27 June 1942, 2 January and 20 February 1943.

50. "Report of the President of the Cleveland NAACP," 12 December 1943, NAACP of Cleveland Papers, box 1.

51. Minutes of special session of Cleveland Metropolitan Council on Fair Employment Practice, 24 October 1942, FEPC microfilm, reel 47.

52. WMC, "Adequacy of Labor Supply in Important Labor Market Areas," 1 September 1943, Frances P. Bolton Papers, box 72; meeting minutes of the Cleveland Urban League, 19 December 1941, 1, Urban League of Greater Cleveland Papers, box 1; memo, Robert C. Goodwin to Robert C. Weaver, 25 October 1943, WMC Records, box 3530; memo, Edward L. Cushman to Robert C. Goodwin and J. Lawrence Duncan, 10 February 1944, WMC Records, box 3530; WMC, *The Negro and What He Can Do to Help Win the War;* and *Cleveland Call and Post,* 20 February and 13 November 1943.

53. Memo, William T. McKnight to Will Maslow, 25 November 1943, FEPC microfilm, reel 50.

54. William T. McKnight's 1969 curriculum vitae, *Cleveland Press* Morgue; *Cleveland Press,* 28 September 1943; *Cleveland Call and Post,* 2 October 1943; and Kesselman, *The Social Politics of FEPC,* 44.

55. Hill, *The FBI's RACON,* 105.

56. Letter, J. Edgar Hoover to Jonathan Daniels, 13 May 1944, FDR Papers, OF 4245 G, box 7; letter, J. Edgar Hoover to Jonathan Daniels, 27 May 1944, FDR Papers, OF 4245 G, box 7; letter, J. Edgar Hoover to Jonathan Daniels, 1 July 1944, FDR Papers, OF 4245 G, box 7; file memo on racial conditions in Cleveland, 24 May 1944, FDR Papers, OF 4245 G, box 5; National Housing Authority, "Tension Area Reports, Cleveland," FEPC microfilm, reel 71; memo, William T. McKnight to Will Maslow, 1 September 1944, FEPC microfilm, reel 40; *Cleveland Union Leader,* 13 August 1943; and Hill, *The FBI's RACON,* 105–9.

57. Memo, Edward M. Swan to Clarence Mitchell, 28 September 1945, FEPC microfilm, reel 37.

58. *Chicago Defender,* 19 February 1944; letter, C. L. Graves and Stuart R. Smith to L. Pearl Mitchell, 2 December 1944, L. Pearl Mitchell Papers, box 72; and Cleveland Urban League, *Annual Report for the Year 1944,* 2–3.

59. Memo, William T. McKnight to Will Maslow, 1 September 1944, FEPC microfilm, reel 40.

60. Memo, Clarence Mitchell to Lawrence W. Cramer, 10 May 1943, FEPC microfilm, reel 4; *Cleveland Call and Post,* 3 October 1942, 13 and 27 February 1943; unidentified file memo, 22 June 1943, Cleveland Mayoral Collection, box 2; "Data on Work Stoppages in which FEPC Aided in the Settlement," FEPC microfilm, reels 4 and 69. Other racially motivated strikes in Cleveland took place at Thompson Products, Cuyahoga Stamping Company, Harsch Bronze, and Euclid Case Foundry.

61. Quillin, *The Color Line in Ohio,* 145.

62. Himes, "Forty Years of Negro Life in Columbus, Ohio," 133–54; Allen, "Interracial Relations in Columbus, Ohio," 161–69; and U.S. Census Bureau, *Sixteenth Census of the United States,* vol. 3, pt. 1, 543.

63. Letter, John W. Lee to Walter White, 24 July 1941, NAACP microfilm, 13-A-11; letter, Walter White to R. J. Thomas, 21 November 1941, NAACP microfilm, 13-A-11; letter, Lawrence W. Cramer to Walter White, 25 November 1941, NAACP microfilm, 13-A-11; memo, C. J. Graym to Wade Hammond, 27 November 1941, William J. Muldoon Papers,

box 1; NAACP press release, 28 November 1941, NAACP microfilm, 13-A-11; James, *The American Addition;* and Murphy, "The Columbus Urban League," 45.

64. Levitt, *World War II Manpower Mobilization and Utilization in a Local Labor Market,* 247.

65. Letter, Barbee W. Durham to Walter White, 19 October 1940, NAACP microfilm, 13-A-11; weekly regional report William T. McKnight to Will Maslow, 21 February 1944, FEPC microfilm, reel 51; meeting minutes of the Industrial Relations Committee of the Columbus Urban League, 18 December 1941, 1, Columbus Urban League Papers, box 17; preliminary constitution of the Columbus Metropolitan Fair Employment Practices Committee, 23 November 1942, Columbus Urban League Papers, box 19; Columbus YWCA board of directors meeting minutes, 10 November 1942 and 14 December 1943, Columbus YWCA Papers, box 16; and *Cleveland Call and Post,* 12 December 1940 and 28 February 1942.

66. FEPC file memo, 15 February 1943, BSCP Papers, box 132; and Meier and Rudwick, *CORE,* 17, 23–24, 27–28, 31–32, 43, and 61.

67. Weekly report, William T. McKnight to Will Maslow, 30 October 1944, FEPC microfilm, reel 53; U.S. Congress, House, *To Prohibit Discrimination in Employment,* 128; and *Cleveland Call and Post,* 30 October 1943 and 5 February 1944.

68. FEPC, *First Report,* 133.

69. Verbatim transcript of Line Material hearing, 12 January 1945, FEPC microfilm, reel 21; and memo, Emanuel H. Bloch to George M. Johnson, 20 March 1945, FEPC microfilm, reel 21.

70. Verbatim transcript of Line Material hearing, 12 January 1945, FEPC microfilm, reel 21.

71. Memo, Emanuel H. Bloch to George M. Johnson, 20 March 1945, FEPC microfilm, reel 21; letter, A. H. Rentner to Emanuel H. Bloch, 26 February 1945, FEPC microfilm, reel 21; memo, George M. Johnson to Eugene Davidson, 25 April 1945; and weekly report, William T. McKnight to Will Maslow, 26 February 1945, FEPC microfilm, reel 21.

72. Quillin, "The Negro in Cincinnati," 401.

73. See Quillin, *The Color Line in Ohio;* and Dabney, *Cincinnati's Colored Citizens.*

74. "Unemployment in Cincinnati," 35.

75. U.S. Census Bureau, *Sixteenth Census of the United States,* vol. 2, pt. 5, 707; and Berry, "The Negro in Cincinnati Industries."

76. Berry, "The Negro in Cincinnati Industries," 363.

77. Kuhn, *Job Discrimination in the Cincinnati Area,* 9.

78. Office of War Information, "Negroes and the War: A Study in Baltimore and Cincinnati," FDR Papers, OF 4245 G, box 7.

79. Letter, Thurgood Marshall to William A. McClain, 13 December 1940, NAACP microfilm, 13-A-17; meeting minutes of the Cincinnati Woman's City Club Race Relations Committee, 4 December 1942, Woman's City Club Papers, box 18; and *Chicago Defender,* 29 January 1944.

80. Industrial Committee of the Division of Negro Welfare (Cincinnati), *Fifth Annual Report, June 1, 1941–May 31, 1942,* 3, Urban League of Greater Cincinnati Papers, box 1.

81. Memo, James M. Baker to E. L. Keenan, 6 December 1943, WMC Records, series 278, box 3532.

82. Letter, J. Harvey Kerns to Clayton Williams, n.d., Urban League of Greater Cincinnati Papers, box 11; letter, J. Harvey Kerns to Thomas Wright, 24 September 1942, Urban League of Greater Cincinnati Papers, box 11; letter, Thomas Wright to J. Harvey Kerns, 3 October 1942, Urban League of Greater Cincinnati Papers, box 11; letter, Thomas Wright to J. Harvey Kerns, 22 October 1942, Urban League of Greater Cincinnati Papers, box 11; Race Relations Field Report, 31 December 1943 and 31 July 1944, Urban League of Greater Cincinnati Papers, box 39; *Cincinnati Post,* 3 March 1942; *Cleveland*

Call and Post, 14 November 1943; and *A Monthly Summary of Events and Trends in Race Relations,* January 1944, 4.

83. Memo, Ernest G. Trimble to George M. Johnson, 10 September 1943, Papers of the President's Committee on Fair Employment Practice, Cincinnati Office General Files, box 2.

84. *Cincinnati Enquirer,* 6 and 14 June 1944.

85. Memo, Ernest G. Trimble to George M. Johnson, 10 September 1943, Papers of the President's Committee on Fair Employment Practice, Cincinnati Office General Files, box 2; "Abstracts Concerning Racial Tension, Cincinnati," FDR Papers, OF 4245 G, box 5; and Hill, *The FBI's RACON,* 101–5.

86. Memo, Emanuel H. Bloch to George M. Johnson, 24 January 1945, FEPC microfilm, reel 8; and *Ohio State News,* 20 May 1944.

87. *Cincinnati Post,* 11 January 1945.

88. Weekly report, Harold James to Will Maslow, 26 February 1945, Papers of the President's Committee on Fair Employment Practice, Cincinnati Office Files, box 1 (quotation); field report of Arnold B. Walker, 26 January 1945, Urban League of Greater Cincinnati Papers, box 39; weekly report Harold James to Will Maslow, 3 March 1945, FEPC microfilm, reel 51; *Ohio State News,* 20 May 1944; and *Cleveland Call and Post,* 17 February 1945.

89. Letter, Harold James to Theodore Berry, 5 March 1945, Papers of the President's Committee on Fair Employment Practice, Cincinnati Office General Files, box 1; verbatim hearing transcripts concerning Crosley Radio, Baldwin, Cambridge Tile, F. H. Lawson, Kirk and Blum Manufacturing, Schaible, Streitmann Biscuit, and Victor Electric, Papers of the President's Committee on Fair Employment Practices, Cincinnati Hearings Records, boxes 1 and 2. Quote from transcript of Crosley Radio hearing, 86. See also FEPC, *Final Report,* 19; *Cincinnati Enquirer,* 15–17 March 1945; *Cincinnati Times-Star,* 15–16 March 1945; and *Cincinnati Post,* 16–17 March 1945. See Kersten, "Publicly Exposing Discrimination."

90. *Cleveland Call and Post,* 19 May 1945; and proposed decision in the matter of Goodyear Aircraft Corporation, Case No. 83, 1–4, FEPC microfilm, reel 22.

91. Verbatim transcript of Goodyear Aircraft Corporation hearing, 84–85, FEPC microfilm, reel 22.

92. Proposed decision in the matter of Goodyear Aircraft Corporation, 5–6, FEPC microfilm, reel 22. The UAW-CIO considered the FEPC the most important part of its civil rights agenda from the 1940s through the 1960s. See Boyle, *The UAW and the Heyday of American Liberalism,* 107–31 and 292 n. 4; Lichtenstein, *The Most Dangerous Man in Detroit,* 208–19; and Zieger, *The CIO,* 152–58. Relations between the FEPC and the UAW were so friendly that in August 1944 officials of the two groups signed an operating agreement to coordinate efforts against employment discrimination. See FEPC, *First Report,* 28.

93. Verbatim transcript of Goodyear Aircraft Corporation hearing, 226–68, FEPC microfilm, reel 22; and letter, George W. Crockett to Richard E. Reisinger, 29 May 1945, FEPC microfilm, reel 57 FR. Akron was the site of intense fighting between the AFL and CIO. In addition to competing for bargaining rights in the Goodyear Aircraft plant, the two labor organizations fought for supremacy in Akron's rubber industries. See Jones, *Life, Liberty, and Property;* and Nelson, *American Rubber Workers and Organized Labor,* 7, 189–90, 312–14. De Bruin's argument was not completely specious. Goodyear's machinists' union did object to fair employment and there had been hate strikes in Akron during the war. See appendix B.

94. Press release from *Cincinnati Voice,* Papers of the President's Committee on Fair Employment Practice, Cincinnati Office General Files, box 2; and Reed, *Seedtime for the Modern Civil Rights Movement.*

Chapter 7: The FEPC and the Motor City

1. See Meier and Rudwick, *Black Detroit and the Rise of the UAW;* Thomas, *Life for Us Is What We Make It;* Thompson, "The Politics of Labor, Race, and Liberalism in the Auto Plants and the Motor City"; and Sugrue, *The Origins of the Urban Crisis.*

2. Boris, "'You Wouldn't Want One of 'Em Dancing with Your Wife'"; and Korstad and Lichtenstein, "Opportunities Found and Lost," 787–801.

3. Hill, *Black Labor and the American Legal System;* Goings and Mohl, "Toward a New African-American Urban History"; and Goings and Mohl, "The Shifting Historiography of African-American Urban History," 435–37.

4. Works Progress Administration, Federal Writers' Project, *Michigan,* 231.

5. Merz, *And Then Came Ford;* Martin, *Detroit and the Great Migration;* and Thomas, *Life for Us Is What We Make It,* 26.

6. Brown, "Why Race Riots," 449.

7. Works Progress Administration, Federal Writers' Project, *Michigan,* 109; Current, "Let's Get Ten Thousand!" 292; and Fine, *Frank Murphy,* 145–70.

8. Janowitz, "Black Legions on the March"; Jackson, *The Ku Klux Klan in the City,* 127–43; Jeansonne, *Gerald L. K. Smith,* 80–100; and Warren, *Radio Priest.*

9. Works Progress Administration, Federal Writers' Project, *Michigan,* 241.

10. Haynes, *Negro New-Comers in Detroit,* 12–19; Thomas, *Life for Us Is What We Make It,* 274; Zieger, *The CIO,* 147–77; Lichtenstein, *The Most Dangerous Man in Detroit,* 209–30; and Capeci, "Black-Jewish Relations in Wartime Detroit," 221–36.

11. Weaver, "Detroit and Negro Skill," 132.

12. Meier and Rudwick, *Black Detroit and the Rise of the UAW,* 11.

13. Letter, Walter White to Charles Houston, 6 May 1941, NAACP microfilm, 13-A-3; White, *A Man Called White,* 211–19; Bailer, "The Automobile Unions and Negro Labor"; and Meier and Rudwick, *Black Detroit and the Rise of the UAW,* 34–107.

14. Lorence, "Controlling the Reserve Army," 25.

15. File memo of Geraldine Bledsoe, 25 September 1945, Francis Albert Kornegay Papers, box 1; OWI press release, 19 April 1944, FEPC microfilm, reel 68; and Clive, *State of War,* 34–42.

16. J. Lawrence Duncan, *Michigan State Conference on Employment Problems of the Negro: Findings, Report, Recommendations* (Detroit, 1940), 39–40, UAW Vertical Files, box 13. See also Michigan State Employment Service, *Survey of the Employment Situation in Wayne County and Adjacent Areas, with Special Reference to Negro Workers* (May 1940), 32–41, Detroit Urban League (DUL) Papers, box 74.

17. "Employment Problems of Negroes in Michigan," 353.

18. Michigan Unemployment Compensation Commission, "Labor Market Bulletin #5: Special Report on Occupational Qualifications of Available Negro Workers Registered with the Michigan State Employment Service, June 18, 1941," UAW President's Office, Walter P. Reuther Collection, box 5; file report, "Employment Opportunities For Negroes in Michigan Industries, 1941," DUL Papers, box 4; War Manpower Commission, "Utilization of Non-White Workers in War Production in the Detroit Area, April 9, 1943," DUL Papers, box 5; and FEPC, *First Report,* 61–62.

19. *Chicago Defender,* 8 March 1941.

20. "Employment Opportunities for Negroes in Michigan Industries, 1941," DUL Papers, box 4; and Capeci, *Race Relations in Wartime Detroit,* 12–14, 25–27.

21. Weaver, "Detroit and Negro Skill," 132; and Thomas, *Life for Us Is What We Make It,* 66–67.

22. "Employment Opportunities for Negroes in Michigan Industries, 1941," DUL Papers, box 4.

23. Letter, Arthur Perry, Christopher C. Alston, and Tom January to Melvin Bishop, 13 November 1941, UAW War Policy Division Collection, box 6.

24. Letter, Curt Murdock to R. J. Thomas, 27 November 1941, UAW War Policy Division Collection, box 6.

25. Letter, Robert C. Weaver to Walter White, 22 January 1941, NAACP microfilm, 13-A-3; letter, R. J. Thomas to Local 190 Executive Board, 21 November 1941, UAW War Policy Division Collection, box 6; Weaver, "Detroit and Negro Skill," 133–36; Meier and Rudwick, *Black Detroit and the Rise of the UAW*, 175–206; Thomas, *Life for Us Is What We Make It*, 166; and Lichtenstein, *The Most Dangerous Man in Detroit*, 207–8.

26. Letter, Albert J. Lucas to FEPC, 18 August 1941, NAACP microfilm, 13-A-3.

27. Memo, Ernest Trimble to Lawrence W. Cramer, 21 July 1942, FEPC microfilm, reel 36; letter, James J. McClendon to Milton P. Webster, 10 January 1942, FEPC microfilm, reel 36; and "The Defense Front," 327.

28. Constitution of Metropolitan Detroit Council on Fair Employment Practices, DUL Papers, box 4.

29. Anderson, *In Support of Fair Employment Practice*, iv; and Anderson, "Metropolitan Detroit FEPC," 43.

30. Memo, Theodore A. Jones to Lawrence Cramer, 20 November 1942, FEPC microfilm, reel 49.

31. Sugrue, *The Origins of the Urban Crisis*, 28; and Thomas, *Life for Us Is What We Make It*, 162–63.

32. FEPC file memo regarding Ford Motor Company, 1 October 1942, FEPC microfilm, reel 49; file memo regarding the Detroit FEP Council's meeting with Harry Bennett, 29 May 1942, UAW War Policy Division Collection, box 6; "Work and Wage Experience of Willow Run Workers"; Wolcott, "The Culture of the Informal Economy"; Thomas, *Life for Us Is What We Make It*, 162–63; and Sugrue, *The Origins of the Urban Crisis*, 28.

33. Capeci, *Race Relations in Wartime Detroit*, 27; and Sugrue, "Crabgrass-Roots Politics."

34. UAW-CIO file memo, 17 May 1942, UAW War Policy Division Collection, box 6.

35. Letter, Horace Sheffield to Victor Reuther, 20 October 1942, WMC Records, series 278, box 3530; letter, Horace L. Sheffield to John C. Dancy, 14 May 1942, DUL Papers, box 4; Resolution of UAW CIO Local 600, 11 October 1942, FEPC microfilm, reel 44; *Chicago Defender*, 8 August 1942; and Bailer, "The Automobile Unions and Negro Labor," 571–77.

36. Handbill for 20 August 1942 Ford demonstration, DUL Papers, box 4; letter, Horace L. Sheffield to Victor Reuther, 20 October 1942, WMC Records, series 278, box 3530; handbill for 15 November 1942 Ford demonstration, DUL Papers, box 4; and Njeru Wa Murage, "Organizational History of the Detroit Urban League."

37. Letter, Walter White to Lawrence W. Cramer, 21 September 1942, NAACP microfilm, 13-A-3; NAACP press release, 25 September 1942, NAACP microfilm, 13-A-7; NAACP press release, 23 October 1942, NAACP microfilm, 13-A-7; memo, J. Lawrence Duncan to Lawrence W. Cramer, 7 December 1942, WMC Records, series 278, box 3530; letter, Zaio A. Woodford to Montague Clark, 13 July 1942, WMC Records, series 278, box 3530; memo, J. Lawrence Duncan to E. L. Keenan, 21 December 1942, WMC Records, series 278, box 3530; letter, M. A. Clark to George Johnson, 27 October 1942, WMC Records, series 278, box 3530; memo, Jack B. Burke to Lawrence Cramer, 22 December 1942, FEPC microfilm, reel 47; and FEPC press release, 27 November 1942, NAACP microfilm, 13-B-10.

38. Telegram, Victor Reuther to Lawrence W. Cramer, 25 November 1942, UAW War Policy Division Collection, box 14.

39. Terkel, *The Good War*, 341–42; Ruchames, *Race, Jobs, and Politics*, 50; and *Chicago Defender*, 16 and 23 January 1943.

40. WMC, "Utilization of Negroes in War Production in the Wayne County Area, 22 January 1943," UAW War Policy Division Collection, box 6.

41. FEPC meeting minutes, Detroit, 6 April 1943, FEPC microfilm, reel 40.

42. Letter, Horace Sheffield to Franklin D. Roosevelt, 19 April 1943, FDR Papers, OF 93, box 5.

43. *Michigan Chronicle*, 23 January 1943; White, *What Caused the Detroit Riot?* 11; Hill, *The FBI's RACON*, 111–54.

44. FEPC meeting minutes, Detroit, 6 April 1943, FEPC microfilm, reel 40; "Negro Women Employees, 5 January 1943," DUL Papers, box 4; "Employment of Women, April 1943," DUL Papers, box 5; "Utilization of Non-White Workers in War Production in the Detroit Area, April 9, 1943," DUL Papers, box 5; and Thomas, *Life for Us Is What We Make It*, 163–64.

45. Handbill for Cadillac Square demonstration, 11 April 1943, DUL Papers, box 5.

46. Letter, Lawrence W. Cramer to Edwin M. Watson, 1 May 1943, FDR Papers, OF 93, box 5; cross-reference file memo concerning Horace L. Sheffield, 19 April 1943, FDR Papers, OF 4245 G, box 4; copy of Cadillac Charter, FDR Papers, OF 93, box 5; letter, Horace L. Sheffield to FDR, 19 April 1943, FDR Papers, OF 93, box 5; letter, Edwin M. Watson to Horace L. Sheffield, 5 May 1943, FDR Papers, OF 93, box 5; *Detroit Free Press*, 12 April 1943; and Glaberman, *Wartime Strikes*, 39–45.

47. Memo, G. James Fleming to Will Maslow, 23 July 1943, FEPC microfilm, reel 40.

48. FEPC meeting minutes, Washington, D.C., 19 April 1943, FEPC microfilm, reel 1; and memo, Maceo W. Hubbard to Lawrence W. Cramer, 14 May 1943, FEPC microfilm, reel 37.

49. Letter, C. Pat Quinn to Milton P. Webster, 3 May 1943, BSCP Papers, box 132; letter, C. Pat Quinn to Earl B. Dickerson, 3 May 1943, FEPC microfilm, reel 44.

50. Memo, Lawrence W. Cramer to Milton P. Webster, 26 February 1943, BSCP Papers, box 132.

51. Letter, Lawrence W. Cramer to John F. Shepherd, 8 May 1943, Civil Rights Congress of Michigan Papers, box 48.

52. Telegram, G. James Fleming to workers in New Steel Plant and Aluminum Foundry, 30 April 1943, FEPC microfilm, reel 40.

53. Memo, G. James Fleming to Lawrence W. Cramer, 26 April 1943, FEPC microfilm, reel 49; memo, Clarence Mitchell to Lawrence W. Cramer, 10 May 1943, FEPC microfilm, reel 38; memo, G. James Fleming to Lawrence W. Cramer, 25 March 1943, FEPC microfilm, reel 49; memo, Clarence Mitchell to Lawrence W. Cramer, 10 May 1943, FEPC microfilm, reel 3; and memo, G. James Fleming to Lawrence W. Cramer, 1 May 1943, FEPC microfilm, reel 49.

54. Letter, J. Lawrence Duncan to Lawrence W. Cramer, 21 June 1943, FEPC microfilm, reel 37; letter, G. James Fleming to Earl B. Dickerson, 15 May 1943, FEPC microfilm, reel 37; letter, Judan Drob to Earl B. Dickerson, 16 May 1943, FEPC microfilm, reel 37; and letter, Charles A. Hill to Lawrence W. Cramer, 20 May 1943, FEPC microfilm, reel 43.

55. White, *What Caused the Detroit Riot?* 7.

56. Ibid.

57. Summary of the 24 May to 3 June Packard strike, n.d., FEPC microfilm, reel 2; memo, G. James Fleming to Lawrence W. Cramer and George M. Johnson, 3 June 1943, FEPC microfilm, reel 1; FEPC staff memo from Francis J. Haas, 4 June 1943, FEPC microfilm, reel 3; NAACP press release, 3 June 1943, NAACP microfilm, 13-A-10; telegram, Walter White to FDR, 4 June 1943, NAACP microfilm, 13-A-10; letter, Walter White to General Henry H. Arnold, 18 June 1943, NAACP microfilm, 13-A-10; letter, Walter White to Col.George E. Strong, 21 June 1943, NAACP microfilm, 13-A-10; KKK at Packard, n.d., Civil Rights Congress of Michigan Papers, box 16; FEPC meeting minutes, Detroit, 6 April 1943, FEPC microfilm, reel 40; letter, Walter White to Philip Murray, 2 July 1942, NAACP microfilm, 13-A-16; letter, Walter White to Ulric Bell, 1 July 1942, NAACP microfilm, 13-A-16; clipping from *Michigan Chronicle*, n.d., NAACP microfilm, 13-A-3; *A Monthly Sum-*

mary of Events and Trends in Race Relations, August 1943, 4; and Meier and Rudwick, *Black Detroit and the Rise of the UAW*, 169–74.

58. Sitkoff, "The Detroit Race Riot of 1943"; Capeci and Wilkerson, *Layered Violence*; Brown, "Why Race Riots"; Polenberg, *War and Society*, 126–29; and White, *What Caused the Detroit Race Riot?*

59. Raushenbush, "How to Prevent Race Riots," 304.

60. White, *What Caused the Detroit Race Riot?* 5.

61. Letter, Leslie to Walter White, 4 May 1943, NAACP microfilm, 13-B-22; memo, Rensis Likert to R. Keith Kane, 14 April 1942, FDR Papers, OF 4245 G, box 5; FEPC press release, 19 April 1944, FEPC microfilm, reel 68; *New York Post*, 16 May 1944; Marshall, "The Gestapo In Detroit"; and Hill, *The FBI's RACON*, 111–54.

62. White, *What Caused the Detroit Race Riot?* 11.

63. FEPC press release, 8 July 1943, FEPC microfilm, reel 1.

64. Memo, G. James Fleming to Will Maslow, 9 July 1943, FEPC microfilm, reel 49.

65. Memo, G. James Fleming to Will Maslow, 31 July 1943, FEPC microfilm, reel 49; memo, G. James Fleming, Jack Burke, and Ernest Trimble to George M. Johnson, 25 September 1943, FEPC microfilm, reel 50; and memo, Clarence Mitchell to George M. Johnson, 28 September 1943, FEPC microfilm, reel 3; and *Michigan Chronicle*, 14 August 1943.

66. Memo, G. James Fleming to Will Maslow, 17 July 1943, FEPC microfilm, reel 49.

67. Memo, Will Maslow to Jack Burke, 26 August 1943, FEPC microfilm, reel 6.

68. Letter, Jack Burke to George M. Johnson, 27 August 1943, FEPC microfilm, reel 6.

69. J. Lawrence Duncan, "Michigan State Conference on Employment Problems of the Negro: Findings, Report, Recommendations, Detroit, 1940," 39–40, UAW Vertical Files, box 13; George W. Crockett Oral Interview with Herbert Hill, 2 February 1968, Blacks in the Labor Movement Oral History Project, 13, 14; memo, Clarence Mitchell to George M. Johnson, 28 September 1943, FEPC microfilm, reel 3; FEPC and meeting minutes, Detroit, 6 April 1943, FEPC microfilm, reel 40.

70. FEPC, *First Report*, 114, 118.

71. Martin, "Detroit—Still Dynamite."

72. *Chicago Defender*, 5 February 1944; and file memo, "Number of Negro Women Employed, September 1943," DUL Papers, box 5.

73. FBI report on Detroit, 20 October 1943, FDR Papers, OF 4245 G, box 6; "Abstracts Concerning Racial Tensions: Detroit," FDR Papers, OF 4245 G, box 5; letter, J. Edgar Hoover to Jonathan Daniels, 19 June 1944, FDR Papers, OF 4245 G, box 6; memo, William T. McKnight to Will Maslow, 25 November 1943, FEPC microfilm, reel 40; letter, Clarence W. Anderson to George E. Strong, 1 October 1943, FEPC microfilm, reel 50; WMC, "Adequacy of Labor Supply in Important Labor Market Areas, 1 September 1943," Frances P. Bolton Papers, box 72; memo, John A. Davis to Alice Kahn, 13 September 1943, FEPC microfilm, reel 49; FEPC, "Employment of Negroes in the Local Transit Industry, 20 October 1943," DUL Papers, box 5; file memo, 7 December 1943, DUL Papers, box 5; *Detroit Free Press*, 16 January 1944; and *A Monthly Summary of Events and Trends in Race Relations*, October 1943, 3. The Detroit Transit System was perhaps a national exception. For the FEPC's more typical experience with transportation industries see Winkler, "The Philadelphia Transit Strike of 1944."

74. Memo, Clarence Mitchell to William T. McKnight, 22 September 1943, FEPC microfilm, reel 40; weekly report Edward M. Swan to Clarence Mitchell, 6 November 1943, FEPC microfilm, reel 51; memo, Edward L. Cushman to J. Lawrence Duncan and Robert C. Goodwin, 10 February 1944, WMC Records, Series 278, box 3530; memo, Edward M. Swan to Will Maslow, 17 March 1944, FEPC microfilm, reel 77; weekly report Edward M. Swan to Clarence Mitchell, 22 April 1944, FEPC microfilm, reel 51; weekly report Edward M. Swan to Clarence Mitchell, 12 July 1944, FEPC microfilm, reel 51; letter, J. Edgar Hoover

to Jonathan Daniels, 14 November 1944, FDR Papers, OF 4245 G, box 6; memo, Lethia W. Clore to Clarence Mitchell, 18 November 1944, FEPC microfilm, reel 51; "Data on Work Stoppages in which FEPC Aided in the Settlement," FEPC microfilm, reels 4 and 69; *Michigan Chronicle*, 25 November 1944; and *A Monthly Summary of Events and Trends in Race Relations*, December 1944, 125.

75. Memo, Edward L. Cushman to J. Lawrence Duncan and Ed Keenan, 25 April 1945, WMC Records, series 278, box 3530.

76. Weekly report Edward M. Swan to Clarence Mitchell, 22 July 1944, FEPC microfilm, reel 51; handbill for Ross speech, 8 October 1944, Pre-1960 Vertical Files, box 13; Anderson, *Unfinished Business;* and Anderson, *In Support of Fair Employment Practices*, 1–11.

77. Memo, Edward L. Cushman to Robert C. Goodwin and J. Lawrence Duncan, 10 February 1944, WMC Records, series 278, box 3530; memo, William T. McKnight to Will Maslow, 29 November 1944, WMC Records, series 278, box 3530; memo, Edward L. Cushman to Robert C. Goodwin and J. Lawrence Duncan, 25 August 1944, WMC Records, series 278, box 3530; memo, J. Lawrence Duncan and E. L. Keenan to William T. McKnight, 15 May 1945, WMC Records, series 278, box 3530; Crockett oral history, Blacks in the Labor Movement Oral History Project, 20; UAW-CIO press release, 13 October 1944, DUL Papers, box 5; UAW-CIO, *First Annual Summary of Activities*, 28; *Detroit Free Press*, 3 September 1944; *A Monthly Summary of Events and Trends in Race Relations*, October 1944, 62–63; and Anderson, *In Support of Fair Employment Practice*, 12–14.

78. Verbatim hearing transcript concerning International Brotherhood of Teamsters, et al., 2 June 1945, FEPC microfilm, reel 22.

79. Letter, J. Edgar Hoover to Jonathan Daniels, 19 August 1944, FDR Papers, OF 4245 G, box 7; letter, Charles M. Hay to Jonathan Daniels, 24 August 1944, FDR Papers, OF 4245 G, box 6; file memo by William T. McKnight, n.d., FDR Papers, OF 4245 G, box 6; file memo by Philleo Nash, 17 August 1944, FDR Papers, OF 4245 G, box 6; weekly report Edward M. Swan to Clarence Mitchell, 6 January 1945, FEPC microfilm, 51; memo, Maceo W. Hubbard to George M. Johnson, 30 April 1945, FEPC microfilm, reel 2; *A Monthly Summary of Events and Trends in Race Relations*, June 1945, 317; *Michigan Chronicle*, 16 September 1944; and Hill, *Black Labor and the American Legal System*, 248–59.

80. Weekly report Edward M. Swan to Clarence Mitchell, 9 June 1945, FEPC microfilm, reel 51.

81. Memo, Edward M. Swan to William T. McKnight, 20 January 1945, UAW Fair Practices and Anti-Discrimination Department Collection, box 1; WMC, "Adequacy of Labor Supply in Important Labor Market Areas," 1 September 1943–1 January 1945, Uniroyal Inc. Papers, box 25; and memo, Edward M. Swan to William T. McKnight, 13 September 1944, FEPC microfilm, reel 40.

82. File memo, n.d., DUL Papers, box 5.

83. FEPC, *Final Report*, 62.

84. *Chicago Defender*, 5 February 1944; and "Employment within (Michigan) Cities, September, 1944," DUL Papers, box 5.

85. Gloster B. Current, "What's Wrong with Detroit?" n.d., Detroit NAACP Papers, box 1.

86. Weaver, *Negro Labor*, 78–81.

87. FEPC, *First Report*, 62, 114.

88. Letter, William H. Leiniger to George Schermer, 19 June 1946, Francis Albert Kornegay Papers, box 1; and *Michigan Chronicle*, 26 May 1945.

89. Clive, *State of War*, 135.

90. U.S. Congress, Senate Committee on Education and Labor, *Fair Employment Practices Act*, 87–98, 212–14; U.S. Congress, House, *To Prohibit Discrimination in Employment*, 66–79, 248–49; *Detroit Free Press*, 31 May 1944 and 2 May 1946; and *Detroit Tribune*, 4 May 1946.

Chapter 8: Stretching the Social Pattern

1. FEPC, *Final Report,* 17–18.
2. Verbatim transcript of McQuay-Norris hearing, FEPC microfilm, reel 20, 33–34.
3. Burnett, *St. Louis at War,* 40.
4. Sterner, *The Negro's Share,* 206; Ross, "They Did It in St. Louis," 9; Adams, "Fighting for Democracy in St. Louis," 58–59; and Corbett and Seematter, "'No Crystal Stair.'"
5. Myrdal, *An American Dilemma,* 528; Catledge, "Racial Employment Problems, 6 August 1943," FDR Papers, OF 4245 G, box 5; Crossland, *Industrial Conditions among Negroes in St. Louis,* 12–23; Christen, "Black St. Louis," 67.
6. Ross, "They Did It in St. Louis," 9.
7. Dowden, "'Over This Point We Are Determined to Fight,'" 32.
8. Weiss, *The National Urban League,* 57, 73, 90–91, 119–20, 184.
9. Badger, *The New Deal,* 25.
10. Dowden, "'Over This Point We Are Determined to Fight,'" 34.
11. U.S. Census Bureau, *Sixteenth Census of the United States,* vol. 2, pt. 4, 455; Kirkendall, *A History of Missouri,* 133–40, 169–73; Weiss, *Farewell to the Party of Lincoln,* 182; and Foner, *Organized Labor and the Black Worker,* 190.
12. Dowden, "'Over This Point We Are Determined to Fight,'" 36.
13. Corbett and Seematter, "'No Crystal Stair,'" 87; Weiss, *The National Urban League,* 251; Northrup, *Organized Labor and the Negro,* 31, 36, 41, 42, 45; and Wolters, *Negroes and the Great Depression,* 177–78.
14. Dowden, "'Over This Point We Are Determined to Fight,'" 38.
15. Letter, Herbert Northrup to John T. Clark, 10 December 1942, St. Louis Urban League Papers, series 4, box 4; letter, John T. Clark to Herbert Northrup, 14 December 1942, St. Louis Urban League Papers, series 4, box 4; Dowden, "'Over This Point We Are Determined to Fight,'" 38–40; Wolters, *Negroes and the Great Depression,* 169–92; Brunn, "Black Workers and Social Movements of the 1930s in St. Louis," 1–13; Zieger, *The CIO,* 70; Jones, *Labor of Love, Labor of Sorrow,* 218; and Paris and Brooks, *Blacks in the City,* 252–54.
16. Jefferson, "Negro Employment in St. Louis War Production," 116; U.S. Census Bureau, *Sixteenth Census of the United States,* vol. 2, pt. 4, 850; and Adams, "Fighting for Democracy in St. Louis," 62.
17. Letter, Sidney R. Williams to "Our Fellow White Citizens," 11 July 1940, Detroit Urban League Papers, box 20.
18. Letter, E. J. Bradley to Frank S. Horne, 20 September 1941, BSCP Papers, box 129; OWI press release, 19 April 1944, FEPC microfilm, reel 68; William H. Stead, "Making Effective Use of Labor Resources in St. Louis, September 1942," FEPC microfilm, reel 19; Weaver, *Negro Labor,* 31, 36; Jefferson, "Negro Employment in St. Louis War Production," 116; Northrup, *Organized Labor and the Negro,* 34; and Harris, *Keeping the Faith,* 128.
19. "Address by Sidney Hillman Associate Director General, OPM, to the First Annual Conference on the Negro in Business, 18 April 1941," NAACP microfilm, 13-A-18; letter, William Sentner to Robert C. Weaver, 13 June 1942, FEPC microfilm, reel 20; *St. Louis American,* 26 November 1942; *St. Louis Argus,* 13 November 1942; and *Chicago Defender,* 5 December 1942 and 4 August 1945.
20. Letter, Delores de Leery to FDR, 18 November 1942, FEPC microfilm, reel 36.
21. Memo, Daniel R. Donovan to Lawrence W. Cramer, 21 December 1941, FEPC microfilm, reel 49; "Report of St. Louis Urban League Industrial Committee Secretary, December 1941," St. Louis Urban League Papers, series 4, box 6; Jefferson, "Negro Employment in St. Louis War Production"; and Adams, "Fighting for Democracy in St. Louis," 63.
22. FEPC, *Final Report,* 17.
23. William H. Stead, "Making Effective Use of Labor Resources in St. Louis, Septem-

ber 1942," FEPC microfilm, reel 19; memo, Will Maslow to All Regional Directors, 28 September 1944, FEPC microfilm, reel 68; and Jefferson, "Negro Employment in St. Louis War Production."

24. Jefferson, "Negro Employment in St. Louis War Production," 117; and statement of David M. Grant of the St. Louis Unit of the March on Washington Movement before Committee on Labor, United States House of Representatives, in U.S. Congress, House, *To Prohibit Discrimination in Employment,* 49–50 (hereafter Grant statement).

25. Letter, St. Louis March on Washington Movement to Malcolm MacLean, 24 July 1942, BSCP Papers, box 130.

26. Grant, "The Saint Louis Unit of the March on Washington Movement," 7.

27. File memo by Roy Wilkins, July 1943, NAACP microfilm, 13-B-23; telegram, T. D. McNeal to Mr. Richard, 20 June 1942, Ernest Calloway Papers, box 50; Theodore D. McNeal Oral History, 22 July 1970, 11–12; *St. Louis Argus,* 26 June 1942; *St. Louis Star-Times,* 20 June 1942; Grant statement, 50–51; Grant, "The Saint Louis Unit of the March on Washington Movement," 8; Burnett, *St. Louis at War,* 40; Weiss, *Farewell to the Party of Lincoln,* 90–94; and Hill, *The FBI's RACON,* 237.

28. Letter, St. Louis March on Washington Movement to Malcolm MacLean, 24 July 1942, BSCP Papers, box 130.

29. Sentner's as well as the UE's support for the St. Louis MOWM waned during the war. See Theodore D. McNeal Oral History, 22 July 1970; David Grant Oral History, 24 August 1970; and "Report of Industrial Committee Secretary, August 1944," St. Louis Urban League Papers, series 4, box 6.

30. Grant statement, 50–51; letter, Lawrence W. Cramer to Franklin O. Nichols, 17 April 1942, St. Louis Urban League Papers, series 1, box 4; letter, St. Louis March on Washington Movement to Malcolm Maclean, 24 July 1942, BSCP Papers, box 130; *St. Louis Star-Times,* 26 June 1942; Zieger, *The CIO,* 144–45, 154–60, 257; and Filippelli, "The United Electrical, Radio, and Machine Workers of America," 98–131.

31. "Negro Employment in War Production Plants, November 27, 1942," St. Louis Urban League Papers, series 4, box 6; unidentified report on blacks in war industries, ca. July 1942, St. Louis Urban League Papers, series 4, box 1; letter, John T. Clark to J. Hutton Hynd, 17 June 1943, St. Louis Urban League Papers, series 1, box 9; Grant statement, 52; *Chicago Defender,* 29 January 1944; and Adams, "Fighting for Democracy in St. Louis," 73.

32. United States Employment Service (St. Louis), "Hopeful Change in Local Attitudes," 16–17.

33. Letter, St. Louis Unit of the March on Washington Movement to Malcolm Maclean, 24 July 1942, FEPC microfilm, reel 43.

34. Ibid.

35. Memo, Ernest G. Trimble to Lawrence W. Cramer, 21 July 1942, FEPC microfilm, reel 36; *Pittsburgh Courier,* 25 July 1942; and Burnett, *St. Louis at War,* 42.

36. Letter, Robert H. Goins to Milton P. Webster, 20 August 1942, BSCP Papers, box 130.

37. *St. Louis Argus,* 21 August 1942.

38. Letter, Theodore D. McNeal to Walter White, 4 August 1942, NAACP microfilm, 13-B-22; *St. Louis Star-Times,* 28 August 1942; *St. Louis Post-Dispatch,* 29 August 1942; Grant, "The Saint Louis Unit of the March on Washington Movement," 136–42; Adams, "Fighting for Democracy in St. Louis," 63; and Burnett, *St. Louis at War,* 41–43.

39. FEPC press release, 27 November 1942, NAACP microfilm, 13-B-10.

40. Turner Catledge, "Race Employment Problems," FDR Papers, OF 4245 G, box 5.

41. Statement of T. L. Gauke, n.d., Fannie Cook Papers, box 9; *St. Louis American,* 21 January 1943; *St. Louis Argus,* 26 February 1943; *St. Louis Star-Times,* 5 February 1943; FBI report on St. Louis, 23 October 1943, FDR Papers, OF 4245 G, box 6; WMC, "Adequacy of Labor Supply in Important Labor Market Areas, September 1, 1943," Frances

P. Bolton Papers, box 72; and Grant, "The Saint Louis Unit of the March on Washington Movement," 50–76.

42. St. Louis Urban League, "A Survey of Negroes in the Chemical Industry, April 1945," 5, DUL Papers, box 20.

43. Grant, "The Saint Louis Unit of the March on Washington Movement," 82–86.

44. Letter, David M. Grant to Oliver Thornton, 12 May 1943, St. Louis MOWM Scrapbook, vol. 1; letter, David M. Grant to Striking Black Workers, 2 June 1943, St. Louis MOWM Scrapbook, vol. 1; *St. Louis Post,* 3 June 1943; *St. Louis Post-Dispatch,* 3 June and 27 October 1943; *Chicago Defender,* 12 June 1943; *St. Louis Star-Times,* 27 October 1943; and *A Monthly Survey of Events and Trends in Race Relations,* May 1944, 6.

45. Grant, "The Saint Louis Unit of the March on Washington Movement," 76.

46. Theodore D. McNeal's 16 June 1943 Southwestern Bell Telephone Bill, St. Louis MOWM Scrapbook, vol. 1.

47. Letter, Orden C. Oechsli to Leyton Weston, 24 June 1943, St. Louis MOWM Scrapbook, vol. 1; "1944 Activities of the St. Louis NAACP Branch," NAACP of Cleveland Papers, box 53; memo, Office of General Counsel to George M. Johnson, 28 September 1942, BSCP Papers, box 130; memo, Evelyn N. Cooper to FEPC, 7 March 1945, FEPC microfilm, reel 8; *St. Louis Argus,* 28 May 1943; *St. Louis Star-Times,* 19 September 1943; *St. Louis Post-Dispatch,* 28 October 1944; and Adams, "Fighting for Democracy in St. Louis," 64–65.

48. FBI report on St. Louis, 23 October 1943, FDR Papers, OF 4245 G, box 6.

49. Letter, John T. Clark to William Dee Becker, 8 July 1942, St. Louis Urban League Papers, series 1, box 5; minutes of St. Louis Race Relations Commission, 18 July 1944, Fannie Cook Papers, box 9; copy of William Sentner's statement before Committee on Labor, United States House of Representatives, June 1944, FEPC microfilm, reel 20; *St. Louis Post-Dispatch,* 26 March 1944; *St. Louis American,* 16 September 1943; file memo, 2 March 1945, Philleo Nash Papers, box 25; Grant, "The Saint Louis Unit of the March on Washington Movement," 82; Adams, "Fighting for Democracy in St. Louis," 67; Burnett, *St. Louis at War,* 112, 117; and Jeansonne, *Gerald L. K. Smith,* 83.

50. St. Louis Race Relations Commission, *Bulletin: Progress Report for 1945,* Fannie Cook Papers, box 9; letter, Richard Jefferson to Lemuel L. Foster, 26 February 1945, St. Louis Urban League Papers, series 4, box 5; and St. Louis Race Relations Commission, "Statement of Purpose, 1 June 1944," Fannie Cook Papers, box 9.

51. Letter, Theodore E. Brown to Milton P. Webster, 7 November 1941, BSCP Papers, box 6; letter, Milton P. Webster to Lawrence W. Cramer, 24 July 1942, BSCP Papers, box 130; letter, Theodore E. Brown to Leyton Weston, 17 January 1944, St. Louis MOWM Scrapbook, vol. 1; and verbatim hearing transcripts concerning Amertorp, Bussman, Carter Carburetor, General Cable, McDonald Aircraft, McQuay-Norris, St. Louis Shipbuilding, United States Cartridge, and Wagner Electric, FEPC microfilm, reels 6, 19, and 20. Although there had been some interest in forming a St. Louis FEP Council in early 1943, such an organization never materialized. See letter, E. G. Steger to Lawrence W. Cramer, 6 January 1943, FEPC microfilm, reel 44.

52. WMC, "Adequacy of Labor Supply in Important Labor Market Areas, June 1944–January 1945," Uniroyal Inc. Papers, box 25; "Data on Work Stoppages in which FEPC Aided in the Settlement," FEPC microfilm, reels 4 and 69; *Chicago Defender,* 29 January and 6 May 1944; *St. Louis Star-Times,* 3 August 1944; and Burnett, *St. Louis at War,* 116.

53. FEPC meeting minutes, 27 May 1944 and 13 June 1944, FEPC microfilm, reel 1; memo, Stanley D. Metzger to Will Maslow, 4 February 1944, FEPC microfilm, reel 49; memo, Stanley D. Metzger to Will Maslow, 5 February 1944, FEPC microfilm, reel 49; memo, Stanley D. Metzger to Will Malsow, 30 March 1944, FEPC microfilm, reel 1; file memo on McDonnell Aircraft, 23 June 1944, FEPC microfilm, reel 3; and Foner, *Women and the American Labor Movement,* 346.

54. Verbatim hearing transcripts concerning Bussman, 31, FEPC microfilm, reel 19.

55. Verbatim hearing transcripts concerning Amertorp, Bussman, Carter Carburetor, McDonald Aircraft, McQuay-Norris, St. Louis Shipbuilding and Steel, Wagner Electric, and United States Cartridge, FEPC microfilm, reels 19 and 20; decisions in the cases of Amertorp, Bussman, Carter Carburetor, McDonald Aircraft, McQuay-Norris, St. Louis Shipbuilding and Steel, Wagner Electric, and United States Cartridge, FEPC microfilm, reel 19; and *St. Louis Post-Dispatch*, 1 and 3 August 1944.

56. Verbatim hearing transcripts concerning McQuay-Norris, 32, FEPC microfilm, reel 20.

57. Decisions in the cases of Amertorp, Bussman, Carter Carburetor, McDonald Aircraft, McQuay-Norris, St. Louis Shipbuilding and Steel, Wagner Electric, and United States Cartridge, FEPC microfilm, reel 19; and *Chicago Defender*, 20 January 1945. See also Graham, *The Civil Rights Era*, 33–34.

58. Letter, Henry Knickmeyer to FDR, 7 August 1944, FEPC microfilm, reel 47; FEPC, *Weekly News Digest*, vol. 1, 11 August 1944, FEPC microfilm, reel 86; *St. Louis Star-Times*, 1 August 1944; *St. Louis Argus*, 4 and 18 August 1944; and *Chicago Defender*, 14 August 1944.

59. Letter, Meta M. Daumer to FDR, 10 August 1944, FEPC microfilm, reel 47.

60. Emanuel Bloch, "Summary of St. Louis non-compliance cases for *Final Report*," n.d., FEPC microfilm, reel 2; "Report from McQuay-Norris Pursuant to Directive Dated 16 December 1944," FEPC microfilm, reel 3; letter, Malcolm Ross to Wagner Electric, 21 February 1945, FEPC microfilm, reel 19; biweekly report, Theodore E. Brown to Will Maslow, 17 February and 30 April 1945, FEPC microfilm, reel 52; letter, Theodore E. Brown to G. B. Evans, 14 April 1945, FEPC microfilm, reel 19; memo, Theodore E. Brown to Clarence Mitchell, 10 February 1945, FEPC microfilm, reel 76; UAW-CIO file memo, 27 April 1945, R. J. Thomas Papers, box 21; letter, George W. Crockett to John W. Livingston, 1 October 1945, R. J. Thomas Papers, box 21; *Chicago Defender*, 20 January 1945; *St. Louis American*, 12 October 1944; and Adams, "Fighting for Democracy in St. Louis," 73.

61. *St. Louis Post-Dispatch*, 18 December 1944.

62. Weekly report Theodore E. Brown to Will Maslow, 23 December 1944, FEPC microfilm, reel 52; memo, Charles H. Houston to Malcolm Ross, 1 December 1944, FEPC microfilm, reel 5; monthly report of the industrial secretary of the St. Louis Urban League, August 1944, St. Louis Urban League Papers, series 4, box 6; *St. Louis Post-Dispatch*, 15 December 1944; *St. Louis Globe-Democrat*, 16 December 1944; and Zieger, *The CIO*, 178–79.

63. Biweekly report Theodore E. Brown to Will Maslow, 3 February–23 July 1945, FEPC microfilm, reel 52; Emanuel Bloch, "Summary of U.S. Cartridge Company, St. Louis, for *Final Report*," n.d., FEPC microfilm, reel 2; memo, Charles H. Houston to Malcolm Ross, 1 December 1944, FEPC microfilm, reel 5; letter, B. E. Bassett to Malcolm Ross, 18 April 1945, FEPC microfilm, reel 20; Grant statement, 54; and *Chicago Defender*, 10 March 1945.

64. Verbatim transcript of General Cable hearing, 11, FEPC microfilm, reel 22.

65. Ross, "They Did It in St. Louis," 11.

66. Ibid., 12.

67. Work Stoppages Report, Theodore E. Brown to Will Maslow, 19 March 1945, FEPC microfilm, reel 63; weekly report Theodore E. Brown to Will Maslow, 2 April 1945, FEPC microfilm, reel 37; letter, Dwight R. G. Palmer to Edwin B. Meissner, 14 April 1945, FEPC microfilm, reel 76; FEPC meeting minutes, 31 March and 11 May 1945, FEPC microfilm, reel 1; Emanuel Bloch, "Summary of General Cable Corporation for *Final Report*," FEPC microfilm, reel 2; Ross, "They Did It in St. Louis," 9–15; Burnett, *St. Louis at War*, 132–33; and Ross, *All Manner of Men*, 67–79. Ross never identified the generals.

68. Ross, "They Did It in St. Louis," 14.

69. Ibid.; memo, Charles H. Houston to Malcolm Ross, 1 December 1944, FEPC microfilm, reel 5; and FEPC, *Final Report*, 18.

Chapter 9: A "Vicious and Destructive Attack"

1. *Congressional Record* 90, pt. 1 (12 January 1944): 132.

2. *St. Louis Star-Times*, 14 June 1945; Maslow, "FEPC—A Case History In Parliamentary Maneuver"; Nuechterlein, "The Politics of Civil Rights"; and Reed, *Seedtime for the Modern Civil Rights Movement*, 321–44. This anti-FEPC coalition resembles the anti–New Deal "conservative coalition" described by Patterson in *Congressional Conservatism and the New Deal*.

3. Letter, Earl B. Dickerson to FDR, 1 March 1943, BSCP Papers, box 132.

4. *Congressional Record* 89, pt. 8 (3 December 1943): 10294–95. On the 1943 riots, see Capeci, *The Harlem Riot of 1943*; Mazon, *The Zoot Suit Riots*; and Capeci and Wilkerson *Layered Violence*.

5. Dierenfield, *Keeper of the Rules*, xi, 47–103.

6. *Congressional Record* 89, pt. 1 (11 February 1943): 872–84; NAACP press release, 3 January 1944, NAACP microfilm, 13-B-12; Porter, *Congress and the Waning of the New Deal*, ix–xiv; and Patterson, *Congressional Conservatism and the New Deal*, 179–81.

7. U.S. Congress, House, *To Investigate Executive Agencies;* Winkler, "The Philadelphia Transit Strike of 1944"; and Reed, *Seedtime for the Modern Civil Rights Movement*, 140–42. The Smith Committee consisted of Representatives Smith, James J. Delaney (D, N.Y.), H. Jerry Voorhis (D, Calif.), Fred A. Hartley (R, N.J.), Clare E. Hoffman (R, Mich.), and Hugh Peterson (D, Ga.).

8. *New York Times*, 17 June, 21 June, and 26 June 1944; "Real Test for FEPC," 104; *Congressional Record* 90, pt. 2 (23 February 1944): 1963; *Congressional Record* 90, pt. 3 (24 March 1944): 3059; *Congressional Record* 90, pt. 5 (20 June 1944): 6344; Nuechterlein, "The Politics of Civil Rights," 182; Fite, *Richard B. Russell*, 180–83, 226–28; and Mann, *The Walls of Jericho*, 40–46.

9. *New York Times*, 29 February 1944.

10. "Communication from the President of the United States, 9 March 1944," *Miscellaneous House Documents*, 78th Cong., 1st sess., doc. 486, 9–10; Roosevelt, *The Complete Roosevelt Presidential Press and Radio Conferences*, v. 23, entry 216; letter, Walter White to Rep. Clarence Cannon, 17 May 1944, NAACP microfilm, 13-B-12; NAACP press release, 16 March 1944, NAACP microfilm, 13-B-12; U.S. Congress, House Committee on Appropriations, *Hearings before the Subcommittee on National War Agencies Appropriation Bill for 1945*, 526–607; and *Chicago Sun*, 2 March 1944.

11. *Congressional Record* 90, pt. 3 (24 March 1944): 3062.

12. Ibid., 3062–67; "Estimate of Appropriation for Committee on Fair Employment Practice of the Office for Emergency Management," *Miscellaneous Senate Documents*, 78th Cong., 2d sess., doc. 486; *Chicago Defender*, 17 June 1944; and "Republicans and FEPC," 193.

13. *Congressional Record* 90, pt. 3 (24 March 1944): 3065.

14. *A Monthly Summary of Events and Trends in Race Relations*, May 1944, 3.

15. *Congressional Record* 90, pt. 4 (26 May 1944): 5028–29; and *New York Times*, 27 May 1944. On early votes, Republicans supported the Tarver amendment, but by the time the final vote was taken many Republicans opposed the amendment.

16. *Congressional Record* 90, pt. 4 (26 May 1944): 5053–58. In the summer of 1944 the FEPC had 105 officials and staff workers. Forty-five were white and sixty were black.

17. Ibid., 5038–57, especially 5043–47.

18. Ibid., 5058–63.

19. *Congressional Record* 90, pt. 5 (20 June 1944): 6263.

20. Ibid., 6263–64.

21. *Congressional Record* 90, pt. 10 (1 and 22 August 1944): A 3484, A 3696; *Congressional Record* 91, pt. 5 (8 June 1945): 5796; "Estimate of Appropriation for Committee on Fair

Employment Practice of the Office for Emergency Management," *Miscellaneous House Documents*, 78th Cong., 2nd sess., doc. 486; U.S. Congress, House Committee on Appropriations, *Hearings before the Subcommittee on National War Agencies Appropriation Bill for 1946*, 70–95; and "Letter to Chairman, House Rules Committee, Concerning the Committee on Fair Employment Practice, 5 June 1945," *Public Papers of Harry S. Truman, 1945*, 104.

22. *Congressional Record* 91, pt. 5 (8 June 1945): 5796–5813; and Scobie, *Center Stage*, 144–45, 184–86, 192–93, 206.

23. *Congressional Record* 91, pt. 5 (30 June 1945): 7058–62.

24. Ibid., 7066.

25. Ibid., 7066–67; and *St. Paul Dispatch*, 17 and 27 May 1944. Although he opposed much of the New Deal, Morse apparently identified with "the underdogs of society," and therefore supported the FEPC. See Smith, *The Tiger in the Senate*, 9, 106.

26. *Congressional Record* 91, pt. 6 (12 July 1945): 7455; letter, Paula Keyes Lewis to Theodore Bilbo, 21 July 1944, FDR Papers, OF 4245 G, box 4; *New York Times*, 28 June 1945; Morgan, *Redneck Liberal*, 249; and Bilbo, *Take Your Choice*. To the best of my knowledge the FEPC employed no Japanese Americans. The committee did handle a few complaints from Japanese Americans, which were less than 1 percent of its entire caseload during the war. See *Congressional Record* 90, pt. 4 (26 May 1944): 5045–47; and FEPC, *First Report*, 126.

27. *Congressional Record* 91, pt. 6 (11 July 1945): 7474; and *Congressional Record* 91, pt. 6 (16 July 1945): 7551, 7636, 7662.

28. FEPC, *Final Report*, 19, 37.

29. FEPC, *First Report*, 114–15; memo, Elmer Henderson to Clarence Mitchell, 15 November 1945, FEPC microfilm, reel 37; memo, Clarence Mitchell to Malcolm Ross, 2 November 1945, FEPC microfilm, reel 37; "Outline for Conduct of FEPC Midwest Hearings," FEPC microfilm, reel 69; *Chicago Defender*, 4 August 1945; *Michigan Chronicle*, 3 November 1945; *Kansas City Call*, 7 December 1945; *Detroit Free Press*, 2 May 1945; and *Detroit Tribune*, 4 May 1945.

30. Letter, FEPC to Harry S. Truman, 18 September 1945, Papers of President Harry S. Truman, Secretary's File, box 119; letter, Charles H. Houston to Harry S. Truman, 3 December 1945, Papers of President Harry S. Truman, OF 40, box 265; Reed, *Seedtime for the Modern Civil Rights Movement*, 333–37; McNeil, *Groundwork*, 171–75; Hamby, *Man of the People*, 365; and McCoy and Reutten, *Quest and Response*, 27.

31. "Executive Order 9664," *Federal Register* 10, no. 250 (20 December 1945): 15301.

32. Telegram, Walter White to Harry S. Truman, 19 December 1945, NAACP microfilm, 13-B-12; and Reed, *Seedtime for the Modern Civil Rights Movement*, 322–43.

33. Ross, "Equal Job Opportunity," 93.

34. FEPC, *First Report*, 114–43; and FEPC, *Final Report*, vii–ix.

35. "War and Post-War Trends in Employment of Negroes" and U.S. Congress, Senate, *Employment and Economic Status of Negroes in the United States*.

36. Ross, "Equal Job Opportunity," 93.

37. Weaver, *Negro Labor*, 78–81.

38. Ibid., 81; Polenberg, *War and Society*, 123; Brody, "The New Deal and World War II," 275–76; and Bernstein, "America in War and Peace," 297–99.

39. Weaver, *Negro Labor*, 78–81; and FEPC, *First Report*, 114.

40. Weaver, *Negro Labor*, 136; Ross, "Equal Job Opportunity," 93; and FEPC, *First Report*, 43, 133, 78–84.

41. Press release from the *Cincinnati Voice*, Papers of the President's Committee on Fair Employment Practice, Cincinnati Office General Files, box 2; and Reed, *Seedtime for the Modern Civil Rights Movement*, 164.

42. FEPC, *Final Report*, 41–95; Weaver, *Negro Labor*, 249–316; National Community Relations Advisory Council, *Postwar Employment Discrimination against Jews;* and Dinnerstein, *Antisemitism in America*, 154–56.

43. FEPC, *Final Report,* 68–70.

44. Monthly report Elmer Henderson to Clarence Mitchell, 15 October 1945, FEPC microfilm, reel 51; memo, Joy Schultz to Elmer Henderson, 10 October 1945, FEPC microfilm, reel 37; Milwaukee Urban League, "A Sample Survey, 1948," Milwaukee Urban League Papers, box 17; and Slocum, *Milwaukee's Negro Community.*

45. Memo, Edward M. Swan to Clarence Mitchell, 28 September 1945, FEPC microfilm, reel 37; memo, Theodore E. Brown to Clarence Mitchell, 8 September 1945, FEPC microfilm, reel 37; monthly report Elmer Henderson to Clarence Mitchell, 15 October 1945, FEPC microfilm, reel 51; National Community Relations Advisory Council, *The Work of Jewish Agencies in the Field of Employment Discrimination,* 7; *A Monthly Summary of Events and Trends in Race Relations,* March 1946, 241; *Ohio State News,* 13 July 1946; and FEPC, *Final Report,* 59, 85.

46. Letter, Harold James to Sara Southall, 24 March 1945, Papers of the President's Committee on Fair Employment Practice, Cincinnati Office General Files, box 4; letter, Harold James to John A. Davis, 10 May 1945, Papers of the President's Committee on Fair Employment Practice, Cincinnati Office General Files, box 2; letter, Marshall H. Bragdon to Malcolm Ross, 13 August 1945, Papers of the President's Committee on Fair Employment Practice, Cincinnati Office General Files, box 1; letter, Edward Swan to Marshall H. Bragdon, 6 September 1945, Papers of the President's Committee on Fair Employment Practice, Cincinnati Office General Files, box 1; *Cincinnati Post,* 27 July 1945; and Mayor's Friendly Relations Committee, *Report: The First Five Years,* 14.

47. Monthly report Edward M. Swan to Clarence Mitchell, 15 January 1946, FEPC microfilm, reel 3.

48. *Detroit Free Press,* 2 May 1946; and letter, Walter Reuther and George F. Addes to all local unions in Regions 1 and 1A, 18 May 1946, Walter Reuther Collection, box 80.

49. Garfinkel, *When Negroes March,* 148–77; Norgen and Hill, *Toward Fair Employment,* 93–148; U.S. Labor Department, *Summary of State Fair Employment Practices Acts,* 1–11; Bureau of National Affairs, *State Fair Employment Laws and Their Administration;* and Mayor's Friendly Relations Committee, *Report: The First Five Years,* 14.

50. Hill, "Twenty Years of State Fair Employment Practice Commissions"; Fine, "'A Jewel in the Crown of All of Us'"; Brindley, "Cleveland's Cooperative Fair Employment Plan"; Bowman, "Fair Employment Practice Legislation"; *A Monthly Summary of Events and Trends in Race Relations,* August/September 1945, 7; *Gary Post-Tribune,* 6 October 1950; Graham, *The Civil Rights Era;* and *Statutes at Large* 78 (1964): 253–66.

Bibliography

Manuscript Collections

Bentley Historical Library, University of Michigan, Ann Arbor, Michigan
    Detroit Urban League Papers
    Francis Albert Kornegay Papers
    G. Mennen Williams Papers
Chicago Historical Society, Chicago, Illinois
    Claude Albert Barnett Papers
    Brotherhood of Sleeping Car Porters Papers
    Flora Juliette Cooke Papers
    Earl B. Dickerson Papers
    Frank W. McCulloch Papers
    St. Louis MOWM Scrapbooks
    Milton P. Webster Papers
Cincinnati Historical Society, Cincinnati, Ohio
    President's Committee on Fair Employment Practice
        Cincinnati Office General Files
        Cincinnati Hearings Records
    Urban League of Greater Cincinnati Papers
    Woman's City Club Papers
Cleveland State University Archives, Cleveland, Ohio
    Cleveland Press Morgue
Illinois Historical Society, Springfield, Illinois
    C. Wayland Brooks Papers
    Illinois Commission on Human Relations Papers
    Illinois Fair Employment Practice Commission Papers
    Illinois State Federation of Labor and Congress of Industrial Organizations Papers
    Scott W. Lucas Papers
    Springfield Urban League Papers
Indiana State Archives, Indianapolis, Indiana
    Federal Employment Security Agency Reports
    Indiana Fair Employment Practices Commission Papers
    Indiana War History Commission Collection

Milwaukee Public Library, Milwaukee, Wisconsin
    Bruno Bitker Papers
    Daniel Hoan Papers
    Carl Zeidler Papers
Milwaukee Urban Archives, University of Wisconsin at Milwaukee, Milwaukee, Wisconsin
    Milwaukee Industrial Council Papers
    Milwaukee NAACP Papers
    Milwaukee Urban League Papers
Missouri Historical Society, St. Louis, Missouri
    Fannie Cook Papers
National Archives and Records Administration, Great Lakes Region, Chicago, Illinois
    Records of the War Manpower Commission
    William J. Muldoon Papers
Ohio State Historical Society, Columbus, Ohio
    John Bricker Papers
    Columbus NAACP Papers
    Columbus Urban League Papers
    Frank Lausche Papers
    David McKelvy Papers
    Vanguard League Papers
    John M. Vorys Papers
Walter P. Reuther Library, Detroit, Michigan
    Blacks in the Labor Movement Oral History Project
    Civil Rights Congress of Michigan Papers
    George W. Crockett Papers
    Detroit Commission on Community Relations Papers
    Detroit Metropolitan AFL-CIO Papers
    Detroit NAACP Papers
    Michigan AFL-CIO Papers
    Walter P. Reuther Collection
    R. J. Thomas Papers
    UAW Fair Practices and Anti-Discrimination Department—Women's Bureau
        Collection
    UAW War Policy Division Collection
    George L-P Weaver Papers
    Vertical File Collection
Franklin D. Roosevelt Library, Hyde Park, New York
    Francis Biddle Papers
    Stephen T. Early Papers
    Eleanor Roosevelt Papers (microfilm)
    Franklin D. Roosevelt Papers
        President's Alphabetical Files
        President's Official Files (93, 391, 2538, 4245, 4905)
        President's Secretary Files
        President's Press Conference Files
        President's Speech Collection
Harry S. Truman Library, Independence, Missouri
    Philleo Nash Papers
    David Niles Papers
    John Ohly Papers
    Oral Interviews located at Truman Library
        Andrew J. Biemiller

Mark Ethridge
Earl Warren
Papers of President Harry S. Truman
Confidential Files
Memoirs Manuscripts
Official Files (40, 40A, 419B, 596A)
Personal Files
Secretary's Files
Speech Files
Public Opinion Mail
Records of the Office of War Mobilization and Reconversion
Records of the President's Committee on Civil Rights
University of Chicago Archives, Chicago, Illinois
Chicago Urban League Papers
University of Cincinnati Archives, Cincinnati, Ohio
Cincinnati Human Relations Committee Papers
University of Wisconsin at Eau Claire Archives, Eau Claire, Wisconsin
Uniroyal Inc. Papers
University of Missouri at St. Louis Archives, St. Louis, Missouri
Ernest Calloway Papers
David Grant Oral History
Theodore D. McNeal Oral History
Washington University Archives, St. Louis, Missouri
Aloys P. Kaufmann Papers
St. Louis Chamber of Commerce Papers
St. Louis Urban League Papers
William Sentner Papers
Western Reserve Historical Society, Cleveland, Ohio
Edward Blythin Papers
Francis P. Bolton Papers
Cleveland Mayoral Collection
Cleveland YWCA Papers
Consumers League of Ohio Papers
Russell H. Davis Papers
Future Outlook League Papers
Frank Lausche Papers
Clifford E. Minton Papers
L. Pearl Mitchell Papers
NAACP of Cleveland Papers
Ohio Committee for Fair Employment Practices Legislation Papers
Urban League of Greater Cleveland Papers
YWCA of Cleveland Papers

Microfilm Consulted

Records of the Fair Employment Practice Committee
Records of the National Association for the Advancement of Colored People

Magazines and Newspapers Consulted, 1940–46

American Federalist
Baltimore Afro-American
Chicago Defender

Chicago Sun
Chicago Tribune
Cincinnati Enquirer
Cincinnati Post
Cincinnati Sun
Cincinnati Times-Star
Cincinnati Union
Cleveland Call and Post
Cleveland Gazette
Cleveland Plain Dealer
Cleveland Press
Cleveland Union Leader
Detroit Free Press
Detroit Tribune
Gary Post-Tribune
Indianapolis Recorder
Industrial Relations Bulletin of the Chicago Urban League
Kansas City Call
Michigan Chronicle
Milwaukee Journal
Minneapolis Spokesman
Minneapolis Star-Journal
Minneapolis Tribune
A Monthly Summary of Events and Trends in Race Relations
New York Times
Ohio State News
Philadelphia Tribune
Pittsburgh Courier
PM
Rhindlander News
St. Louis American
St. Louis Argus
St. Louis Dispatch
St. Louis Globe-Democrat
St. Louis Post
St. Louis Post-Dispatch
St. Louis Star-Times
St. Paul Dispatch
New York Times

Books, Chapters, Journal Articles, and Theses

Abdell, John B. "The Negro in the Industries in Cleveland." *Trade Winds*, March 1924, 17–20.
Adams, Patricia L. "Fighting for Democracy in St. Louis: Civil Rights during World War II." *Missouri Historical Review* 80 (1985): 58–75.
"AFL Slams Door Again." *Crisis* (November 1941): 343.
Albert, Michael Daniel. "Japanese-American Communities in Chicago and the Twin Cities." Ph.D. diss., University of Minnesota, 1980.
Alford, Albert Lee. "FEPC: An Administrative Study of Selected State and Local Programs." Ph.D. diss., Princeton University, 1953.
"Along the N.A.A.C.P. Battlefront." *Crisis* (March 1943): 87.

Allen, Nimrod B. "Interracial Relations in Columbus, Ohio." *Southern Workman* 55 (April 1926): 161–69.

Ambrose, Stephen E. *D-Day, June 6, 1944: The Climatic Battle of World War II.* New York: Simon and Schuster, 1994.

Anderson, Alan B., and George W. Pickering. *Confronting the Color Line: The Broken Promises of the Civil Rights Movement in Chicago.* Athens: University of Georgia Press, 1986.

Anderson, Clarence W. "Metropolitan Detroit FEPC: A History of the Organization and Operation of a Citizen's Action Group to Encourage Practices without Regard to Race, Creed, Color or National Origin." M.A. thesis, Wayne University, 1947.

———. *In Support of Fair Employment Practice.* Detroit: Metropolitan Detroit FEPC, 1944.

———. *Unfinished Business: A Fair Employment Handbook.* Detroit: Metropolitan Detroit FEPC, 1944.

Anderson, Jervis. *A. Philip Randolph: A Biographical Portrait.* New York: Harcourt, Brace, Jovanovich, 1973.

Anderson, Karen T. "Last Hired, First Fired: Black Women Workers during World War II." *Journal of American History* 69 (June 1982): 82–97.

Arnesen, Eric. "Up from Exclusion: Black and White Workers, Race, and the State of Labor History." *Reviews in American History* 26 (March 1998): 146–74.

Arroyo, Luis L. "Chicano Participation in Organized Labor: The CIO in Los Angeles, 1938–1950. An Extended Research Note." *Aztlan* 6 (1975): 277–303.

Ayer, Hugh M. "Hoosier Labor in the Second World War." *Indiana Magazine of History* 59 (1963): 95–120.

Ayers, Edward L., Patricia Nelson Limerick, Stephen Nissenbaum, and Peter S. Onuf. *All Over the Map: Rethinking American Regions.* Baltimore: Johns Hopkins University Press, 1996.

Badger, Anthony J. *The New Deal: The Depression Years, 1933–1940.* New York: Hill and Wang, 1989.

Bailer, Lloyd H. "The Automobile Unions and Negro Labor." *Political Science Quarterly* 59 (Autumn 1944): 548–77.

Bailey, Robert. "Theodore G. Bilbo and the Fair Employment Practices Controversy: A Southern Senator's Reaction to a Changing World." *Journal of Mississippi History* 42 (1980): 27–42.

Barnett Claude A. "We Win a Place in Industry." *Opportunity* 7 (March 1929): 82–86.

Bates, Beth Tompkins. "A New Crowd Challenges the Agenda of the Old Guard in the NAACP, 1931–1941." *American Historical Review* 102 (April 1997): 340–77.

Beecher, John. "This Is the Picture." *Common Ground* 4 (Summer 1943): 11–16.

———. "8802 Blues." *New Republic,* 22 February 1943, 249.

Berger, Morroe. *Equality by Statute: Legal Controls over Group Discrimination.* New York: Columbia University Press, 1952.

———. "Fair Employment Practices Legislation." *Annals of the American Academy of Political and Social Science* 275 (May 1951): 34–40.

Bernstein, Alison R. *American Indians and the Second World War: Toward a New Era in Indian Affairs.* Norman: University of Oklahoma Press, 1991.

Bernstein, Barton J. "The Ambiguous Legacy: The Truman Administration and Civil Rights." In *Politics and Policies of the Truman Administration,* ed. Barton J. Bernstein, 269–314. Chicago: Quadrangle Books, 1970.

———. "America in War and Peace: The Test of Liberalism." In *Towards a New Past: Dissenting Essays in American History,* ed. Barton J. Bernstein, 289–321. New York: Vintage Books, 1968.

———. "The New Deal: The Conservative Achievements of Liberal Reform." In *Towards a New Past: Dissenting Essays in American History,* ed. Barton J. Bernstein, 263–88. New York: Vintage Books, 1968.

Berry, Theodore M. "The Negro in Cincinnati Industries: A Survey Summary." *Opportunity* 8 (December 1930): 361–78.

Bieder, Robert E. *Native American Communities in Wisconsin, 1600–1960: A Study in Tradition and Change.* Madison: University of Wisconsin Press, 1995.

Bigham, Darrel E. *We Ask Only a Fair Trial: A History of the Black Community of Evansville, Indiana.* Bloomington: Indiana University Press, 1987.

Bilbo, Theodore G. *Take Your Choice: Separation or Mongrelization.* Poplarville, Miss.: Dream House Publishing Company, 1947.

Biles, Roger. *Big City Boss in Depression and War: Mayor Edward J. Kelly of Chicago.* DeKalb: Northern Illinois University Press, 1984.

Blake, I. George. *Paul V. McNutt: Portrait of a Hoosier Statesman.* Indianapolis: Central Publishing Company, 1966.

Blantz, Thomas E. *A Priest in Public Service: Francis J. Haas and the New Deal.* Notre Dame: University of Notre Dame Press, 1982.

Blum, John M. *V Was for Victory: Politics and American Culture during World War II.* New York: Harcourt, Brace, Jovanovich, 1976.

Bodenhamer, David J., and Robert G. Barrows, eds. *The Encyclopedia of Indianapolis.* Indianapolis: Indianapolis Historical Society, 1994.

Boris, Eileen. "'You Wouldn't Want One of 'Em Dancing with Your Wife': Racialized Bodies on the Job in World War II." *American Quarterly* 50 (March 1998): 77–108.

Boryczka, Raymond, and Lorin Lee Cary. *No Strength without Union: An Illustrated History of Ohio Workers, 1803–1980.* Columbus: Ohio Historical Society, 1982.

Bowman, John Hemphill. "Fair Employment Practice Legislation: An Evaluation of the Ohio Experience, 1959–1964." M.A. thesis, Ohio State University, 1965.

Boyle, Kevin. *The UAW and the Heyday of American Liberalism, 1945–1968.* Ithaca, N.Y.: Cornell University Press, 1996.

———. "There Are No Union Sorrows That the Union Can't Heal: The Struggle for Racial Equality in the United Automobile Workers, 1940–1960." *Labor History* 36 (Winter 1995): 5–23.

Bracey, John H., and August Meier. "Allies or Adversaries? The NAACP, A. Philip Randolph and the 1941 March on Washington." *Georgia Historical Quarterly* 75 (September 1991): 1–17.

Branson, Herman. "The Training of Negroes for War Industries in World War II." *Journal of Negro Education* 12 (1943): 376–85.

Brindley, Margaret Mary. "Cleveland's Cooperative Fair Employment Plan." M.A. thesis, Catholic University, 1951.

Brinkley, Alan. *American History: A Survey.* 9th Ed. New York: McGraw Hill, 1995.

———. *The End of Reform: New Deal Liberalism in Recession and War.* New York: Vintage Books, 1995.

Brody, David. "The New Deal and World War II." In *The New Deal: The National Level,* ed. John Braeman, Robert H. Bremner, and David Brody, 267–309. Columbus: Ohio State University Press, 1975.

Brophy, John. *A Miner's Life.* Madison: University of Wisconsin Press, 1964.

Broussard, Albert S. *Black San Francisco: The Struggle for Racial Equality in the West, 1900–1954.* Lawrence: University Press of Kansas, 1993.

Brown, Earl. "Why Race Riots: Lessons from Detroit." In *A Documentary History of The Negro People in the United States, 1933–1945,* ed. Herbert Aptheker, 443–53. Secaucus, N.J.: Citadel Press, 1974.

Brunn, Paul. "Black Workers and Social Movements of the 1930s in St. Louis." Ph.D. diss., Washington University, 1975.

Buni, Andrew. *Robert L. Vann of the Pittsburgh Courier.* Pittsburgh: University of Pittsburgh Press, 1974.

Bureau of National Affairs. *State Fair Employment Laws and Their Administration: Texts, Federal-State Cooperation, Prohibited Acts.* Washington D.C.: Bureau of National Affairs, 1964.

Bureau on Jewish Employment Problems. *The Extent of Employment Discrimination against Jewish Workers in the Chicago Area: Report to the President's Committee on Fair Employment Practices, March 28, 1946.* Chicago: Bureau on Jewish Employment Problems, 1946.

———. *Employment Barriers in Wartime: Report of Activity, May 1, 1942.* Chicago: Bureau on Jewish Employment Problems, 1942.

———. *Manpower and Minorities: Annual Report, April 1943.* Chicago: Bureau on Jewish Employment Problems, 1943.

Burnett, Betty. *St. Louis at War: The Story of a City, 1941–1945.* St. Louis: Patrice Press, 1987.

Burnham, Robert A. "The Mayor's Friendly Relations Committee: Cultural Pluralism and the Struggle for Black Advancement." In *Race and the City: Work, Community, and Protest in Cincinnati, 1820–1970,* ed. Henry Louis Taylor Jr., 258–79. Urbana: University of Illinois Press, 1993.

Burstein, Paul. *Discrimination, Jobs, and Politics: The Struggle for Equal Employment Opportunity since the New Deal.* Chicago: University of Chicago Press, 1986.

Capeci, Dominic J. "Black-Jewish Relations in Wartime Detroit." *Jewish Social Studies* 47 (Summer/Fall 1985): 221–42.

———. "Wartime FEPCs: The Governor's Committee and the First FEPC in NYC, 1941–1943." *Afro-Americans in New York Life and History* 9 (1985): 45–63.

———. *Race Relations in Wartime Detroit: The Sojourner Truth Housing Controversy of 1942.* Philadelphia: Temple University Press, 1984.

———. *The Harlem Riot of 1943.* Philadelphia: Temple University Press, 1977.

Capeci, Dominic J., and Martha Wilkerson. *Layered Violence: The Detroit Rioters of 1943.* Jackson: University of Mississippi Press, 1991.

Cardozier, V. R. *The Mobilization of the United States in World War II: How the Government, Military, and Industry Prepared for War.* Jefferson, N.C.: McFarland, 1995.

Cavnes, Max Parvin. *The Hoosier Community at War.* Bloomington: Indiana University Press, 1961.

Cayton, Andrew R. L., and Peter S. Onuf. *The Midwest and the Nation: Rethinking the History of an American Region.* Bloomington: Indiana University Press, 1990.

Cayton, Horace R., and George S. Mitchell. *Black Workers and the New Unions.* Chapel Hill: University of North Carolina Press, 1939.

Chadakoff, Rochelle, ed. *Eleanor Roosevelt's My Day.* New York: Pharos Books, 1989.

Chafe, William H. *The Unfinished Journey: America since World War II.* New York: Oxford University Press, 1995.

Chalmer, Frances K., and Dorothy Height. *Fair Practice in Employment.* New York: Women's Press, 1948.

Chavous, Arthur Melton. "Industrial Education for Negroes in Ohio." Ph.D. diss., Ohio State University, 1945.

Chesnutt, Charles W. "The Negro in Cleveland." *The Clevelander* 25 (November 1930): 3–4, 24, 26–27.

Chicago Commission on Race Relations. *The Negro in Chicago: A Study of Race Relations and a Race Riot.* Chicago: University of Chicago Press, 1922.

Chicago Conference on Civic Unity. *Human Relations in Chicago, 1949: Inventory in Human Relations, 1945–1948.* Chicago: Mayor's Commission on Human Relations, 1949.

Christen, Lawrence O. "Black St. Louis: A Study in Race Relations, 1865–1916." Ph.D. diss., University of Missouri, 1972.

Civilian Production Administration. *Industrial Mobilization for War.* Vol. 1. Washington, D.C.: Government Printing Office, 1947.

———. *Labor Policies of the National Defense Advisory Commission and the Office of Production Management.* Washington, D.C.: Government Printing Office, 1946.

Clark, Jeanne. "Indian Women Harness Old Talents to New War Jobs." *Indians at Work* 10 (September 1942): 25–28.

Clark, Kenneth B. "Morale of the Negro on the Home Front: World Wars I and II." *Journal of Negro Education* 12 (1943): 417–28.

Clarke, Jeanne Nienaber. *Roosevelt's Warrior: Harold L. Ickes and the New Deal.* Baltimore: Johns Hopkins University Press, 1996.

Cleveland Urban League. *The Negro in Cleveland, 1950–1963.* Cleveland: Cleveland Urban League, 1964.

———. *Annual Report for the Year 1944.* Cleveland: Cleveland Urban League, 1944.

Clive, Alan. *State of War: Michigan in World War II.* Ann Arbor: University of Michigan Press, 1979.

Cobb, Charles W. Jr. "The Outlook Regarding State FEPC Legislation." *The Journal of Negro History* 31 (July 1946): 247–53.

Cohen, Lizabeth. *Making a New Deal: Industrial Workers in Chicago, 1919–1939.* New York: Cambridge University Press, 1990.

Community Relations Board. *Interim Report on the Administration of the Cleveland FEP Law.* Cleveland: Community Relations Board, 1950.

———. *Report on Hearings Held by the Law Committee on Employment Discrimination.* Cleveland: Community Relations Board, 1947.

Connery, Robert H. *The Navy and Industrial Mobilization in World War II.* Princeton, N.J.: Princeton University Press, 1951.

Corbett, Katharine T., and Mary E. Seematter. "'No Crystal Stair': Black St. Louis, 1920–1940." *Gateway Heritage* 16 (Fall 1995): 82–88.

Cramer, Lawrence W. "The Committee on Fair Employment Practice." In *National Conference of Social Work Proceedings,* 57–68. New York: Oxford University Press, 1943.

Crossland, William August. *Industrial Conditions among Negroes in St. Louis.* St. Louis: Mendle Printing Company, 1914.

Current, Gloster. "Let's Get Ten Thousand!" *Crisis* 33 (September 1942): 292–94.

Dabney, William Phillips. *Cincinnati's Colored Citizens.* 1926. New York: Johnson Reprint Company, 1970.

Dalfiume, Richard M. *Desegregation of the United States Armed Forces: Fighting on Two Fronts, 1939–1953.* Columbia: University of Missouri Press, 1969.

———. "The 'Forgotten Years' of the Negro Revolution." *Journal of American History* 55 (1968): 90–106.

Dancy, John Campbell. *Sand against the Wind: The Memoirs of John C. Dancy.* Detroit: Wayne State University Press, 1966.

Daniel, Cletus E. *Chicano Workers and the Politics of Fairness: The FEPC in the Southwest, 1941–1946.* Austin: University of Texas Press, 1990.

Daniels, Jonathan. *White House Witness, 1942–1945.* Garden City, N.Y.: Doubleday, 1975.

Daniels, Roger. "Bad News from the Good War: Democracy at Home during World War II." In *The Home-Front War: World War II and American Society,* ed. Kenneth Paul O'Brien and Lynn Hudson Parsons, 157–72. Westport, Conn.: Greenwood, 1995.

———. *Prisoners without Trial: Japanese Americans in World War II.* New York: Hill and Wang, 1993.

Darden, Joe T., ed. *Detroit, Race, and Uneven Development.* Philadelphia: Temple University Press, 1987.

Davies, Richard O. *Defender of the Old Guard: John Bricker and American Politics.* Columbus: Ohio State University Press, 1993.

Davis, John A. "Non-Discrimination in the Federal Agencies." *Annals of the American Academy of Political and Social Science.* 244 (March 1946): 64–74.

———. "Educational Programs for the Improvement of Race Relations: Organized Labor and Industrial Organizations." *Journal of Negro Education* 13 (1944): 340–48.

———. "The Negro Outlook Today." *Survey Graphic* 31 (1942): 500–503, 562–63.

Davis, John A., and Cornelius A. Golightly. "Negro Employment in the Federal Government." *Phylon* 6 (1945): 337–46.

Davis, John A., and Marjorie McKenzie Lawson. "Postwar Employment and the Negro Worker." *Common Ground* 7 (Spring 1946): 3–15.

Davis, Lenwood G. *Blacks in the State of Ohio, 1800–1976.* Monticello, Ill.: Council of Planning Libraries, 1976.

Davis, Russell H. *Black Americans in Cleveland from George Peake to Carl B. Stokes, 1796–1969.* Washington, D.C.: Associated Publishers, 1972.

Dawley, Alan, and Joe William Trotter Jr. "Race and Class." *Labor History* 35 (Fall 1994): 486–94.

"The Defense Front." *Crisis* (October 1941): 327.

"Defense Jobs." *Crisis* (August 1941): 247.

Dickerson, Dennis C. *Out of the Crucible: Black Steelworkers in Western Pennsylvania, 1875–1980.* New York: State University of New York Press, 1986.

Dickerson, Earl B. "The Participation of Negro Labor in Our War Effort." *Lawyers Guild Review* 3 (May 1942): 24–32.

Dierenfield, Bruce J. *Keeper of the Rules: Congressman Howard W. Smith of Virginia.* Charlottesville: University Press of Virginia, 1987.

Dinnerstein, Leonard. *Antisemitism in America.* New York: Oxford University Press, 1994.

"Discrimination against Negro Workers." *Monthly Labor Review* 24 (November 1941): 1218–19.

"Discrimination in Employment—The FEPC." *Lawyers Guild Review* 4 (1943): 32–36.

Dittmer, John. *Local People: The Struggle for Civil Rights in Mississippi.* Urbana: University of Illinois Press, 1994.

Dowden, Priscilla A. "'Over This Point We Are Determined to Fight': The Urban League of St. Louis in Historical Perspective." *Gateway Heritage* 13 (Spring 1993): 32–47.

Drake, J. G. St. Clair. "Profiles: Chicago." *Journal of Educational Sociology* 18 (January 1944): 261–71.

Drake, J. G. St. Clair, and Horace R. Cayton. *Black Metropolis: A Study of Negro Life in a Northern City.* New York: Harcourt, Brace, and Company, 1945.

Drury, Allen. *A Senate Journal, 1943–1945.* New York: McGraw-Hill, 1963.

Dubofsky, Melvin. *The State and Labor in Modern America.* Chapel Hill: University of North Carolina Press, 1994.

DuBois, W. E. B. "Race Relations in the United States, 1917–1947." *Phylon* 9 (1948): 234–47.

Duis, Perry R., and Scott La France. *We've Got a Job to Do: Chicagoans and World War II.* Chicago: Chicago Historical Society, 1992.

Duncan, Otis Dudley, and Beverly Duncan. *The Negro Population of Chicago.* Chicago: University of Chicago Press, 1957.

Dykeman, Wilma, and James Stokeley. *The Seeds of Southern Change: The Life of Will Alexander.* Chicago: University of Chicago Press, 1962.

Eagles, Charles W. *Jonathan Daniels and Race Relations: The Evolution of a Southern Liberal.* Knoxville: University of Tennessee Press, 1982.

Ellis, John. *World War II: A Statistical Survey.* New York: Facts on File, 1993.

"Employability of Persons on Relief in Marion County, Indiana." *Monthly Labor Review* 24 (June 1941): 1397–1401.

"Employment of Negroes by Federal Government." *Monthly Labor Review* 26 (May 1943): 889–90.

"Employment Problems of Negroes in Michigan." *Monthly Labor Review* 24 (February 1941): 350–54.

Ethridge, Mark F. "Jobs for Everyone." *American Federationalist* 49 (February 1942): 23–24.

Evans, Peter B., Dietrich Rueschemeyer, and Theda Skocpol, eds. *Bringing the State Back In.* Cambridge: Cambridge University Press, 1985.

Fair Employment Practice Committee. *Final Report.* Washington, D.C.: Government Printing Office, 1947.

———. *First Report.* Washington, D.C.: Government Printing Office, 1945.

———. *FEPC: How It Operates.* Washington, D.C.: Government Printing Office, 1944.

———. *Minorities in Defense.* Washington, D.C.: Government Printing Office, 1941.

Federal Security Agency. *Workers and the National Defense Program.* Washington, D.C.: Government Printing Office, 1941.

Filippelli, Ronald L. "The United Electrical, Radio, and Machine Workers of America, 1933–1949." Ph.D. diss., Pennsylvania State University, 1970.

Fine, Sidney. "'A Jewel in the Crown of All of Us': Michigan Enacts a Fair Employment Practices Act, 1941–1955." *Michigan Historical Review* 22 (Spring 1996): 19–66.

———. *Frank Murphy: The Detroit Years.* Ann Arbor: University of Michigan Press, 1975.

Fink, Leon. *Workingmen's Democracy: The Knights of Labor and American Politics.* Urbana: University of Illinois Press, 1983.

Finkle, Lee. *Forum for Protest: The Black Press during World War II.* Rutherford, N.J.: Fairleigh Dickinson University Press, 1975.

———. "The Conservative Aims of Militant Rhetoric: Black Protest during World War II." *Journal of American History* 60 (December 1973): 692–713.

Fite, Gilbert C. *Richard B. Russell, Jr.: Senator from Georgia.* Chapel Hill: University of North Carolina Press, 1991.

Flynn, George Q. *The Mess in Washington: Manpower Mobilization in World War II.* Westport, Conn.: Greenwood Press, 1979.

Foner, Philip S. *Women and the American Labor Movement: From the First Trade Unions to the Present.* New York: Free Press, 1980.

———. *Organized Labor and the Black Worker, 1619–1973.* New York: International Publisher's Press, 1976.

Franklin, John Hope. *George Washington Williams: A Biography.* Chicago: University of Chicago Press, 1985.

Fraser, Steven. *Labor Will Rule: Sidney Hillman and the Rise of American Labor.* New York: Basic Books, 1991.

Frazier, E. Franklin. "Ethnic Minority Groups in Wartime, with Special Reference to the Negro." *American Journal of Sociology* 48 (November 1942): 369–77.

Freidel, Frank. *Franklin D. Roosevelt: A Rendezvous with Destiny.* Boston: Little, Brown, 1991.

Friend, Bruce I. *Guide to the Microfilm Record of Selected Documents of the Committee on Fair Employment Practice in the Custody of the National Archives.* Glen Rock, N.J.: Microfilm Publishing Corporation of America, 1970.

Funigiello, Philip J. *The Challenge to Urban Liberalism: Federal-City Relations during World War II.* Knoxville: University of Tennessee Press, 1978.

Garfinkel, Herbert. *When Negroes March: The March on Washington and the Organizational Politics for FEPC.* Glencoe, Ill.: Free Press, 1959.

Gavett, Thomas W. *Development of the Labor Movement in Milwaukee.* Madison: University of Wisconsin Press, 1965.

Gelfand, Mark I. *A Nation of Cities: The Federal Government and Urban America, 1933–1965.* New York: Oxford University Press, 1975.

Gibbs, Wilma L., ed. *Indiana's African-American Heritage: Essays from Black History News and Notes.* Indianapolis: Indiana Historical Society, 1993.

Giffin, William. "Black Insurgency in the Republican Party of Ohio, 1920–1932." *Ohio History* 82 (Winter–Spring 1973): 25–45.

———. "The Negro in Ohio, 1914–1939." Ph.D. diss., Ohio State University, 1968.

Girard, Robert A., and Louis L. Jaffe. "Some General Observations on Administration of State Fair Employment Practice Laws." *Buffalo Law Review* 14 (Fall 1964): 114–20.

Glaberman, Martin. *Wartime Strikes: The Struggles against the No-Strike Pledge in the UAW during World War II.* Detroit: Bewick, 1980.

Gleason, Philip. "Americans All: World War II and the Shaping of American Identity." *Review of Politics* 43 (1981): 483–518.

Goings, Kenneth W., and Raymond A. Mohl. "The Shifting Historiography of African-American Urban History." *Journal of Urban History* 22 (May 1995): 435–37.

———. "Toward a New African-American Urban History." *Journal of Urban History* 22 (March 1995): 283–95.

Goldfield, Michael. "Race and the CIO: The Possibilities for Racial Egalitarianism during the 1930s and 1940s." *International Labor and Working Class History* 44 (Fall 1993): 1–32.

Golightly, Cornelius L. "Negro Higher Education and Democratic Negro Morale." *Journal of Negro Education* 11 (July 1942): 324–28.

Goodwin, Doris Kearns. *No Ordinary Time: Franklin and Eleanor Roosevelt: The Home Front in World War II.* New York: Simon and Schuster, 1994.

Goodwin, E. Marvin. *Black Migration in America from 1915 to 1960: An Uneasy Exodus.* Lewiston, N.Y.: E. Mellen Press, 1990.

Gould, Helen M. "The Negro and the CIO." *Common Ground* 6 (Winter 1945): 73–75.

Gould, William B. *Black Workers in White Unions: Job Discrimination in the United States.* Ithaca, N.Y.: Cornell University Press, 1977.

Governor's Interracial Commission (Minnesota). *The Negro Worker in Minnesota.* St. Paul: Interracial Commission, 1945.

Grabowski, John J., and David D. Van Tassel. *The Encyclopedia of Cleveland History.* Bloomington: Indiana University Press, 1987.

Graham, Hugh Davis. *The Civil Rights Era: Origin and Development of National Policy.* New York: Oxford University Press, 1990.

Graham, Otis L., and Meghan Robinson, eds. *Franklin D. Roosevelt: His Life and Times, an Encyclopedic View.* Boston: G. K. Hall, 1985.

Granger, Lester B. "No Short-Cut to Democracy." *Common Ground* 5 (Winter 1944): 13–17.

———. "Techniques in Race Relations." *Survey Graphic* 32 (December 1943): 323–26.

———. "Barriers to Negro War Employment." *Annals of the American Academy of Political and Social Science* 223 (Sept 1942): 72–80.

———. "Negroes and War Production." *Survey Graphic* 31 (1942): 468–71, 543–44.

Grant, Louise Elizabeth. "The St. Louis Unit of the March on Washington Movement: A Study in Conflict." M.A. thesis, Fisk University, 1944.

Grantham, Dewey W. *The South in Modern America: A Region at Odds.* New York: HarperCollins Publishers, 1994.

Graves, W. Brooke. *Fair Employment Practice Legislation in the United States, Federal-State-Municipal.* Washington, D.C.: Government Printing Office, 1953.

Gray, Chester J. *Job Opportunities for Negro Youth in Columbus.* Columbus: National Youth Administration in Ohio, 1938.

Green, Howard Whipple. *Population Characteristics by Census Tracts, Cleveland, Ohio—1930.* Cleveland: Plain Dealer Publishing Company, 1931.

Greer, Edward. *Big Steel: Black Politics and Corporate Power in Gary, Indiana.* New York: Monthly Review Press, 1979.

Grossman, James R. *Land of Hope: Chicago, Black Southerners, and the Great Migration.* Chicago: University of Chicago Press, 1989.

Haas, Francis J., and G. J. Fleming. "Personal Practices and Wartime Changes." *Annals of the American Academy of Political and Social Science* 244 (March 1946): 48–56.

Halpern, Rick. *Down on the Killing Floor: Black and White Workers in Chicago's Packing-houses, 1904–54.* Urbana: University of Illinois Press, 1997.

Hamby, Alonzo L. *Man of the People: A Life of Harry S. Truman.* New York: Oxford University Press, 1995.

———. *Beyond the New Deal: Harry S. Truman and American Liberalism.* New York: Oxford University Press, 1973.

Hamilton, Charles V. *Adam Clayton Powell, Jr.: The Political Biography of an American Dilemma.* New York: Atheneum, 1991.

Hardin, Frances Anne. "The Role of Presidential Advisors: Roosevelt Aides and the FEPC, 1941–1943." M.A. thesis, Cornell University, 1975.

Harris, Abram L. *The Negro Population in Minneapolis: A Study of Race Relations.* Minneapolis: Urban League and Phyllis Wheatley Settlement House, 1927.

Harris, William H. *Keeping the Faith: A. Philip Randolph, Milton P. Webster, and the Brotherhood of Sleeping Car Porters, 1925–37.* Urbana: University of Illinois Press, 1984.

———. "Federal Intervention in Union Discrimination: FEPC and West Coast Shipyards during World War II." *Labor History* 22 (Summer 1981): 325–47.

Harrison, William Jefferson. "The New Deal in Black St. Louis, 1932–1940." Ph.D. diss, St. Louis University, 1976.

Haynes, George E. *The Negro at Work during the World War and during Reconstruction.* Washington, D.C.: Government Printing Office, 1921.

———. *Negro New-Comers in Detroit.* New York: Home Mission Council, 1918.

Henderson, Alexa B. "FEPC and the Southern Railway Case: An Investigation into the Discriminatory Patterns of Railroads during World War II." *Journal of Negro History* 61 (1976): 172–87.

Henderson, Elmer. "Employment of Negroes in the Federal Government." *Monthly Labor Review* 26 (May 1943): 889–91.

———. "Negroes in Government Employment." *Opportunity* 21 (1943): 113–21, 142–43.

Hess, Gary. *The United States at War, 1941–1945.* Arlington Heights, Ill.: Harlan Davidson, 1986.

Hill, Herbert. "The Problem of Race in American Labor History." *Reviews in American History* 24 (June 1996): 189–208.

———. *Black Labor and the American Legal System.* Madison: University of Wisconsin Press, 1985.

———. "Twenty Years of State Fair Employment Practice Commissions: A Critical Analysis with Recommendations." *Buffalo Law Review* 14 (1964): 22–69.

Hill, Herbert, and James E. Jones Jr., eds. *Race in America: The Struggle for Equality.* Madison: University of Wisconsin Press, 1993.

Hill, Robert A., comp. *The FBI's RACON: Racial Conditions in the United States during World War II.* Boston: Northeastern University Press, 1995.

Himes, J. S. Jr. "Forty Years of Negro Life in Columbus, Ohio." *Journal of Negro History* 27 (April 1942): 133–54.

Honey, Michael K. *Southern Labor and Black Civil Rights: Organizing Memphis Workers.* Urbana: University of Illinois Press, 1993.

Hope, John II. *Equality of Opportunity: A Union Approach to Fair Employment.* Washington, D.C.: Public Affairs Press, 1956.

Horowitz, Roger. *"Negro and White, Unite and Fight!": A Social History of Industrial Unionism in Meatpacking, 1930–90.* Urbana: University of Illinois Press, 1997.

Huddle, Frank P. "Fair Practice in Employment." *Editorial Research Reports* 36 (January 1945): 1–51.

Hunt, A. Bruce. "The Proposed Fair Employment Practice Act: Facts and Fallacies." *Virginia Law Review* 32 (1945): 1–38.

Huthmacher, J. Joseph. *Senator Robert F. Wagner and the Rise of Urban Liberalism.* Cambridge, Mass.: Harvard University Press, 1968.

Ickes, Harold L. *The Secret Diary of Harold L. Ickes.* Vol. 2, *The Inside Struggle, 1936–1939.* New York: Simon and Schuster, 1954.

Illinois Fair Employment Practices Commission. *Rules and Regulations of Procedure under Fair Employment Practices Act of Illinois.* Chicago: Illinois FEP Commission, 1962.

———. *Report.* Chicago: Illinois FEP Commission, n.d.

Illinois Human Relations Commission. *Report of the Commission on Human Relations.* Springfield: Illinois Human Relations Commission, 1953.

Illinois Interracial Commission. *Third Report, 1947–1949.* Springfield: Illinois Interracial Commission, 1949.

———. *Memorandum.* Springfield: Illinois Interracial Commission, 1948.

———. *Special Report on Employment Opportunities in Illinois.* Springfield: Illinois Interracial Commission, 1948.

———. *Second Report, 1945–1947.* Springfield: Illinois Interracial Commission, 1947.

———. *First Report, 1943–1945.* Springfield: Illinois Interracial Commission, 1945.

———. *Annual Report of the Illinois Interracial Commission.* Springfield: Illinois Interracial Commission, 1943.

Imse, Thomas. "The Negro Community in Milwaukee." M.A. thesis, Marquette University, 1942.

Indiana State Defense Council and Indiana State Chamber of Commerce. *Job Opportunities for Negroes—The Goal of Indiana's Bi-Racial Cooperation Plan.* Indianapolis: Indiana State Defense Council, 1943.

———. *The Indiana Plan of Bi-Racial Cooperation.* Indianapolis: Indiana State Defense Council, 1942.

———. *The Action toward a Solution.* Indianapolis: Indiana State Defense Council, 1941.

———. *The Story of House Bill No. 445 and the Problem of the Negro in Industry.* Indianapolis: Indiana State Defense Council, 1941.

Indiana Fair Employment Practices Commission. *Civil Rights in Indiana.* Indianapolis: Indiana FEPC, 1961.

———. *Progress Report.* Indianapolis: Indiana FEPC, n.d.

"Indians in War Industries." *Indians at Work* 10 (April 1942): 8.

Jackson, Kenneth T. *The Ku Klux Klan in the City, 1915–1930.* Chicago: University of Chicago Press, 1992.

James, Cyril L. R. et al. *Fighting Racism in World War II.* New York: Monad Press, 1980.

James, Felix. *The American Addition: History of a Black Community.* Washington, D.C.: University Press of America, 1979.

Janeway, Eliot. *The Struggle for Survival: A Chronicle of Economic Mobilization.* New Haven, Conn.: Yale University Press, 1951.

Janken, Kenneth Robert. *Rayford W. Logan and the Dilemma of the African-American Intellectual.* Amherst: University of Massachusetts Press, 1993.

Janowitz, Morris. "Black Legions on the March." In *America in Crisis,* ed. Daniel Aaron, 305–25. New York: Knopf, 1952.

January, Alan F. *A Century of Achievement: Black Hoosiers in the Indiana General Assembly.* Indianapolis: Indiana Historical Bureau, 1986.

Jeansonne, Glen. *Gerald L. K. Smith: Minister of Hate.* New Haven, Conn.: Yale University Press, 1988.

Jeffries, John W. *Wartime America: The World War II Home Front.* Chicago: Ivan R. Dee, 1996.

Jeffrey, Kirk. "The Major Manufacturers: From Food and Forest Products to High Technology." In *Minnesota in a Century of Change: The State and Its People since 1900,* ed. Clifford E. Clark, 223–59. St. Paul: Minnesota Historical Society, 1989.

Jefferson, Richard R. "Negro Employment in St. Louis War Production." *Opportunity* 22 (Summer 1944): 116–17.

Jenkins, Lou Ella. "The Fair Employment Practice Committee and Mexican-Americans in the Southwest." M.A. thesis, Georgia State University, 1974.

Jennings, John K. *The War Manpower Commission in Indiana, 1943–1945.* Indianapolis: War Manpower Commission of Indiana, 1946.

Jewish Bureau on Employment Problems. *Some Aspects of Employment Discrimination: An American Problem, First Annual Report.* Cleveland: Jewish Welfare Federation, 1940.

Jirran, Raymond J. "Cleveland and the Negro following World War II." Ph.D. Diss., Kent State University, 1972.

Johnson, Charles. "Negro Internal Migration, 1940–1943: An Estimate." *A Monthly Summary of Events and Trends in Race Relations,* August 1943, 12–12.

Jones, Alfred W. *Life, Liberty, and Property: A Story of Conflict and a Measurement of Conflicting Rights.* New York: Octagon Books, 1941.

Jones, Jacqueline. *Labor of Love, Labor of Sorrow: Black Women, Work, and the Family from Slavery to the Present.* New York: Basic Books, 1985.

Jones, Leroi. *Blues People.* New York: W. Morrow, 1963.

Kapur, Sudarshan. *Raising Up a Prophet: The African-American Encounter with Gandhi.* Boston: Beacon Press, 1992.

Kelley, William V. "Don't Be Touchy." *Latest News from the Milwaukee Urban League* (February 1943): 4–5.

Kellogg, Peter. "Civil Rights Consciousness in the 1940s." *The Historian* 42 (1979): 18–41.

Kerns, J. Harvey. *A Study of the Social and Economic Conditions of the Negro Population of Gary, Indiana.* New York: National Urban League, 1944.

Kersten, Andrew E. "Jobs and Justice." *Michigan Historical Review* 25 (Spring 1999): 77–101.

———. "Stretching the Social Pattern: The President's Fair Employment Practice Committee and St. Louis." *Missouri Historical Review* 43 (January 1999): 149–64.

———. "Fighting for Fair Employment: The FEPC in the Midwest, 1941–1946." Ph.D. diss., University of Cincinnati, 1997.

———. "Publicly Exposing Discrimination: The 1945 FEPC Hearings in Cincinnati, Ohio." *Queen City Heritage* 52 (Fall 1994): 9–22.

Kesselman, Louis C. *The Social Politics of FEPC: A Study in Reform Pressure Movements.* Chapel Hill: University of North Carolina Press, 1948.

———. "The Fair Employment Practice Movement in Perspective." *Journal of Negro History* 31 (January 1946): 30–46.

Kessner, Thomas. *Fiorello H. La Guardia and the Making of Modern New York.* New York: McGraw-Hill, 1989.

Kilar, Jeremy W. "The Great Lakes Industrial Region." In *The Encyclopedia of American Social History,* ed. Mary Kupice Cayton, Elliot J. Gorn, and Peter W. Williams, 973–86. New York: Scribner, 1993.

King, Desmond. *Separate and Unequal: Black Americans and the U.S. Federal Government.* New York: Oxford University Press, 1995.

Kirby, John B. *Black Americans in the Roosevelt Era: Liberalism and Race.* Knoxville: University of Tennessee Press, 1980.

Kirk, Russell, and James McClellan. *The Political Principles of Robert A. Taft.* New York: Fleet Press Corporation, 1967.

Kirkendall, Richard S. *A History of Missouri.* Vol. 5. Columbia: University of Missouri Press, 1986.

Korstad, Robert, and Nelson Lichtenstein. "Opportunities Found and Lost: Labor, Radicals, and the Early Civil Rights Movement." *Journal of American History* 75 (1988): 786–811.

Krislov, Samuel. *The Negro in Federal Employment: The Quest for Equal Opportunity.* Minneapolis: University of Minnesota Press, 1967.

Kruman, Marie W. "Quotas for Blacks: The Public Works Administration and the Black Construction Worker." *Labor History* 16 (Winter 1975): 37–51.

Kuhn, Alfred. *Job Discrimination in the Cincinnati Area.* Cincinnati: Stephen H. Wilder Foundation, 1952.

Kusmer, Kenneth L. *A Ghetto Takes Shape: Black Cleveland, 1870–1930.* Urbana: University of Illinois Press, 1976.

Lane, James B. *City of the Century: A History of Gary, Indiana.* Bloomington: Indiana University Press, 1978.

Lawson, Steven. "Freedom Then, Freedom Now: The Historiography of the Civil Rights Movement." *American Historical Review* 96 (April 1991): 456–71.

Leonard, Kevin Allen. "Years of Hope, Days of Fear: The Impact of World War II on Race Relations in Los Angeles, California." Ph.D. diss., University of California at Davis, 1992.

Lett, Harold A. "Have FEPC Laws Increased Opportunities for Negroes?" In *National Conference of Social Work Proceedings,* 130–41. New York: Oxford University Press, 1950.

Leuchtenberg, William E. *The FDR Years: Roosevelt and His Legacy.* New York: Columbia University Press, 1996.

———. *In the Shadow of FDR: From Harry Truman to Bill Clinton.* Ithaca, N.Y.: Cornell University Press, 1992.

Levitt, Theodore. *World War II Manpower Mobilization and Utilization in a Local Labor Market.* Columbus: Ohio State University Press, 1951.

Lewis, E. S. "An Evaluation of the Fair Employment Practice Committee." *Opportunity* 20 (May 1942): 135–36.

Lewis, Dottie L., ed. *Cincinnati Goes to War: A Community Responds to World War II.* Cincinnati: Cincinnati Historical Society, 1991.

Lichtenstein, Nelson. *The Most Dangerous Man in Detroit: Walter Reuther and the Fate of American Labor.* New York: Basic Books, 1995.

———. *Labor's War at Home: The CIO in World War II.* Cambridge: Cambridge University Press, 1982.

Lieberman, Robert C. *Shifting the Color Line: Race and the American Welfare State.* Cambridge, Mass.: Harvard University Press, 1998.

Lipsitz, George. *Rainbow at Midnight: Labor and Culture in the 1940s.* Urbana: University of Illinois Press, 1994.

Lloyd, Kent Murdock. "Solving an American Dilemma. The Role of the FEPC Official: A Comparative Study of State Civil Rights Commissions." Ph.D. diss., Stanford University, 1964.

Loeb, Charles H. *The Future is Yours: The History of the Future Outlook League, 1935–1946.* Cleveland: The Future Outlook League, 1947.

Lorence, James L. "Controlling the Reserve Army: The United Automobile Workers and Michigan's Unemployed, 1933–1941." *Labor's Heritage* 5 (Spring 1994): 18–37.

Lorwin, Lewis L. *The American Federation of Labor: History, Policies, and Prospects.* Washington, D.C.: The Brookings Institute, 1933.

Lowry, Herbert J., and Mary J. Drucker. *Vocational Opportunities for Negroes in Cleveland.* Columbus: National Youth Administration in Ohio, 1938.

Madison, James H. "Hoosiers at War, 1941–1945." *Traces of Indiana and Midwestern History* 7 (Fall 1995): 4–7.

———. *Indiana through Tradition and Change.* Bloomington: Indiana University Press, 1982.

Mangum, Charles S. *The Legal Status of the Negro.* Chapel Hill: University of North Carolina Press, 1940.

Mann, Robert. *The Walls of Jericho: Lyndon Johnson, Hubert Humphrey, and Richard Russell and the Struggle for Civil Rights.* New York: Harcourt Brace, 1996.

Marabel, Manning. "A. Philip Randolph and the Foundations of Black American Socialism." *Radical America* 14 (1980): 6–32.

Mark, Mary Louise. *Negroes in Columbus.* Columbus: Ohio State University Press, 1928.

Marshall, Thurgood. "The Gestapo In Detroit." *Crisis* 34 (August 1943): 232–34.

Martin, Elizabeth Anne. *Detroit and the Great Migration, 1916–1929.* Ann Arbor, Mich.: Bentley Historical Library, 1993.

Martin, Louis. "Detroit—Still Dynamite." *Crisis* (35 January 1944): 9–10.

———. "Prelude to Disaster: Detroit." *Common Ground* 4 (Autumn 1943): 21–26.

Maslow, Will. "FEPC—A Case History in Parliamentary Maneuver." *University of Chicago Law Review* 13 (1946): 407–44.

———. "The Law and Race Relations." *Annals of the American Academy of Political and Social Science* 244 (March 1946): 75–80.

Mayor's Friendly Relations Committee. *Report.* Cincinnati: Mayor's Friendly Relations Committee, 1953.

———. *Report: The First Five Years.* Cincinnati: Mayor's Friendly Relations Committee, 1948.

Mayor's Commission on Race Relations. *City Planning in Race Relations.* Chicago: Mayor's Commission on Race Relations, 1945.

———. *Race Relations in Chicago, December, 1944.* Chicago: Mayor's Commission on Race Relations, 1944.

Mazon, Mauricio. *The Zoot Suit Riots: The Psychology of Symbolic Annihilation.* Austin: University of Texas Press, 1984.

McCoy, Donald R., and Richard T. Reutten. *Quest and Response: Minority Rights and the Truman Administration.* Lawrence: University Press of Kansas, 1973.

McNeil, Genna Rae. *Groundwork: Charles Hamilton Houston and the Struggle for Civil Rights.* Philadelphia: University of Pennsylvania Press, 1983.

McShane, Stephen G. "Boom! The World War II Home Front in the Calumet Region." *Traces of Indiana and Midwestern History* 3 (Fall 1991): 22–25.

McWilliams, Carey. "Minneapolis: The Curious Town." *Common Ground* 7 (Autumn 1946): 61–65.

Meier, August, and Elliot Rudwick. *Black Detroit and the Rise of the UAW.* New York: Oxford University Press, 1979.

———. *CORE: A Study in the Civil Rights Movement, 1942–1968.* New York: Oxford University Press, 1973.

———. "Negro Protest at the Chicago World's Fair, 1933–1934." *Journal of the Illinois State Historical Society* 59 (Summer 1966): 161–71.

Meier, August, and John H. Bracey Jr. "The NAACP as a Reform Movement, 1909–1965: 'To Reach the Conscience of America.'" *Journal of Southern History* 59 (February 1993): 3–30.

Meister, Richard Julius. "A History of Gary, Indiana, 1930–1940." Ph.D. diss., Notre Dame University, 1966.

Merz, Charles. *And Then Came Ford.* Garden City, N.Y.: Doubleday, 1929.

Meyer, Gerald. *Vito Marcantonio: Radical Politician, 1902–1954.* Albany: State University of New York Press, 1989.

Meyer, Stephen. "*Stalin over Wisconsin": The Making and Unmaking of Militant Unionism, 1900–1950.* New Brunswick, N.J.: Rutgers University Press, 1992.

Michigan Fair Employment Practices Commission. *Four Years on the Job in Michigan.* Lansing: Michigan FEPC, 1960.

———. *Report.* Lansing: Michigan FEPC, n.d.

"Migration to War-Industry Areas." *Monthly Labor Review* 25 (July 1942): 58–61.

Minneapolis Fair Employment Practice Commission. *Annual Report.* Minneapolis: Minnesota FEPC, 1955–61.

———. *Two-year Report of Operations of the City of Minneapolis Fair Employment Practice Commission, June 1, 1947–June 30, 1949.* Minneapolis: Minnesota FEPC, 1949.

Minor, Richard. "Negroes in Columbus." Ph.D. diss., Ohio State University, 1936.

Minton, Clifford E. *Summary Report on the Activities of the Department of Industrial Relations of the Cleveland Urban League.* Cleveland: Cleveland Urban League, 1948.

Modell, John. "World War II in the Lives of Black Americans." *Journal of American History* 76 (1989): 838–48.

Mohl, Raymond A., and Neil Betten. *Steel City: Urban and Ethnic Patterns in Gary, Indiana, 1906–1950.* New York: Holmes and Meier, 1986.

Moore, Jesse Thomas. *A Search for Equality: The National Urban League, 1910–1961.* University Park: Pennsylvania State University Press, 1981.

Moore, Deborah Dash. *At Home in America: Second Generation New York Jews.* New York: Columbia University Press, 1981.

Moore, William Franklin. "Status of the Negro in Cleveland." Ph.D. Diss., Ohio State University, 1953.

Moreno, Paul. *From Direct Action to Affirmative Action: Fair Employment Law and Policy in America, 1933–1972.* Baton Rouge: Louisiana University Press, 1997.

Morgan, Chester A. *Redneck Liberal: Theodore G. Bilbo and the New Deal.* Baton Rouge: Louisiana State University Press, 1985.

Morrison, Allan. "The Secret Papers of FDR." *Negro Digest* 9 (January 1951): 3–13.

Morton, Mary A. "The Federal Government and Negro Morale." *Journal of Negro Education* 12 (1943): 452–63.

"Municipal FEPC in Minneapolis." *Survey Graphic* 36 (March 1947): 86.

Murage, Njeru Wa. "Organizational History of the Detroit Urban League, 1916–1960." Ph.D. diss., Michigan State University, 1993.

Murphy, Melvin L. "The Columbus Urban League: A History, 1917–1967." Ph.D. diss., Ohio State University, 1970.

Myrdal, Gunnar. *An American Dilemma: The Negro Problem and Modern Democracy.* New York: Harper and Brothers, 1944.

National Community Relations Advisory Council. *FEPC Reference Manual.* New York: National Community Relations Advisory Council, 1948.

———. *The Work of Jewish Agencies in the Field of Employment Discrimination: A Survey Report.* New York: National Community Relations Advisory Council, 1947.

———. *Postwar Employment Discrimination against Jews.* New York: National Community Relations Advisory Council, 1946.

"National Defense Labor Problems: The Weaver Appointment." *Crisis* (October 1940): 319, 322.

National Negro Congress. *Negro Workers after the War.* New York: National Negro Congress, 1945.

National War Labor Board. *Termination Report of the National War Labor Board.* Washington, D.C.: Government Printing Office, 1949.

"The Negro's War." *Fortune* 13 (June 1942): 77–79, 157–58, 160–62.

Nelson, Daniel. *Farm and Factory: Workers in the Midwest, 1880–1990.* Bloomington: Indiana University Press, 1995.

———. *American Rubber Workers and Organized Labor.* Princeton, N.J.: Princeton University Press, 1988.

Nelson, Donald. *Arsenal of Democracy: The Story of American War Production.* New York: Harcourt, Brace, Jovanovich, 1946.

Nelson, Bruce. "Organizing Labor and the Struggle for Black Equality in Mobile during World War II." *Journal of American History* 80 (December 1993): 952–88.

Neuchterlein, James A. "The Politics of Civil Rights: The FEPC, 1941–1946." *Prologue* 10 (1978): 171–91.

"The New FEPC." *Crisis* (August 1943): 231.

Newman, Roger K. *Hugo Black: A Biography.* New York: Pantheon, 1994.

Norgen, Paul, and Samuel Hill. *Toward Fair Employment.* New York: Columbia University Press, 1964.

Northrup, Herbert R. *Organized Labor and the Negro.* New York: Harper and Brothers, 1944.

Nunnerlly, William A. *Bull Connor.* Tuscaloosa: University of Alabama Press, 1991.

Odum, Howard. *Race and Rumors of Race.* Chapel Hill: University of North Carolina Press, 1943.

Ohio General Assembly. *Journal of the House of Representatives.* 95th General Assembly. Columbus: State of Ohio, 1943.

"One of Those Things?" *Employment Security Review* 9 (July 1942): 12.

O'Reilly, Kenneth, and David Gallen, eds. *Black Americans: The FBI Files.* New York: Carroll and Graf, 1994.

Ottley, Roi. *"A New World A-Coming": Inside Black America.* Boston: Houghton Mifflin Company, 1943.

"Out in the Cold." *Crisis* (July 1940): 209.

Paris, Guichard, and Lester Brooks. *Blacks in the City: A History of the National Urban League.* Boston: Little, Brown, 1971.

Patterson, James T. *Mr. Republican: A Biography of Robert A. Taft.* Boston: Little, Brown, 1972.

———. *Congressional Conservatism and the New Deal.* Lexington: University of Kentucky Press, 1967.

Pfeffer, Paula F. *A. Philip Randolph: Pioneer of the Civil Rights Movement.* Baton Rouge: Louisiana State University Press, 1990.

Pifer, Richard L. "A Social History of the Home Front: Milwaukee Labor during World War II." Ph.D. diss., University of Michigan, 1986.

Polenberg, Richard. "The Good War? A Reappraisal of How World War II Affected American Society." *Virginia Magazine of History and Biography* 100 (July 1992): 295–322.

———. *One Nation Divisible: Class, Race, and Ethnicity in the United States since 1938.* New York: Viking Press, 1980.

———. *War and Society: The United States, 1941–1945.* New York: J. P. Lippincott, 1972.

———. *America at War: The Home Front, 1941–1945.* Englewood Cliffs, N.J.: Prentice-Hall, 1968.

———. *Reorganizing Roosevelt's Government: The Controversy over Executive Reorganization, 1936–1939.* Cambridge, Mass.: Harvard University Press, 1966.

Porter, David L. *Congress and the Waning of the New Deal.* Port Washington, New York: Kenikat Press, 1980.

Powell, Dorothy M. "The Negro Worker in Chicago Industry." *University of Chicago Journal of Business* 20 (January 1947): 21–32.

Prucha, Francis P. *Atlas of American Indian Affairs.* Lincoln: University of Nebraska Press, 1990.

Public Papers of the Presidents: Harry S. Truman, April 12, 1945 to January 20, 1953. Washington, D.C.: Government Printing Office, 1961.

Quillin, Frank U. *The Color Line in Ohio.* Ann Arbor: University of Michigan, 1913.

———. "The Negro in Cleveland, Ohio." *Independent* 70 (7 March 1912): 518–20.

———"The Negro in Cincinnati." *Independent* 68 (24 February 1910): 399–403.

Randolph, A. Philip. "Why Should We March." *Survey Graphic* 31 (November 1942): 488–89.

Raushenbush, Winifred. *Jobs without Creed or Color.* New York: Worker Defense League, 1945.

———. "Green Light for the FEPC." *Survey Graphic* 32 (December 1943): 498–503.

———. "How to Prevent Race Riots." *American Mercury* 57 (September 1943): 302–9.

"Real Test for FEPC." *Crisis* (March 1944): 104.

Reed, Christoper R. *The Chicago NAACP and the Rise of Black Professional Leadership.* Bloomington: Indiana University Press, 1997.

Reed, Merl E. *Seedtime for the Modern Civil Rights Movement: The President's Committee on Fair Employment Practice, 1941–1946.* Baton Rouge: Louisiana State University Press, 1991.
———. "Black Workers, Defense Industries, and Federal Agencies in Pennsylvania, 1941–1945." *Labor History* 27 (1986): 356–84.
———. "FEPC and the Federal Agencies in the South." *Journal of Negro History* 65 (1980): 43–56.
———. "The FEPC, the Black Worker, and the Southern Shipyards." *South Atlantic Quarterly* 74 (1975): 446–67.
Reid, Ira De A. "Special Problems of Negro Migration during the War." *Milbank Memorial Fund Quarterly* 25 (July 1947): 284–92.
"Republicans and FEPC." *Crisis* (July 1945): 193.
Research Committee of the Evansville Postwar Planning Council. *Postwar Employment: Survey of the Desires of Evansville War Workers.* Evansville: The Council, n.d.
Ricks, John Addison. "Mr. Integrity and McCarthyism: Senator Robert A. Taft and Senator Joseph R. McCarthy." Ph.D. diss., University of North Carolina, 1974.
Robertson, David. *Sly and Able: A Political Biography of James F. Byrnes.* New York: Norton, 1994.
Rodabaugh, James H. "The Negro in Ohio." *Journal of Negro History* 31 (1946): 9–29.
Roosevelt, Franklin D. *The Complete Roosevelt Presidential Press Conferences.* 25 vols. New York: Da Capo Press, 1972.
Rosenman, Samuel I., ed. *The Public Papers and Addresses of Franklin D. Roosevelt, 1940: War and Aid to Democracies.* New York: Random House, 1941.
Ross, Malcolm. *All Manner of Men.* New York: Reynal and Hitchcock, 1948.
———. "They Did It in St. Louis: One Man against Folklore." *Commentary* 3 (July 1947): 9–16.
———. "The Outlook for a New FEPC." *Commentary* 3 (April 1947): 301–8.
———. "Equal Job Opportunity." *Common Ground* 7 (Winter 1946): 91–96.
———. "Results Obtained by Fair Employment Practice Committee Warrant Legislation to Make it Permanent." *Congressional Digest* 24 (June 1945): 180.
Rotnem, Victor W. "Civil Rights during the War: The Role of the Federal Government." *Iowa Law Review* 29 (1944): 409–14.
"Roundtable: Post-War Prospects for Negroes." *Negro Digest* 2 (November 1944): 27–35.
"Roundtable: Should Government Guarantee Job Equality for All Races?" *Negro Digest* 3 (February 1945): 21–26.
"Roundtable: Should Negroes Be Given War Jobs?" *Negro Digest* 1 (January 1943): 27–31.
"Roundtable: Solving the Race Problem: A State or Federal Issue?" *Negro Digest* 2 (April 1944): 35–37.
"Roundtable: Which Union is Fairer: AFL or CIO?" *Negro Digest* 3 (June 1945): 39–50.
Ruchames, Louis. *Race, Jobs, and Politics: The Story of the FEPC.* New York: Columbia University Press, 1953.
Ruddy, Michael T. *Mobilizing for War: St. Louis and the Middle Mississippi during World War II.* St. Louis: U.S. Army Corps of Engineers, 1983.
Rudwick, Elliot M. *Race Riot at East St. Louis, July 2, 1917.* Carbondale: Southern Illinois University Press, 1964.
———. "Fifty Years of Race Relations in East St. Louis: The Breaking Down of White Supremacy." *Midcontinent American Studies Journal* 6 (Spring 1965): 3–15.
Rustin, Bayard. *Down the Line: The Collected Writings of Bayard Rustin.* Chicago: Quadrangle Books, 1977.
Saint Louis Fair Employment Practices Division. *Report.* St. Louis: St. Louis FEPD, 1965.
Salmond, John A. *A Southern Rebel: The Life and Times of Aubrey Willis Williams, 1890–1965.* Chapel Hill: University of North Carolina Press, 1983.

Schonberger, Rebecca. "Employer Changes Hiring Policy." *Employment Security Review* 9 (July 1942): 18.

Scobie, Ingrid Winther. *Center Stage: Helen Gahagan Douglas: A Life.* New York: Oxford University Press, 1992.

Scott, Emmett J. *Negro Migration during the War.* New York: Oxford University Press, 1920.

Seidman, Joel. *American Labor from Defense to Reconversion.* Chicago: University of Chicago Press, 1953.

"Seniority by Race Banned by FEPC: Employers Ordered to Discontinue Use of Separate White and Negro Seniority Lists." *Labor Relations Reporter* 15 (8 January 1945): 565–66.

Shapiro, Herbert. *White Violence and Black Response: From Reconstruction to Montgomery.* Amherst: University of Massachusetts Press, 1988.

Shortridge, James R. *The Middle West: Its Meaning in American Culture.* Lawrence: University Press of Kansas, 1989.

Shryock, Henry S., and Hope Tisdale Eldridge. "Internal Migration in Peace and War." *American Sociological Review* 12 (1947): 27–39.

Sitkoff, Harvard. *A New Deal for Blacks: The Emergence of Civil Rights as a National Issue: The Depression Decade.* New York: Oxford University Press, 1978.

———. "Racial Militancy and Interracial Violence in the Second World War." *Journal of American History* 58 (December 1971): 661–81.

———. "The Detroit Race Riot of 1943." *Michigan History* 53 (1969): 183–206.

Slocum, A. Lester. *Milwaukee's Negro Community.* Milwaukee: Citizen's Government Research Bureau, 1946.

Smith, A. Robert. *The Tiger in the Senate: The Biography of Wayne Morse.* Garden City, N.Y.: Doubleday, 1962.

Smith, Alonzo N., and Quintard Taylor. "Racial Discrimination in the Workplace: A Study of Two West Coast Cities during the 1940s." *Journal of Ethnic Studies* 8 (1980–81): 35–54.

Smith, R. Elberton. *The Army and Economic Mobilization.* Washington, D.C.: Center for Military History, 1959.

Sobel, Irwin. *The Negro in the St. Louis Economy, 1954.* St. Louis: St. Louis Urban League, 1954.

Sosna, Morton. *In Search of the Silent South: Southern Liberals and the Race Issue.* New York: Columbia University Press, 1977.

Southall, Sarah E. *Industry's Unfinished Business.* New York: Harper, 1950.

Spangler, Earl. *The Negro in Minnesota.* Minneapolis: T. S. Denison, 1961.

Spear, Allan H. *Black Chicago: The Making of a Negro Ghetto, 1890–1920.* Chicago: University of Chicago Press, 1967.

Steele, Richard W. "'No Racials': Discrimination against Ethnics in American Defense Industry, 1940–1942." *Labor History* 32 (Winter 1991): 66–90.

———. "The War on Intolerance: The Reformulation of American Nationalism, 1939–1941." *Journal of American Ethnic Studies* 9 (Fall 1989): 9–35.

Stein, Judith. "Race and Class Consciousness Revisited." *Reviews in American History* 19 (December 1991): 551–60.

Sterner, Richard. *The Negro's Share.* New York: Harper and Brothers, 1943.

Stevenson, Marshall Field. "Points of Departure, Acts of Resolve: Black-Jewish Relations in Detroit, 1937–1962." Ph.D. diss., University of Michigan, 1988.

Stockton, Edward Jerome. "Negro Employment in Metropolitan Columbus." M.A. thesis, Ohio State University, 1956.

Strickgold, Simon. *Memorandum #1: Specific Methods for Promoting Good Will among Racial Groups in Illinois.* Springfield: Illinois Interracial Commission, 1943.

Strickland, Arvarh E. *History of the Chicago Urban League.* Urbana: University of Illinois Press, 1966.

Suggs, Henry Lewis. *P. B. Young, Newspaperman: Race, Politics, and Journalism in the New South, 1910–1962.* New York: State University of New York Press, 1988.

Sugihara, Ina. "Our Stake in a Permanent FEPC." *Crisis* 36 (January 1945): 14–15, 29.

Sugrue, Thomas J. *The Origins of the Urban Crisis: Race and Inequality in Postwar Detroit.* Princeton, N.J.: Princeton University Press, 1996.

———. "Crabgrass-Roots Politics: Race, Rights, and the Reaction against Liberalism in the Urban North, 1940–1964." *Journal of American History* 82 (September 1995): 551–78.

Sullivan, Patricia. *Days of Hope: Race and Democracy in the New Deal.* Chapel Hill: University of North Carolina Press, 1996.

Taylor, Quintard. *The Forging of a Black Community: Seattle's Central District from 1870 through the Civil Rights Era.* Seattle: University of Washington Press, 1994.

Terkel, Studs. *Hard Times: An Oral History of the Great Depression.* New York: Pantheon, 1986.

———. *The Good War: An Oral History of World War Two.* New York: New Press, 1984.

Thomas, Richard Walter. *Life for Us Is What We Make It: Building Black Community in Detroit, 1915–1945.* Bloomington: Indiana University Press, 1992.

Thompson, Heather Ann. "The Politics of Labor, Race, and Liberalism in the Auto Plants and the Motor City, 1940–1980." Ph.D. diss., Princeton University, 1995.

Thompson, William F. *The History of Wisconsin.* Vol. 6, *Continuity and Change, 1940–1965.* Madison: State Historical Society of Wisconsin, 1988.

Thornbrough, Emma Lou. *The Negro in Indiana: A Study of a Minority.* Indianapolis: Indiana Historical Bureau, 1993.

———. *Since Emancipation: A Short History of Indiana Negroes, 1863–1963.* Indianapolis: Indiana Division of the American Negro Emancipation Centennial Authority, 1963.

Timbers, Edwin. "Labor Unions and Fair Employment Practices Legislation." Ph.D. diss., University of Michigan, 1954.

Trent, Dover P. "The Use of Indian Manpower." *Indians at Work* 13 (January–February 1945): 6–9.

Trotter, Joe William Jr. "African Americans in the City: The Industrial Era, 1900–1950." *Journal of Urban History* 21 (May 1995): 438–57.

———. "African-American Workers: New Directions in U.S. Labor Historiography." *Labor History* 35 (Fall 1994): 495–523.

———. *Black Milwaukee: The Making of an Industrial Proletariat, 1915–45.* Urbana: University of Illinois Press, 1985.

Trotter, Joe W. Jr., and Earl Lewis. *African Americans in the Industrial Age: A Documentary History, 1915–1945.* Boston: Northeastern University Press, 1996.

Turner, Lynn W. "Indiana in World War II—A Progress Report." *Indiana Magazine of History* 52 (March 1955): 1–20.

Turner, Lynn W., comp. *Indiana at War: A Directory of Hoosier Civilians Who Held Positions of Responsibility in Official, Volunteer, and Cooperating War-Time Organizations.* Bloomington, Ind.: War History Commission, 1951.

Tuttle, William M. *Race Riot: Chicago in the Red Summer of 1919.* New York: Atheneum, 1970.

UAW-CIO. *First Annual Summary of Activities: International UAW-CIO Fair Practices Committee.* Detroit: UAW-CIO, 1946.

"Unemployment in Cincinnati, May 1930." *Monthly Labor Review* 13 (July 1930): 35.

United States. Congress. House. *Appropriation for Terminating Functions and Duties of Committee on Fair Employment Practice.* 79th Congress, 1st session, Serial Set Document 786.

———. *Estimate of Appropriation for Committee on Fair Employment Practice of the Office for Emergency Management.* 78th Congress, 2d session, Serial Set Document 486.

————. *The Fair Employment Practice Act.* 79th Congress, 1st session, Serial Set Document 187.

————. *The Fair Employment Practice Act: Report to Accompany H.R. 2232.* Washington, D.C.: Government Printing Office, 1945.

————. *To Investigate Executive Agencies: Hearings before the Special Committee to Investigate Executive Agencies.* 78th Congress, 1st and 2d sessions. Washington, D.C.: Government Printing Office, 1943–44.

————. *To Prohibit Discrimination in Employment: Hearings on H.R. 3986, 1–16 June 1944.* 78th Congress, 2d session. Washington, D.C.: Government Printing Office, 1944.

————. *Prohibiting Discrimination in Employment Because of Race, Color, Religion, or National Origin.* 78th Congress, 2d session, Serial Set Document 2016.

————. *Proposed Provision Pertaining to an Appropriation for the Committee on Fair Employment Practice of the Office for Emergency Management.* 78th Congress, 2nd session, Serial Set Document 719.

United States. Congress. House Committee on Appropriations. *Hearings before the Subcommittee on National War Agencies Appropriation Bill for 1946.* Washington, D.C.: Government Printing Office, 1945.

————. *Hearings before the Subcommittee on National War Agencies Appropriation Bill for 1945.* Washington, D.C.: Government Printing Office, 1944.

United States. Congress. House Committee on Rules. *To Prohibit Discrimination in Employment Because of Race, Creed, Color, National Origin or Ancestry: Hearings on H.R. 2232, 8 March, 19–26 April 1945.* 79th Congress, 1st session. Washington, D.C.: Government Printing Office, 1945.

————. *Prohibiting Discrimination in Employment Because of Race, Color, Religion, or National Origin: Report to Accompany H.R. 3986.* Washington, D.C.: Government Printing Office, 1944.

United States Congress. Senate Committee on Education and Labor. *Fair Employment Practices Act: Hearings Before a Subcommittee of Committee on Education and Labor on S. 101 and S. 459, 12–14 March 1945.* 78th Congress, 1st session. Washington, D.C.: Government Printing Office, 1945.

————. *Fair Employment Practices Act, S. 2048: Hearings before a Subcommittee of Committee on Education and Labor, 30–31 August, 6–8 September, 1944.* 78th Congress, 2d session. Washington, D.C.: Government Printing Office, 1944.

————. *Prohibiting Discrimination in Employment Because of Race, Creed, Color, National Origin or Ancestry: Report to Accompany S. 101.* 78th Congress, 1st session. Washington, D.C.: Government Printing Office, 1945.

————. *Prohibiting Discrimination in Employment Because of Race, Creed, Color, National Origin or Ancestry: Report to Accompany S. 2048.* 78th Congress, 2d session. Washington, D.C.: Government Printing Office, 1944.

————. *Prohibiting Discrimination in Employment Because of Race, Creed, Color, National Origin, or Ancestry.* 78th Congress, 2d session, Serial Set Document 1109.

————. *Prohibiting Discrimination in Employment Because of Race, Creed, Color, National Origin, or Ancestry.* 79th Congress, 1st session, Serial Set Document 290.

United States. Congress. Senate. *Employment and Economic Status of Negroes in the United States: Staff Report to the Subcommittee on Labor and Labor-Relations of the Committee on Labor and Public Welfare.* 82d Congress, 2d session. Serial Set Document 14.

United States Employment Service (St. Louis). "Hopeful Change in Local Attitudes." *Employment Security Review* 9 (July 1942): 16–17.

U.S. Census Bureau. *Historical Statistics of the United States: Colonial Times to 1957.* Washington, D.C.: Government Printing Office, 1976.

————. *Statistical Abstract of the United States, 1948.* Washington, D.C.: Government Printing Office, 1949.

———. *Statistical Abstract of the United States, 1943.* Washington, D.C.: Government Printing Office, 1944.

———. *Sixteenth Census of the United States.* Washington, D.C.: Government Printing Office, 1943.

U.S. Labor Department. *Summary of State Fair Employment Practices Acts: Labor Law Series No. 6-A, August 1966.* Washington, D.C.: Government Printing Office, 1966.

"U.S.A. Needs Sharp Break with the Past." *Crisis* (May 1942): 151.

Verge, Arthur G. "The Impact of the Second World War on Los Angeles." *Pacific Historical Review* 63 (August 1994): 289–314.

Wallace, James F. "Wisconsin Puts Minorities to Work." *Employment Security Review* 9 (July 1942): 15–16.

"War and Post-War Trends in Employment of Negroes." *Monthly Labor Review* 28 (July 1945): 1–5.

War Manpower Commission. *History of the Mobilization of Labor for War Production during World War II.* Washington, D.C.: Government Printing Office, 1946.

———. "The Negro and What He Can Do to Win the War." Cleveland: War Manpower Commission, 1943.

Warren, Donald I. *Radio Priest: Charles Coughlin, the Father of Hate Radio.* New York: Free Press, 1996.

Watson, Denton L. *Lion in the Lobby: Clarence Mitchell, Jr.'s Struggle for the Passage of Civil Rights Laws.* New York: Morrow, 1990.

Watters, Mary. *Illinois in the Second World War.* 2 vols. Springfield: Illinois State Historical Library, 1951–52.

Weaver, Robert C. *Negro Labor: A National Problem.* New York: Harcourt, Brace, Jovanovich, 1946.

———. "The Employment of the Negroes in United States War Industries." *International Labour Review* 1 (1944): 141–59.

———. "Detroit and Negro Skill." *Phylon* 4 (1943): 131–43.

———. "The Employment of Negroes in War Industries." *Journal of Negro Education* 12 (1943): 386–87.

———. "Racial Tensions in Chicago." In *Social Service Year Book,* 1–8. Chicago: Council of Social Agencies, 1943.

———. "The Negro Comes of Age in Industry." *Atlantic Monthly,* September 1943, 54–59.

———. "Racial Employment Trends in National Defense." *Phylon* 3 (1942): 22–30.

———. "With the Negro's Help." *Atlantic Monthly,* June 1942, 696–707.

———. "Defense Industries and the Negro." *Annals of the American Academy of Political and Social Science* 233 (September 1942): 60–66.

———. "Racial Employment Trends in National Defense." *Phylon* 2 (1941): 337–58.

———. "The Defense Program and the Negro." *Opportunity* 18 (November 1940): 324–27.

Wechsler, James A. "Pigeonhole for Negro Equality." *Nation,* 23 January 1943, 121–22.

Weiss, Nancy. *Farewell to the Party of Lincoln: Black Politics in the Age of F.D.R.* Princeton, N.J.: Princeton University Press, 1983.

———. *The National Urban League, 1910–1940.* New York: Oxford University Press, 1974.

Wesley, Charles Harris. *Negro-Americans in Ohio.* Wilberforce, Ohio: Central State University, 1953.

White, Graham, and John Maze. *Harold Ickes of the New Deal: His Private Life and Public Career.* Cambridge, Mass.: Harvard University Press, 1985.

White, Walter F. *A Man Called White: The Autobiography of Walter White.* New York: Viking Press, 1948.

———. *What Caused the Detroit Riot? An Analysis.* Washington, D.C.: NAACP, 1943.

———. "It's Our Country, Too: The Negro Demands the Right to Be Allowed to Fight for It." *Saturday Evening Post,* 14 December 1940, 27, 61, 63, 66, 68.

Winkler, Allan M. *Home Front U.S.A.: America during World War II.* Arlington Heights, Ill.: Harlan Davidson, 1986.

———. "The Philadelphia Transit Strike of 1944." *Journal of American History* 59 (June 1972): 73–89.

Wirth, Louis. "Morale and Minority Groups." *American Journal of Sociology* 47 (1941): 415–33.

Wisconsin Industrial Commission, Fair Employment Division. *Biennial Report, 1948–1950.* Madison: Wisconsin FEPC, 1950.

———. *Fair Employment.* Madison: Wisconsin FEPC, 1948.

Wolcott, Victoria W. "The Culture of the Informal Economy: Numbers Runners in Inter-War Black Detroit." *Radical History Review* 69 (Fall 1997): 46–75.

Wolters, Raymond. *Negroes and the Great Depression: The Problem of Economic Recovery.* Westport, Conn.: Greenwood Press, 1970.

"Work and Wage Experience of Willow Run Workers." *Monthly Labor Review* 28 (December 1945): 1074–90.

Works Progress Administration. Federal Writers' Project. *Michigan: A Guide to the Wolverine State.* 1941. New York: Oxford University Press, 1974.

———. *Wisconsin: A Guide to the Badger State.* New York: Duell, Sloan, and Pearce, 1941.

———. *The Calumet Region Historical Guide.* Gary, Ind.: German Printing Company, 1939.

World Almanac and Book of Facts. New York: Press Publishing Company, 1940.

Woytinsky, W. S. "Interstate Migration during the War." *State Government* 19 (1946): 81–84.

Wye, Christopher G. "Midwest Ghetto: Patterns of Negro Life and Thought in Cleveland, Ohio, 1929–1945." Ph.D. diss., Kent State University, 1973.

Wynn, Neil A. *The Afro-American and the Second World War.* New York: Holmes and Meier, 1993.

Zaid, Charles. *Records of the Committee on Fair Employment Practice.* Washington, D.C.: Government Printing Office, 1962.

Zieger, Robert H. *The CIO, 1935–1955.* Chapel Hill: University of North Carolina Press, 1995.

Index

Index

ANDREW EDMUND KERSTEN is an assistant professor of American history and humanistic studies at the University of Wisconsin at Green Bay. He has published several articles on the FEPC and is working on a history of the American Federation of Labor during World War II.

Typeset in 10.5/12.5 Adobe Minion
Composed by Celia Shapland
for the University of Illinois Press
Manufactured by Thomson-Shore, Inc.

University of Illinois Press
1325 South Oak Street
Champaign, IL 61820-6903
www.press.uillinois.edu